McCLANE'S FIELD GUIDE

TO FRESHWATER FISHES

OF NORTH AMERICA

McCLANE'S

Field Guide to

Freshwater Fishes

OF

NORTH AMERICA

EDITED BY

A. J. McClane

A project of The Gamefish Research Association

ILLUSTRATIONS BY
Dr. Frances Watkins,
Richard E. Younger,
and Ned Smith

An Owl Book

Henry Holt and Company
New York

Copyright © 1965 by Holt, Rinehart and Winston, Inc.
Copyright © 1974, 1978 by A. J. McClane
All rights reserved, including the right to reproduce
this book or portions thereof in any form.
Published by Henry Holt and Company, Inc.,
115 West 18th Street, New York, New York 10011.
Published in Canada by Fitzhenry & Whiteside Limited,
195 Allstate Parkway, Markham, Ontario L3R 4T8

Library of Congress Cataloging in Publication Data
McClane, Albert Jules, 1922–
McClane's Field guide to freshwater fishes of North America.
Portions originally published in McClane's standard fishing encyclopedia
and international angling guide (1965) and McClane's new standard fishing
encyclopedia and international angling guide (1974).
Includes index.
1.   Fishes, Freshwater—North America.
2.   Fishes—North America. I. Title. II. Title:
Field guide to freshwater fishes of North America.
QL625.M3   597'.09297   77-11967
ISBN 0-8050-0194-8 (An Owl book: pbk.)

Henry Holt books are available at special discounts
for bulk purchases for sales promotions, premiums,
fund raising, or educational use. Special editions
or book excerpts can also be created to specification.

    For details contact:

    Special Sales Director
    Henry Holt and Company, Inc.
    115 West 18th Street
    New York, New York 10011

Printed in Hong Kong

10   9   8   7   6   5

CONTENTS

PREFACE

The source volume of this guidebook, *McClane's New Standard Fishing Encyclopedia* (Holt, Rinehart and Winston, 1974), itself a revised and expanded edition of *McClane's Standard Fishing Encyclopedia* (Holt, Rinehart and Winston, 1965), is a book of 1,156 two-column pages, hardly of a size suitable for field identification. To meet the demand for a handy "tackle box" reference, descriptions of the most important game-, food-, and foragefishes found in North American waters have been divided into two small volumes, *McClane's Field Guide to Saltwater Fishes of North America* and *McClane's Field Guide to Freshwater Fishes of North America.* Much of this material has again been revised with respect to new information concerning life histories and the inevitable changes in scientific names. To make fish identification easier, those fish portraits which appeared in black and white in the encyclopedia have been replaced with color.

These field guides are designed for the angler, and while the family arrangement generally follows scientific order, exceptions were made to relate text to the illustrations or to group species that are similar in appearance for quick comparison. Thus, in the freshwater guide a jawless fish (Class Agnatha), the lamprey, will be found adjacent to the American eel, one of the bony fishes (Class Osteichthyes); to an angler discovering a dead lamprey in the stream, which happens with some frequency, the "eellike" form is primary and the class secondary.

It is not practical to include every freshwater and saltwater species endemic to North America in a tackle-box-size field guide, but all those of angling importance are encompassed. In our continental waters there are about 200 minnows and 136 sculpins, for example, and most of these are of very local distribution. However, many of the "minor" fishes that are of special interest to the angler, and those having an especially wide range, are included. Anadromous species such as the salmon and shad are treated as freshwater fishes, while certain marine species which enter freshwater or have become established as inland populations such as the tarpon and snook appear in both volumes with annotations.

The following authors contributed in part or whole to descriptions of various fish species: Dr. John C. Briggs, Keen Buss, Robert A. Jones, Darrel Louder, A. J. McClane, Dr. John Rayner, Luis Rivas, James T. Shields, and Dr. Donald deSylva.

Special thanks are due to Mr. John Rybovitch of the Gamefish Research Association and Mrs. Wayne Hicklin for their financial support in making the color plates possible. A prorated share of the sales of these guides will be contributed to funding the association's ongoing research projects.

The common and scientific names of fishes used in this guide are those recognized by the American Fisheries Society (*Common and Scientific Names of Fishes from the United States and Canada.* 3rd ed., Washington, D.C., 1970).

GLOSSARY

ADIPOSE FIN A small fleshy fin without rays located dorsally on the caudal peduncle. It is typical of the salmonids but occurs on other species.

AMMOCETE The larval stage of a lamprey.

ANADROMOUS Any fish that migrates from the sea into freshwater rivers for the purpose of spawning. Some anadromous species are the salmon, striped bass, alewife, and shad. Fishes that migrate in the reverse direction from freshwater into the sea for their spawning are catadromous.

ANAL FIN The unpaired or single fin on the ventral surface of the body.

ANDATE Attached to, or grown together.

ANTERIOR Toward the front; the opposite of posterior.

AXIL The region behind the pelvic or pectoral fin base.

AXILLARY PROCESS An elongate structure at the base of the pelvic or pectoral fins.

BAND A diagonal or curved marking on a fish's body.

BAR A vertical marking on a fish's body, with more or less straight sides.

BARBEL A threadlike structure or "whisker" on the head near the mouth.

BASIBRANCHIAL TEETH Very small teeth on the basibranchial plate near the base of the tongue.

BRANCHIOSTEGAL RAYS Slender bones in the gill membrane, located below the gill cover at the edge of the gill opening.

CANINE TEETH Long pointed teeth; they may be straight or curved, and are often fanglike.

CARDIFORM TEETH Short pointed teeth in multiple rows.

CATADROMOUS Any fish that migrates from freshwater to the sea for purposes of spawning, as does the American eel. Catadromous is the opposite of anadromous.

CAUDAL Toward the tail, or pertaining to the tail.

CAUDAL FIN The tail or tail fin.

CAUDAL PEDUNCLE That portion of a fish's body immediately preceding the tail, from the base of the anal fin to the base of the caudal fin.

CIRCULUS (pl. circuli) One of a series of concentric ridges that form rings or arcs on the scales of fishes.

CONICAL TEETH Short pointed teeth.

CTENOID SCALES Scales with pointed projections (teeth or ctenii) on their posterior margin. In some species the ctenii are microscopic; in others they are pronounced and make the fish feel rough to the touch.

CYCLOID SCALES   Smooth scales with an evenly curved posterior margin.

DORSAL FIN   The prominent fin on the back. Some species have 2 or more dorsal fins; most cods, for example, have 3 dorsal fins.

EMARGINATE   A tail fin that is concavely curved but not definitely forked (such as the tails of trouts).

FALCATE   A tail fin shaped like a sickle (such as the tails of jacks); it is deeply concave, with the middle rays much shorter than the anterior or posterior rays.

FRENUM   The connecting membrane that holds the upper jaw to the snout.

GANOID SCALES   Hard, diamond-shaped scales that occur on the more primitive bony fishes such as the gars and on the upturned lobe of the tail in sturgeons and paddlefish.

GAS BLADDER   A membranous structure occurring under the kidney in most but not all fishes, also known as the swim or air bladder. The gas bladder acts as a flotation organ to adjust the weight of the fish to equalize water displacement so that the fish neither rises nor sinks. It can also serve as a noise-producing organ and acts as a resonator in hearing. Species that do not possess or have only a rudimentary gas bladder, such as the darters or Atlantic mackerel, sink to the bottom if they stop swimming.

GONADS   The reproductive organs of either sex.

HETEROCERCAL   A tail having a long upper lobe and a shorter lower lobe. The vertebral column extends into the upper lobe. It is typical of sharks.

HOMOCERCAL   A symmetrical tail with lobes of equal length. The vertebral column ends at the base of the tail and does not extend into the upper lobe. It is typical of sunfishes.

INCISIFORM TEETH   Flattened chisellike teeth.

ISTHMUS   The throat or fleshy area that separates the gill chambers.

KEEL   Scales or tissue that form a sharp ridge.

LATERAL LINE   Pored scales extending from the head along the side of the body usually to the base of the caudal fin. Some species do not have a lateral line while in others it may be incomplete or branched or may extend into the caudal fin.

LINE   A very narrow marking on a fish's body; it may be oriented in any direction.

LUNATE   A tail that is sickle in shape but not as deeply concave as falcate. It is typical of the tunas.

MANDIBLE   The lower jaw.

MAXILLARY   Pertaining to or denoting the upper jaw.

MOLARIFORM TEETH   Broad, low, flattened teeth used for grinding and crushing.

NAPE   The back of the "neck" from the occiput to the first ray of the dorsal fin.

NARES   The nostrils.

NUCHAL   Pertaining to the nape.

NUCHAL BAND   A band of color transversing the nape.

OCCIPUT   The back of the head.

OCELLUS   A usually round marking on a fish's body surrounded by a halo of a lighter color.

OMNIVOROUS   Eating both plant and animal foods.

OPERCLE   The large posterior bone of the head covering the gills; also called gill cover or operculum.

ORBIT   The bony eye socket.

PALATINES   Paired bones on each side of the roof of the mouth.

PALATINE TEETH   Teeth occurring on the palatine bones.

PARR   Specifically, a juvenile trout or salmon distinguished by dark vertical blotches or parr marks on its side.

PECTORAL FINS   The anterior paired fins behind the gill openings.

PELAGIC   A fish that spends most of its life close to the surface of the sea, such as the tunas. Fish of pelagic habits are opposed to demersal species, which live close to the bottom, such as the cods.

PELVIC FINS   The posterior paired fins on the ventral surface of the body.

pH   A measure of acidity or alkalinity based on a 0–14 scale. Neutral is 7; below 7 acidity increases, and above 7 alkalinity increases.

PHARYNX   The alimentary canal between the mouth and the esophagus.

PLACOID SCALES   These are dermal denticles, resembling a tooth in structure, which form the rough skin covering of most sharks, skates, and rays.

PLANKTON   Animals that float and drift passively in the water of the seas, lakes, and rivers as distinct from animals that are attached to, or crawling on the bottom. Plankton are mostly of microscopic size and have a large surface area in relation to their weight. Many crustaceans, some mollusks, a few worms, a variety of small larvae, and minute plants (phytoplankton) compose a plankton population.

PREOPERCLE   The anterior bone of the gill cover in front of the opercle, behind and below the eye.

PYLORIC CAECA   Dead-end pouchlike projections attached to the intestinal tract just ahead of the stomach.

SPINE   The stiff but sometimes flexible rod that acts as a supporting structure in the fins; it is without cross striations and is unbranched.

SPIRACLE   An opening on the posterior portion of the head, above and behind the eye.

SPOT   A round or nearly round marking on a fish's body.

STRIATED   Marked with narrow lines or grooves that are usually parallel.

STRIPE   A horizontal marking on a fish's body.

SUBTERMINAL MOUTH   A mouth that opens ventrally with the lower jaw closing within the upper jaw.

TERETE A cylindrical and tapering body with a circular cross section.

THORACIC Pertaining to the chest or thorax.

TOOTH COUNT In identifying minnows, the number and arrangement of the pharyngeal teeth is a diagnostic character. A formula of 5-4, for example, means that there is a single row of 5 teeth on the left arch and 4 on the right arch. A formula of 2, 4-4, 2 means there are 2 teeth in the left outer row, 4 teeth in the left inner row, 4 teeth in the right inner row, and 2 teeth in the right outer row. This identification requires careful dissection and is difficult for anyone except an ichthyologist.

TRUNCATE A tail having a vertical and straight posterior margin, such as the tails of groupers.

TUBERCLES Hornlike projections on the skin which develop on some species during the breeding season, notably many minnows; sometimes called pearl organs.

VERMICULATIONS Wormlike color patterns on the skin, which occur on species such as the brook trout and Spanish mackerel.

VENTRAL Relating to the abdomen or underside of the fish; opposed to dorsal.

VILLIFORM TEETH Small conical teeth in several rows.

VOMER A median bone at the front of the roof of the mouth.

YEAR CLASS The fishes spawned in any one calendar year.

ZOOPLANKTON Protozoa and other animal microorganisms living unattached in water. These include small crustacea such as daphnia and cyclops.

MEASUREMENTS AND IDENTIFICATION OF FISHES

Measurements of a Fish

For various purposes a fish may be measured in different ways. Of primary importance to the angler is the total length, because this determines the legality of his catch. However, the fishery biologist may use the fork length, while the ichthyologist may use the standard length in his research operations. In the *Field & Stream* fishing contest only the fork length is valid. For identification purposes the angler may also want to measure depth of body, depth of head, and length of body.

Standard length: Length of the body of a fish from the tip of the snout with the mouth closed to the end of the vertebral column (base of caudal fin).

Fork length: Length of the fish from tip of snout with the mouth closed to tip of the shortest ray of the caudal fin (or to the center of the fin if the tail is not forked).

Total length: The overall length of a fish, measured from the tip of the jaw with the mouth closed and extending to the tip of caudal fin. The caudal rays are sometimes squeezed together to give the greatest overall measurement, but this is of no scientific value.

Depth of body: The greatest body depth measured at right angles to the long axis of the body; the number of times the greatest depth is contained in the standard length.

Depth of head: The depth of the head measured vertically from the occiput ("neck"); the number of times the depth of the head is contained in the length of the head.

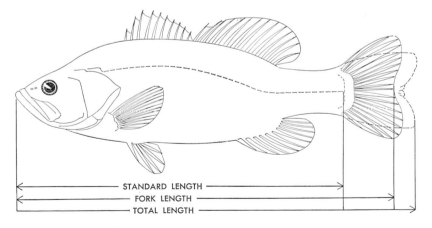

Measurements of a Fish

Scale Counts in Identification

The number of scales on certain parts of a fish's body is a useful aid in identification. The lateral-line count is the most important measurement; while it is seldom constant it will fluctuate within certain limits. In species where the lateral line is incomplete, the number of scale rows above or below the lateral line can be used (see morphology diagram). While it is not practical for the angler in the field to determine counts on finely scaled species of very small fish, particularly without magnification, the method is applicable to species with large scales such as the sunfishes, herrings, snappers and many of the larger cyprinids (minnows and carps).

In any population of northern spotted bass, for example, the lateral-line count varies from 60–68 scales. A small percentage will have 59 or 69 lateral-line scales and the rare individual will have less or more, but the great majority of northern spotted bass fall within the 60–68 range. This would separate the species from the more finely scaled smallmouth with 69–77. One bass whose scale counts overlap the northern spotted is the northern largemouth, but these are readily separated by the fin-ray counts as well as the absence of scales on the interradial membrane at the base of the tail, second dorsal, and anal fins on the largemouth.

Scale counts should be made on a dry specimen. If the bass is large it's fairly easy to count the pored scales in the lateral line while it's still fresh. The above-and-below-lateral-line scale counts run on an angle with the first dorsal and first anal spines as reference points. To make certain that you follow the body contours use the edge of a sheet of paper as a guide in paralleling the correct sequence from the spines to the lateral line. It helps to raise or move each scale as you count and this can be done with a thin-bladed penknife; however, don't "pick" at the scales too much or they will pop out and confuse any recounting. The scales on the interradial membranes of the fins are often very hard to see, as these are frequently embedded and it may require considerable picking under a magnifying glass to establish their presence.

Fin-Ray Count in Identification

The kind and number of rays are characteristic of a species and may be used in identification. A fin ray is a bony rod, usually connected to other rays by a membrane (interradial membrane) to form one of the fins of a fish. Rays are generally of two kinds, spines and softrays. Softrayed fishes are exemplified by the trouts, minnows, and suckers, which have only softrays in their fins. Spinyrayed fishes such as the sunfishes and perches have one or more spines in their dorsal, anal, and pelvic fins, with the remainder of these fins usually

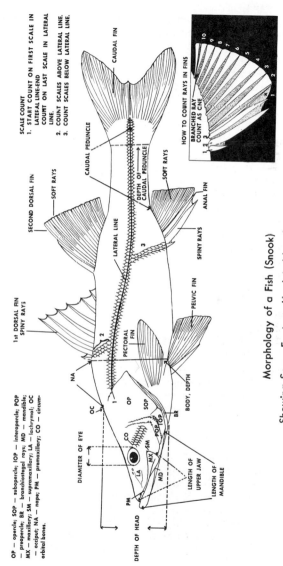

Morphology of a Fish (Snook)
Showing Some Features Used in Identification

OP — opercle; SOP — subopercle; IOP — interopercle; POP — preopercle; BR — branchiostegal rays; MD — mandible; MX — maxillary; SM — supramaxillary; LA — lachrymal; OC — occiput; NA — nape; PM — premaxillary; CO — circumorbital bones.

SCALE COUNT
1. START COUNT ON FIRST SCALE IN LATERAL LINE-END COUNT ON LAST SCALE IN LATERAL LINE.
2. COUNT SCALES ABOVE LATERAL LINE.
3. COUNT SCALES BELOW LATERAL LINE.

HOW TO COUNT RAYS IN FINS
BRANCHED RAY COUNT AS ONE

CAUDAL FIN

CAUDAL PEDUNCLE

SECOND DORSAL FIN

SOFT RAYS

DEPTH OF CAUDAL PEDUNCLE

SOFT RAYS

ANAL FIN

LATERAL LINE

SPINY RAYS

1st DORSAL FIN
SPINY RAYS

PELVIC FIN

PECTORAL FIN

BODY, DEPTH

NA

OC

OP

SOP

POP

BR

DIAMETER OF EYE

CO

SM
MX

LA

MD

LENGTH OF UPPER JAW

LENGTH OF MANDIBLE

PM

DEPTH OF HEAD

LENGTH OF HEAD

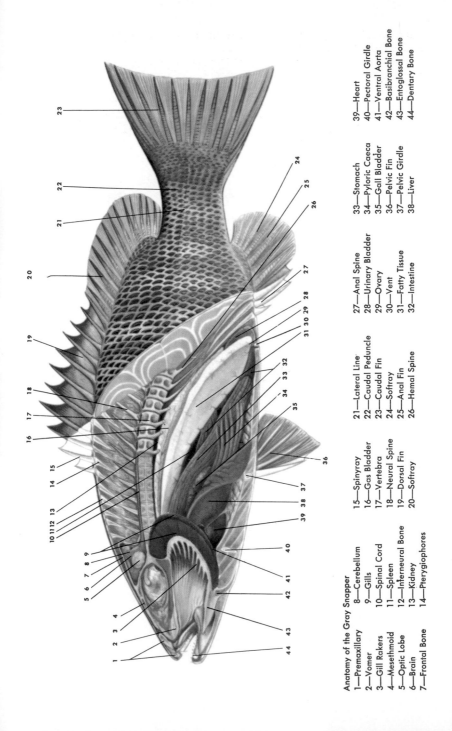

Anatomy of the Gray Snapper

1—Premaxillary
2—Vomer
3—Gill Rakers
4—Mesethmoid
5—Optic Lobe
6—Brain
7—Frontal Bone
8—Cerebellum
9—Gills
10—Spinal Cord
11—Spleen
12—Interneural Bone
13—Kidney
14—Pterygiophores
15—Spinyray
16—Gas Bladder
17—Vertebra
18—Neural Spine
19—Dorsal Fin
20—Softray
21—Lateral Line
22—Caudal Peduncle
23—Caudal Fin
24—Softray
25—Anal Fin
26—Hemal Spine
27—Anal Spine
28—Urinary Bladder
29—Ovary
30—Vent
31—Fatty Tissue
32—Intestine
33—Stomach
34—Pyloric Caeca
35—Gall Bladder
36—Pelvic Fin
37—Pelvic Girdle
38—Liver
39—Heart
40—Pectoral Girdle
41—Ventral Aorta
42—Basibranchial Bone
43—Entoglossal Bone
44—Dentary Bone

made up of softrays (some fish have one spine in each pectoral fin; spines do not occur in the caudal fin).

Spines and softrays take different forms in various kinds of fishes, and a strict definition of either kind of ray is not possible. In some species, such as the mullets, one of the softrays in young juveniles regularly transforms into a spine. In the usual case a spine is rigid, pointed at the tip, and nonsegmented and nonbranched. Softrays are usually flexible, not pointed at the tip (fimbriated), and segmented, and often they are branched.

McCLANE'S FIELD GUIDE
TO FRESHWATER FISHES
OF NORTH AMERICA

HERRING FAMILY   Clupeidae

ALEWIFE *Alosa pseudoharengus*   The alewife differs, along with the blueback herring and shad, from the skipjack herring and hickory shad, in its lower jaw, which does not project noticeably beyond the upper. It has a deep notch in the upper jaw, as has the shad, from which it differs by the presence of a small patch of teeth on the tongue and a relatively low number of gillrakers (33—40) on the lower part of the first gill arch in the adult. The eyes are larger than in other species of the genus. The alewife is bluish above with silvery sides, and faint dark stripes along the sides.

In saltwater, this species grows to a length of over 1 foot, but the landlocked or freshwater form reaches only 3—6 inches. It is found along the Atlantic coast from Florida to Labrador, throughout the St. Lawrence River drainage, recently occurring in Lakes Huron and Michigan through the Welland Canal. The saltwater form of the species begins its migration in February and April, returning to the sea in May. Some fish may stay in the shallow waters of the estuaries

Alewife

as late as early winter but most disappear in the fall. The freshwater form migrates upstream in April and May and then returns to the larger bodies of water, where the fish spend the fall and winter in deepwater. During the summer, large numbers of landlocked ale-wives die and float up on the beaches, creating considerable nuisance to property owners. This mass mortality is believed to be related to changes in water temperature. The alewife feeds primarily on plankton, including shrimps, small fishes, diatoms, and copepods..

The marine form of the alewife is of some commercial importance, with a landing of over 15 million pounds annually. Most are canned, salted, or smoked, although the bony flesh is of poor quality. The roe is excellent. Landlocked populations are an important forage species for trouts and salmon, particularly in Lake Michigan. The alewife is also used as bait.

AMERICAN SHAD *Alosa sapidissima*   The American or white shad is an anadromous fish, and like the salmon it ascends coastal rivers to spawn. It can be separated from its nearest look-alike rela-

1

tive, the hickory shad, by its lower jaw: The hickory has a long, projected lower jaw; the lower jaw of the American shad is entirely enclosed within the upper when the two are pressed together. The American shad is the largest member of its genus and the most widely distributed on our continent. It averages 3–5 pounds, though fish of 13 pounds have been netted from the Connecticut River. In the southern portion of its range the shad rarely attains 6 pounds in size, an environmental limitation predicated on ambient water temperatures.

All white shad are 4–5 years old when they appear on their first spawning run, and as many as 30 percent will become repeat spawners in rivers from Chesapeake Bay north—living to 8–9 years. The biggest fish are the older, second-time migrants and, in lesser numbers, those fish on their third or fourth spawning run. In recent years, fish authenticated to weigh 8 pounds or more were caught from the Wicomico River in Maryland north to the Palmer River in Massachusetts. South of Cape Hatteras, postspawning survival is virtually unknown, and the entire population dies after reproducing at the latitude of Florida's St. Johns River. These deaths are correlated with energy demands at higher stream temperatures; adult shad, like the salmon, do not eat while in freshwater. After a long migration and a tremendous loss in body weight, often as much as 40 percent, the fish simply lack the fat reserves to return to the ocean. In the colder northeastern rivers and those of the Pacific coast, a substantial number of shad are able to make the downstream journey. While at sea, shad remain offshore in deepwaters at the temperature range of 55°–65°F, which causes the schools to travel in a northerly direction in spring and a southerly one in the fall. They have been caught by trawlers at distances over 100 miles from shore and at depths below 400 feet, so these movements occur over a wide area. When spawning time approaches and the colder coastal rivers begin to warm, the fish seek their natal waters, entering the currents at about 55°F. Most shad return to their home streams, oriented by light intensity and an

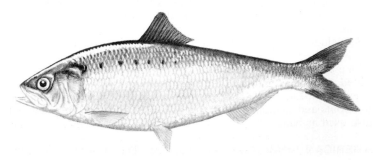

American Shad

olfactory ability to taste/smell the familiar chemical substances of individual rivers.

In their extreme southerly range, the movement is reversed. Southern rivers normally are over 65°F throughout most of the year, so shad begin entering Florida's St. Johns, for example, when the river becomes "cool" after the first chill winds of late November. Thus, the farther north the shad stream, the later its run begins. The peak migrations, when shad are most abundant, occur in the temperature range 62°–67°F. Broadly speaking, the best fishing is in January at the latitude of the St. Johns River, during May in Chesapeake tributaries north to Massachusetts, and in late June around the Gulf of St. Lawrence. This timetable is paralleled on the Pacific coast, where the shad migration in California's Feather River peaks in late May, and the Columbia River far to the north is shad-filled during the first week in July. Small buck shad dominate the earliest catches, with the percentage of roe, or female, shad increasing as the season progresses. The newly hatched fish remain in the river until fall, then spend 2–5 years in saltwater before returning to repeat the cycle. Little is known of their marine existence except that they eat plankton almost exclusively.

BLUEBACK HERRING *Alosa aestivalis*   Like the other members of the herring family, the blueback is a slab-sided, silvery species with a small, terminal mouth. It differs from the other herrings in having a black peritoneum (abdominal lining) and a darker, more slender body. A weight of almost 1 pound and a length of about 15 inches have been reported. The blueback is found along the Atlantic coast from Maine

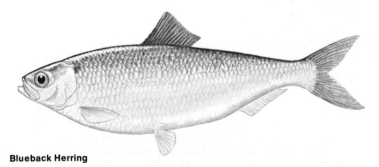

Blueback Herring

to Florida, being more common in the southern part of its range. Like the other species of the genus *Alosa,* it ascends tributaries in the spring for spawning. The young feed on plankton; the adults eat fishes and small crustaceans. The blueback is not particularly important commercially, most of the catch being reported in the catch for the alewife. The flesh has little value commercially.

3

GIZZARD SHAD *Dorosoma cepedianum*   This species is separated from other herrings by the elongated last ray of the dorsal fin; the small mouth, which is located on the lower part of the head; and the gizzardlike stomach. It is a deep-bodied species, generally silver with bluish above and brassy to reddish reflections on the side. The young have a large, dark shoulder spot, which may be absent in large adults. The gizzard shad swims in fresh- and brackish water, in bays, lakes, bayous, and large rivers, occurring in clear or turbid water. It is widespread from the Mississippi River and its drainage, from Minnesota south to the Gulf of Mexico, and from New Jersey southward; it also occurs in northeastern Mexico.

Unlike most shad and herrings, the gizzard is not a migratory species, and although it does mill about in large schools it tends to stay in about the same locality throughout the year. It is primarily a fish of lakes and large streams, where the flow is sluggish. Spawning occurs during the early summer, the young attaining a length of about 4−5 inches by October. Adults reach a length of about $1^1/_2$ feet and a weight of approximately 3 pounds, but seldom exceed 12 inches.

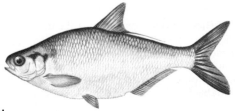

Gizzard Shad

Unlike other shad, the gizzard is not a plankton feeder; rather, it strains small organisms from the mud with its gillrakers. Most of its food is made up of plant material and organic debris. The food is ground in the gizzardlike stomach and the long intestine. Because of this apparatus, the species is extremely important as a foragefish, converting organic matter and plant material directly to fish flesh, which then becomes food for predatory fishes. The gizzard shad is thus an important link in the food web, and this fact is pertinent for fishermen because such species as striped bass, largemouth bass, and white bass feed on the gizzard shad heavily. However, in some waters the gizzard shad has created a serious management problem owing to its extreme abundance where no large predator population exists. The gizzard shad is a poor live bait because it dies quickly on the hook; it is used as a dead bait.

HICKORY SHAD *Alosa mediocris*   Similar to the skipjack herring, the hickory shad differs chiefly in the absence of weak teeth and the

4

presence of faint longitudinal stripes on the sides. The shallow-notched upper jaw, small eyes, and strongly projecting lower jaw also distinguish it from the skipjack herring. The adult has a row of black spots behind each gill cover. The hickory's body is grayish-green above, with silver sides. In the adult the upper rows of scales have well-defined dark lines forming faint lines on the fish's sides. The hickory shad has a lower number of gillrakers on the lower part of the first gill arch (19–21) than its relatives, which generally have in excess of 21.

One of the larger of the shad, it attains a length of 2 feet and a weight of 2½ pounds, although specimens of 5 pounds have been reported. The hickory shad occurs along the Atlantic coast from Florida to the Bay of Fundy.

In the thermal cycle of a season, hickories migrate into freshwater when the river temperature is 50°–52°F, usually preceding the run of white shad by about 2 weeks. And unlike the larger species, which remains to spawn in the main stream, hickory shad prefer small tributaries. The migrations of the hickory are not wholly understood; those

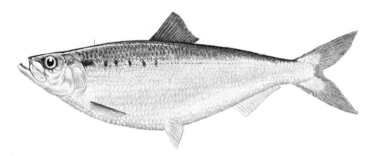

Hickory Shad

entering the streams that drain into Pamlico Sound, for example, are known to be spawning fish, whereas the stocks coming into Chesapeake tributaries evidently reproduce in brackish water even though they school densely in what appears to be a spawning run.

The hickory shad is a popular gamefish in southern U.S. rivers.

SKIPJACK HERRING *Alosa chrysochloris* This species has a strongly compressed body, thin scales, and a curved belly edged with a row of scutes (sharp-edged scales). The upper jaw is notched, and the lower jaw projects far beyond the upper. The young and, usually, the adults have weak teeth in the lower jaw. The back is green with bluish reflections, and the sides are silvery. Usually there are no dark spots behind the gill covers, as in the closely related hickory shad. The skipjack reaches 21 inches and 3½ pounds, usually 12–16 inches.

This species is found from the marine waters of the Gulf coast from Texas to Florida, up the Mississippi River and its larger tributaries, north to Minnesota and Pennsylvania. This large-river fish spawns in late April during upstream migrations; it probably drifts downstream during the fall.

On light tackle, the skipjack herring is an excellent fighter, and is taken on flies, on small spinners or spoons, or on live minnows. It eats insects and crustaceans, as well as small fishes. It is not valued for food, largely because of its bony flesh.

THREADFIN SHAD *Dorosoma petenense* This species closely resembles the gizzard shad, *D. cepedianum,* but differs from it in the coloration of the back and the caudal fin, which are yellowish, and in having a shorter anal fin (20−23 rays in the threadfin compared with about 31 in the gizzard). The adult threadfin has a distinct spot on the shoulder, which is usually not seen in the gizzard shad. The threadfin shad is generally smaller than the gizzard shad, the adult reaching only 6−8 inches.

It is found along the Gulf coast from Florida to Texas, and northward into the Mississippi valley to Tennessee and southern Arkansas and Oklahoma. Taken as far south as British Honduras, this fish was recently introduced in California and Arizona as a foragefish for more desirable sport fishes.

MOONEYE FAMILY Hiodontidae

The Hiodontidae are characterized by having large eyes and mouths edged by small teeth; thus the common name toothed herring is often applied to this family.

GOLDEYE *Hiodon alosoides* The goldeye is a freshwater panfish distributed from the Ohio River into southern Canada. The northern limit of its range is not precisely known, but it has been taken in the Nelson River.

The goldeye is bluish above; the sides and belly are silvery with some gold reflections. It has a sharp margin on the belly anterior to the pelvic fins. There are 9 (rarely 10) softrays in the dorsal fin and 30

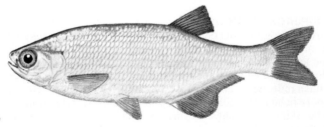

Goldeye

in the anal fin. The lateral line is incomplete and contains 56–58 scales. Unlike most fishes, goldeyes do not spawn every year after reaching sexual maturity. A certain proportion of any population drops its eggs on gravel bars some time between May and July, but the rest of the females carry immature eggs.

Being insectivorous in feeding habits, the goldeye provides excellent fly-fishing. It usually averages less than 1 pound in weight (12 inches in length), but 2-pounders (16 inches) are not uncommon in some lakes.

A large market for smoked goldeye exists in Canada, where it is commonly sold as Lake Winnipeg goldeye. This name no longer identifies the fish with the lake, but rather with the city where it is processed. Most of the goldeyes received in Winnipeg are caught in Clair Lake, Alberta, which is in the Wood Buffalo National Park. A smaller amount comes from the Churchill River and Lake Winnipegosis.

MOONEYE *Hiodon tergisus* This freshwater panfish closely resembles the goldeye. Another species, the southern mooneye (*H. selenops*), differs mainly in lacking a keel on the belly in front of or behind the pelvic fins.

The dorsal surface of the mooneye is olivaceous with dark blue reflections and the sides are silvery. The anterior margin of the dorsal fin is inserted in front of the anterior margin of the anal fin (the dorsal fin of the goldeye originates behind the anterior margin of the anal). There are 11–12 softrays in the dorsal fin and 28 in the anal fin. The lateral line is complete and contains 52–55 scales. The mooneye generally attains a slightly larger size than the goldeye; individuals of 2 pounds are not uncommon, but the species seldom exceeds 2 pounds.

The mooneye is distributed from the Hudson Bay area (in tributary watersheds) to the Lake Champlain drainage system and west through Lake Erie and the Mississippi River to Alabama, Arkansas, Oklahoma, and Kansas.

Although not commonly taken by anglers, the mooneye will rise readily to small flies when feeding near the surface of a large lake.

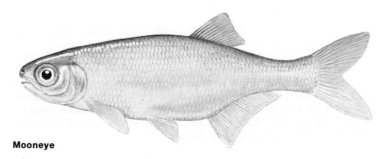

Mooneye

7

TROUT FAMILY Salmonidae

Salmonids are divided into 5 groups: trouts, including the Atlantic salmon (*Salmo*); char (*Salvelinus*); Pacific salmon (*Oncorhynchus*); whitefishes (*Coregonus, Stenodus, Prosopium*); and grayling (*Thymallus*). All salmonids have an adipose fin and an axillary process at the base of each pelvic fin. The family is divided into 3 subfamilies: (1) the Salmoninae subfamily encompassing the black-spotted trouts having 12 or less anal rays, the char with pale or red spots and 12 or less anal rays, the Pacific salmon with black spots present or absent and 13 or more anal rays; (2) the Coregoninae subfamily encompassing the whitefishes, ciscoes, and inconnus, which are distinguished by 1−2 flaps on the septum dividing the nostrils; and (3) the Thymallinae subfamily, which is limited in North America to a single species, the American grayling, easily recognized by its large saillike dorsal fin. The salmonids are described below in the 5-group order.

APACHE TROUT *Salmo apache*   Also called Arizona trout, this species has in years past been confused with the Gila trout. In most characters the Gila and Apache trouts resemble the cutthroat species more than the rainbow, but in the absence of basibranchial (hyoid) teeth they are similar to rainbows. Both the Apache and Gila are chunky, deep-bodied fishes with long heads and jaws, long fins with the origin of the dorsal slightly more posterior than half the standard length. The obvious distinction between the two, however, is the pres-

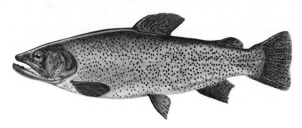

Apache Trout

ence of smaller, more profuse spots on the Gila trout, especially on the dorsal and caudal fins.

In the 1960s the Apache trout's range had been reduced to only a few streams on the Fort Apache Indian Reservation in the White Mountains of Arizona. To save the trout from extinction the Arizona Game and Fish Department implemented an artificial propagation program from a brood stock of a pure-strain wild population. The recovery program has been very successful, with some 20,000 fish released in public waters during 1971.

8

ATLANTIC SALMON *Salmo salar* This best-known member of the Salmonidae is found in the northern part of the Atlantic Ocean. Along North American shores it occurs from Greenland to Cape Cod. In Europe it is found from Russia to Portugal. The species is migratory for the most part, but some lakes in Maine, southeastern Canada, and Argentina contain resident races known as Sebago salmon, ouananiche, or landlocked salmon. Unlike the Pacific salmon, the Atlantic salmon can spawn more than once.

The body of the Atlantic salmon is 5 times as long as it is deep. There are 8–10 rays in the anal fin. The dentaries become large and sharp in the spawning season, and the lower jaw of the male develops a cartilaginous protuberance in the form of a hook, known as a kype. Teeth are also present on the vomer. The scales are large, and there are 120–130 on the lateral line. The body color is variable. Stream-dwelling fish are brownish-olive; the young have red spots on the sides, 2 (rarely 3) dark spots on the operculum, and parr marks, and look very similar to the young brown trout. Sea-run fish are blue-black dorsally and bright silver on the sides. During the long journey to the spawning ground, the silvery flanks of the male become a dirty red and those of the female black. Although weights to 100 pounds have

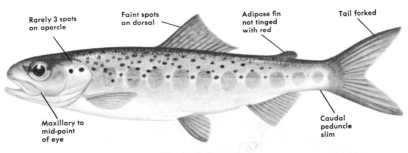

Rarely 3 spots on opercle

Faint spots on dorsal

Adipose fin not tinged with red

Tail forked

Maxillary to mid-point of eye

Caudal peduncle slim

Atlantic Salmon Parr

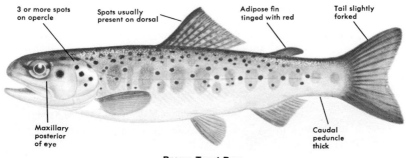

3 or more spots on opercle

Spots usually present on dorsal

Adipose fin tinged with red

Tail slightly forked

Maxillary posterior of eye

Caudal peduncle thick

Brown Trout Parr

9

been reported, the average is probably closer to 12 pounds. Many attempts have been made to transplant Atlantic salmon to the Pacific, but without success. Fish of sea-run origin have been stocked in Oregon lakes with no outlet to the sea, and this landlocked form does provide a token fishery in the western United States.

The salmon spawns in the fall in the upper reaches of streams, and the young remain in freshwater from 1 to 4 or 5 years, migrating then to sea and reaching maturity at 3–5 years of age or more. They may spawn two or three times, but usually less than 10 percent of adults entering freshwater have spawned before. The nest, or redd, is dug by the female in gravel that has been carefully selected. Powerful strokes of the tail when she is on her side move the gravel by means of the resulting hydraulic action of water currents, and a pocket is formed. After the eggs are deposited in the pocket and fertilized, the female covers them and in doing so may instantly cut another depression and deposit eggs in it also. Each spawning act is accompanied by the male lying at her side, who fertilizes the ova with a cloud of milt. Sometimes a redd is several yards in length and as much as 18 inches deep—depending on the size of the female. Parr may also assist in fertilization by lying in close proximity to the redd and releasing milt at the same time as the adult male. The periods of rest between several ovipositions vary considerably, as does the number of ovipositions.

Wherever their river of origin, the parrs disguise their first fragile years under silvery scales and start off to the ocean when 5–6 inches in length. They are now called smolts. The age at which smolts migrate depends on how fast they have grown; some begin their jour-

Atlantic Salmon, 28-pound Male

Atlantic Salmon, Male, Head Showing Kype

ney at 3 years, but the largest 2-year-olds migrate also; still others, the smallest of their year group, remain in freshwater until they are 4 years old. With this apparent attempt at a somewhat uniform beginning, one would expect Atlantic salmon to reach a common weight before returning to their rivers. But eventual size may be a hereditary trait, and geographically the fish divide themselves into 2–4 different age classes that may return at independent seasons. The smallest of these is the grilse, which is ordinarily 3–5 years old. Grilse live through just 1 winter in the ocean, during which time they grow from the 6-inch smolt size to 4 pounds or more (this includes prewinter and postwinter growth). Most rivers have grilse runs, but some regions, like the east coast of the Province of Newfoundland, are dominated by grilse, while other regions have runs of both grilse and older salmon. Older salmon, having passed 2 winters at sea, return as small adults 4–5 years in age, weighing 9–12 pounds. The third group consists of large adult fish 5 and 6 years old, with 3 winters of ocean feeding, weighing 18–30 pounds. The fourth and least common group consists of very large fish that have passed 4, 5, or even 6 winters in the ocean and weigh 35–45 pounds. In this same age class and endemic to certain areas are really big salmon weighing 50–70 pounds. These trophy fish are more common in Europe and appear most often in the rivers of Norway. The world's record rod-caught Atlantic salmon, a Norwegian fish, weighed $79^1/_2$ pounds.

With rare exceptions, all salmon return to their parent rivers for spawning. To what extent they travel in the ocean or what determines the pattern of their marine existence is not known. There is ample evidence that salmon from both sides of the Atlantic share a common feeding ground near Greenland.

The Atlantic salmon is a highly prized game- and foodfish.

BROWN TROUT *Salmo trutta* This is the native trout of Europe, found in streams from the Mediterranean basin to the Black Sea and north to Arctic Norway and Siberia. Widely introduced to North America beginning in 1883, and subsequently to New Zealand, parts of Asia, South America, and Africa, the brown trout has become a favorite of fly-fishermen the world over. The species is less tolerant of warmwater than the rainbow trout, but, because it persists in streams more than native species, where the habitat is favorable it enjoys a reputation for being able to resist environmental change.

The body of the brown trout is usually $4^1/_2$–5 times as long as it is deep. All fins are softrayed; the dorsal has 10–13 rays; the anal fin has 9–10 rays. This trout is generally a golden-brown in color with large brown or black spots on its sides, back, and dorsal fin. These spots are usually surrounded by faint halos of a lighter shade than the body. A lesser number of red or orange spots is generally evident along the lateral surface; the dorsal and adipose fins are often fringed or spotted

Brown Trout, 4½-pound Female, Lake Form

Brown Trout, 6½-pound Male

with bright orange or red. The belly color is dusky-yellow, but may be creamy-white in small stream-born trout. The tail, which is slightly forked in young fish, is more nearly square in old trout; it is yellowish-brown and may be indistinctly spotted near its borders. The pectoral, ventral, and anal fins are usually yellowish-brown and without markings. The vomerine teeth are the most useful character for distinguishing the brown trout from the landlocked salmon, the only other salmonid with which it might be confused in United States waters; in the brown trout these teeth are well developed in the form of a double zigzag row on the vomer. The vomerine teeth of the salmon are poorly developed and exist as a single row; the shaft may even be without teeth, as these are deciduous in a salmon and easily broken off. Brown trout found in large lakes (notably in the Great Lakes, New York, New Hampshire, and Maine) as well as sea-run populations, may otherwise resemble landlocked salmon in that they become very silvery in color and are spotted with black.

The brown trout is slightly less tolerant of warmwater (with lethal limits at 84°–86° F) than the rainbow. However, there are frequent exceptions to the rule for both species, depending on the strain of fish and the rate of temperature change. By comparison, sensitivity to heat is more marked in the brook trout and other chars, with the lethal limits normally given at 77° F. Their preferred temperature range is 54.3°–63.6° F. Brown trout can survive a considerable pH range from 4.5 to 9.8, but in acid or moderately acid waters the fish tend to be quite small; those in highly alkaline water (pH 8.2 or more) display the best growth. This species has been known to reach a weight of 40 pounds, although fish over 10 pounds are considered exceptional in most waters. The brown trout caught in most United States streams weighs less than 1 pound; however, some of the better eastern and western fisheries produce a substantially higher average than this to the skilled angler.

The brown trout feeds on both aquatic and terrestrial insects. It also eats mollusks, crayfishes, and other fishes. Large trout occasionally feed on frogs, birds, and on mice and other small mammals; however, these food forms are not part of its ordinary diet. The brown trout forages freely on the surface when mayflies, caddisflies, and stoneflies are emerging and thus becomes a significant quarry of the fly-fisherman. It is very active at night, and some of the largest brown trout are caught after dark, particularly in the summer months.

CUTTHROAT TROUT *Salmo clarki* There are many subspecies or races of this species, and the various names indicate the areas in which they are found. Endemic to the West, it is the so-called native trout, an appellation also used for the brook trout in eastern states. The cutthroat is distributed on the coast from Prince William Sound, Alaska, to northern California and inland throughout the western United States and Canada, exhibiting varied habits and appearance.

13

Cutthroat Trout, 16-inch Male, Yellowstone River Form

Cutthroat Trout, 15-inch Male, Snake River Form

The body of the cutthroat is usually 5 times as long as it is deep. The tail is slightly forked. All fins are softrayed; the anal fin has 8–12 rays and there are 9–12 branchiostegals supporting the gill membranes. The red markings that give this trout its common name are visible outside and below the lower jaw. Teeth are located at the base of the tongue. Considerable color variation occurs. The adult inland forms may have cadmium coloring along the sides and belly, as in the Piute trout. The Yellowstone cutthroat is a yellowish-green with red on the sides of the head and body and sparse but large dark spots most numerous on the posterior portion of the body. The Snake River cutthroat is more heavily spotted, and this black pigmentation is much smaller. These two forms do not exist in a pure state in many habitats, as there has been a great deal of intermingling. The cutthroat trout hybridizes with the rainbow trout, and in many streams in Wyoming and Montana the cutthroat-rainbow cross is very common. Although the rainbow characteristics remain dominant (including the reddish lateral band), the hybrid is easily recognized by the same bright orange or vivid red "cut" marks under the dentary bone. The cutthroat trout also hybridizes with the golden trout, and in areas where these two species are present, such as the high-altitude lakes of the Jim Bridger Wilderness in Wyoming, these unusually colored crosses occur. The anadromous and nonmigratory coastal subspecies of the cutthroat trout are usually greenish-blue with numerous heavy black spots on the head, body, tail, dorsal fin, and anal fin, as well as with a silvery sheen on the sides.

Cutthroat trout are found in rivers and lakes, and the anadromous form enters saltwater. In most instances, the species does not compete well with other fish, and this factor, coupled with its tendency to hybridize and its inability to withstand heavy fishing pressure, has seriously depleted many populations. A few attempts have been made to introduce cutthroat trout to eastern waters, but without success.

All subspecies exhibit the redd-forming habits of most of the Salmonidae, but they spawn in the winter and spring, the majority of the coastal forms in February and March, and those inland in April and May. Yellowstone cutthroat trout generally spawn at 4 years of age but usually only in alternate years, rarely every year. The life span of this form is about 6 years and possibly 9 years.

The anadromous fish go to sea as young in the second or third year and return after 1–2 years in saltwater. They can spawn repeatedly, and one tagged 10-year-old was caught by an angler in Sand Creek on the Oregon coast.

Although the cutthroat trout has been recorded to a weight of 41 pounds, taken from Pyramid Lake, the inland form seldom exceeds 5 pounds. The coastal subspecies has been recorded to 17 pounds, but 4 pounds is considered large for a sea-run fish.

Numerous subspecies of cutthroat trout are found from the Rocky Mountains west to the Pacific coast into tidewater, and from northern California to Alaska. Each form, with few exceptions, seems to maintain itself best in its natural habitat. These subspecies probably evolved separately by isolation from the parent type.

Some of the recognized subspecies of cutthroat trout are:

Colorado cutthroat	*Salmo c. pleuriticus*
Lahontan cutthroat	*Salmo c. henshawi*
Piute cutthroat	*Salmo c. seleniris*
Rio Grande cutthroat	*Salmo c. virginalis*
Utah cutthroat	*Salmo c. utah*
Yellowstone cutthroat	*Salmo c. lewisi*

Cutthroat trout feed extensively on freshwater shrimps (*Gammarus*) and insect larvae. In a study made on Henrys Lake in Idaho, which is unusually productive though fairly typical of native cutthroat waters, it was found that shrimps, damselfly nymphs, and midges composed 90 percent by number of the food utilized by the trout.

While in saltwater cutthroats feed on sand lances, shrimps, and various fishes in relatively shallow areas. There, the trout can be caught by trolling or casting small silver spoons close to rocky shores, particularly where there is some dropoff.

GILA TROUT *Salmo gilae* This unique member of the Salmonidae was first described in 1950. Earlier systematists and casual observers had considered it to be a cutthroat trout because of its existence in the headwaters of the Gila River in New Mexico and Arizona and owing to its general appearance. A closer look discloses attributes that set it apart as unique. It has an extremely long adipose fin; the head and upper jaws are long; there is a high number of scales (usually about 32 above the lateral line); the distance from tip of snout to occiput is

Gila Trout

great. The Gila trout is dark olive-green along the back, shading to a golden-yellow belly. This yellow-gold color is always found in the pure strains and frequently in hybrid strains. It has small black spots. Gila trout seldom reach a length of more than 8 inches, although rare fish run to 12 inches.

The Gila trout is of no significance as a gamefish. Its tendency to hybridize with the rainbow trout has reduced the range of the pure strain to a very limited area. Originally the trout was endemic to the Gila River drainage. Subsequently a pure strain was found in Ord Creek of the upper White River drainage. Some of these Gila trout were transferred to Grant Creek in the Graham Mountains, where they should not be subject to hybridization. A pure strain also exists in Spruce, Diamond, and McKenna creeks in New Mexico. Plans call for stocking them in isolated streams of both states in order to perpetuate the species. At present, the Gila trout is completely protected and not available to angling.

GOLDEN TROUT *Salmo aguabonita*   The most beautiful of the Salmonidae is the golden trout. Those in streams are most brilliantly colored. The species has cadmium along the belly, a carmine stripe along the middle of each side, yellow on the lower sides, rosy opercles, about 10 parr marks, an orange-tipped dorsal fin, white-tipped anal and ventral fins, spotted caudal, adipose, and dorsal fins. Its head and body are spotted to the lateral line; the caudal peduncle is usually wholly spotted. In lakes, older fish develop a carmine stripe along the lateral line and a brassy overall color except for olive on the back. When the species is reared at low altitudes, it tends to assume a steely-blue appearance, losing the brilliant coloring.

Golden Trout, 10-inch Male

Originally the fish was found only in headwaters of the Kern River in California. Sustaining populations are to be found in Wyoming, Idaho, and Washington, at least. Its weight is to about 11 pounds, but in streams a weight of 1 pound is usually maximal.

Goldens differ from the common species of trouts in being limited to high-altitude lakes and streams, and consequently the techniques of fishing for them are more specialized. In the coldwaters of the Sierra Nevada, large food forms are scarce or absent. Their natural forage consists principally of small insects, notably caddisflies and midges. Small crustaceans are also of varying importance, as are terrestrial insects.

LANDLOCKED SALMON *Salmo salar*   This is a superior freshwater gamefish, highly prized by United States anglers. The anadromous Atlantic salmon is considered by ichthyologists to be structurally the

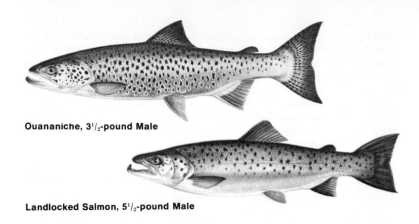

Ouananiche, 3$^1/_2$-pound Male

Landlocked Salmon, 5$^1/_2$-pound Male

same fish with essentially identical taxonomic characteristics. Nevertheless, populations vary in appearance according to environment, and the methods of fishing are dissimilar. A significant landlocked-salmon fishery exists in Maine, where the species is considered the state's most important gamefish.

Four different river systems contained the original Maine populations—the St. Croix drainage in Washington County, Union River drainage in Hancock County, Piscataquis River subdrainage of the Penobscot in Penobscot County, and the Presumpscot River drainage in Cumberland County. Sebago Lake is located in the last-named county. The world's record rod-and-reel catch of 22$^1/_2$ pounds was taken from this lake in 1907. That same year, a specimen of 36 pounds was reportedly netted by some hatchery personnel seining salmon to strip. Occasional landlocks of 9–10 pounds are caught presently in such Maine waters as the West Branch of the Penobscot, Long Lake in Aroostook County, and East Grand Lake in Washington-Aroostook counties. However, the average in Maine has been closer to 2 pounds in recent years.

Landlocked salmon have been widely introduced in other lakes in Maine. New Hampshire has limited populations, and New York has established the fish in a few large lakes.

In the Maritime Provinces of Canada the landlocked salmon is called ouananiche. It was formerly recognized on the subspecific level, *Salmo s. ouananiche*, as was the landlocked salmon of Maine, *Salmo s. sebago*. However, there is no evidence to support a distinction between these forms except their nonmigratory behavior. The ouananiche is highly regarded as a sport fish and in general appearance differs in shape and color from an Atlantic salmon. The fins of the ouananiche are larger in relation to total length and girth. The fish is more elongate and generally darker in color, and its body is heavily covered with black or dark brown spots or crosses. Ouananiche are found in Quebec, Labrador, and Newfoundland.

Landlocked-salmon fry feed on small aquatic insects and other invertebrates, and the young (parrs) stay in the river or stream where they are hatched for 1–2 years before migrating into a lake. Their diet then becomes largely foragefishes (in Maine), such as smelts, young alewives, sticklebacks, yellow perch, and minnows, and occasionally other fishes.

MEXICAN GOLDEN TROUT *Salmo chrystogaster* This trout was first described by Needham and Gard in 1959 and named in 1964. The name *chrystogaster* is derived from the Greek meaning "golden belly." A striking characteristic of this species when alive is the bright orange color below the jaw and on the belly. The Mexican golden trout has the smallest number of vertebrae and pyloric caeca found in any North American member of the genus *Salmo*.

The known range of *S. chrystogaster* is an area 35 by 45 miles in the Fuerte, Sinaloa, and Culiacán river systems in southwestern Chihuahua and northwestern Durango, Mexico.

Descriptive characters of the Needham and Gard holotype are number of vertebrae, 57; scales in lateral line, 108; scales above lateral line, 21; scales 2 rows above lateral line (lateral series), 147; scales below lateral line, 18; branchiostegal rays, 9 (both sides); gillrakers, 17; pyloric caeca, 19; pectoral rays, 14; dorsal rays, 10; pelvic rays, 9; anal rays, 10; caudal rays, 19; basibranchials smooth.

RAINBOW TROUT *Salmo gairdneri* This native American trout is high on the list of gamefishes of the world. Its natural range is from the mountains of northern Mexico to the Aleutian Islands and perhaps into the eastern USSR as the Kamchatka trout.

Nonmigratory rainbows show extreme variation in outward appearance. Those in clear lakes lack spots and are blue or green on the back, silver on the sides grading to whitish on the belly when immature. Stream dwellers tend to be heavily spotted on the body, upper fins, and tail. Mature fish become darker and have a red lateral band. The rainbow has no hyoid teeth; this absence of teeth on the back of its tongue is the most reliable character distinguishing the rainbow from the cutthroat trout. The anal fin has no more than 12 rays; this distinguishes the rainbow from the Pacific salmon (13 or more). The maximum weight for rainbow trout exceeds 50 pounds; a 52½-pound fish was netted in Jewel Lake, British Columbia, during spawn-taking operations. However, average weights vary greatly according to locale.

The temperature tolerance of rainbow trout is from below 32°F to over 80°F, with the preferred level below 70°F. Survival at lethal temperatures in the mid-80s depends on the size of the fish, the rate of change, and how well the trout are acclimatized. In lakes rainbows may be found near the surface if the temperature is below 70°F, but as the upper layer warms they tend to seek a level between 56.5°F and 60°F. They will also tolerate a considerable pH range: 5.8–9.5, or from acid to highly alkaline water.

Rainbow Trout, 2-pound Male

Rainbow Trout, 6¹/₂-pound Female

The life span of the rainbow is 7–11 years depending on the race and locality. Among interior stocks the rainbows of Eagle Lake, California, a recognized subspecies (*Salmo g. aquilarum*), are the longest-lived, attaining at least 11 years. Although 7 years is considered maximum for the anadromous form, 8- and 9-year-olds have been recorded. A 9-year-old female steelhead with newly developing eggs was gillnetted in the eastern North Pacific (1969); it probably would have survived to its tenth year; scale studies indicated that it had a freshwater age of 3 years and an ocean age of 2 years before the first of 4 successive spawnings, plus an additional summer growth.

Inland populations of rainbow trout spawn from January to June in North America and even later (early August) in some coldwater lakes at high elevation. By selective reproduction in hatcheries strains have been isolated that can breed at all months of the year.

Races of nonmigratory rainbows are legion; they bear such names as Kamloops, Nelson trout, red-band, Eagle Lake, Kern River, Shasta, San Gorgonio, and Royal Silver. Nevertheless, various strains of trout, whether wild or domesticated, have potential management implications in terms of catchability, life span, and adaptability to specialized environments.

Rainbow trout readily hybridize with both the golden and cutthroat trouts. The rainbow × golden is perhaps more common in Wyoming, where the golden was introduced in high-altitude lakes that already held rainbow, than in the isolated alpine waters of California, where the golden existed without other trout species. However, hybrids occur in both states. These resemble highly colored rainbows with a brilliant orange lateral blotch and a similar bright color along the ventral surface. The largest golden cross reported is a 9-pound fish from Washakie Lake, Wyoming. The so-called golden trout originally stocked by West Virginia, which has gained some distribution in the eastern United States, is neither a true golden trout nor a hybrid; despite its coloration it is simply a mutation of the rainbow isolated by selective breeding.

The migratory rainbow, whether anadromous or lake type, is known as a steelhead. The sea-run fish resembles the lake-dwelling form in color as it comes from the sea, but as it proceeds up the rivers and nears spawning time it becomes dark and spotted; the red band appears; and it resembles the mature nonmigratory form, though its body is generally slimmer. The largest steelhead on record weighed 42 pounds and was taken at Bell Island, Alaska. Owing to the wide range of habitat over a large area in Pacific coastal streams, it is probable that the steelhead evolved from early geological times into season-differentiated spawning populations in order to occupy viable breeding areas as they became available after each succeeding glaciation or volcanic action.

The ocean migrations and habits of the steelhead are becoming better known because of the attention focused on the Japanese fisheries in the North Pacific Ocean. Marked steelhead have been released from Oregon, tagged in the Gulf of Alaska, and again taken in Oregon at the place of original release. There have been recoveries of tagged or marked steelhead to indicate that the limit of western migration in the ocean for the majority of fish may be somewhat west of 175°W. A steelhead tagged by a Japanese research vessel at 177°W south of Kiska Island in the Aleutians in September 1970 was recaptured by an angler in the Wynoochee River of Washington in March 1971. The fish had returned 2,200 nautical miles to its parent stream. However, Japanese fishery workers report steelhead as far west as 168°E. The Japanese have not been fishing for salmonids in the Pacific Ocean east of 175°W longitude by international agreement (1953) but continue to catch some steelhead. No trout have been taken below latitude 48°N.

ARCTIC CHAR *Salvelinus alpinus* This salmonid is found in the coldwaters of the northern hemisphere. Anadromous and landlocked char are common to parts of northern Canada, Baffin Island, Greenland, Iceland, northern Norway, northern Siberia, and Alaska. In addition, the landlocked form occurs south of this range in the lakes of southern Norway, Sweden, Finland, England, Ireland, Scotland, west-central Europe, and the USSR.

This char is similar to the brook trout in appearance, but without the wormlike markings (vermiculations) on its back. The dorsal surface is usually olive-green or blue or sometimes brown; the sides may be pale or bright red or orange. The fish is not heavily spotted like a trout and sometimes may not be spotted at all, but when present the spots are large, cream, pale pink, or orange markings. Sea-run chars are almost entirely silver when they first arrive in the river. The Arctic char has a slightly forked tail and a more rounded body than the brook trout, but its pectoral, pelvic, and anal fins often have the same cream-trimmed leading edges and bright carmine color as do those of the adult male squaretail. The Arctic char usually weighs 2–8 pounds; however, there are dwarf landlocked and nonmigratory populations as well as giants among the sea-run fish, and the maximum size is over 25 pounds.

To separate the Arctic char from a brook trout, the key points in field identification are:

1. Absence of vermiculations on the back. Faint markings may be suggested on a char, but they are not developed.
2. Absence of any markings on the dorsal fin. Brook trout have irregular dark or blackish markings.
3. Absence of red spots surrounded by bluish halos. Char often have red spots, but lack the blue halos.
4. Absence of any markings on the caudal fin. Nearly all brook trout have irregular black markings or spotting on the tail.

Arctic Char.
18-pound Male in Breeding Colors

Arctic Char, 6½-pound Sea-run Male

The Arctic char is one of a number of salmonids that apparently evolved from a common ancestor in the Pleistocene age, when the Pacific Ocean was separated from the Arctic Ocean by a land bridge. It has been speculated that the bridge isolated a population of char to the south, which we know today as the Dolly Varden, and another population to the north, which followed a circumpolar path across Asia, Europe, and North America and which became the Arctic char. In many waters the Dolly Varden is so similar to the char that it is difficult to separate them. Their range overlaps in Alaska, but the Dolly Varden or bull trout is distributed as far south as northern California and inland to Idaho and Montana.

BLUEBACK TROUT *Salvelinus alpinus* The blueback trout is very similar to the Sunapee trout and is presently considered a landlocked population of Arctic char. Blueback trout were once common in the Rangely Lakes of Maine, but they became extinct here in the early 1900s. Their natural distribution is limited to less than a dozen ponds in Maine.

Blueback Trout

Despite its present taxonomic status, the blueback trout (formerly *S. oquassa*) has very specific habitat and food requirements that are distinct from those of the ordinary Arctic char and its natural associate, the brook trout. This char occupies an ecological niche not utilized by the brook trout. In Maine lakes the upper limit of the blueback's depth distribution is correlated with the coldwaters of the hypolimnion, where it feeds on benthic organisms, mainly plankton. It is a longer-lived fish than the brook trout in Maine, attaining at least 6 years. Owing to its relatively small size (6–12 inches) and limited distribution, the blueback has had little angling value. While attempting to extend their range in recent years, bluebacks to a surprising 4 pounds in weight (Basin Pond) have been caught, implying that they grow to a larger size outside their natural range, and indicating a need for more intensive study.

BROOK TROUT *Salvelinus fontinalis* This beautiful gamefish is distinguished by red spots with blue aureoles on the sides, dark wavy lines (vermiculations) on the back and dorsal fin, pink or reddish lower fins edged with white on the leading edge, and teeth on the head of the vomer. Males at spawning time often have orange on the belly and black on the lower sides. In its native range there are brilliantly colored races with cadmium-colored sides and belly. The body is about 5 times as long as it is deep. The caudal fin is only slightly forked or square; thus the name squaretail is often applied. All fins are softrayed; the dorsal has 10 rays; the anal fin 9 rays. Teeth are well developed on the maxillary, premaxillary, and vomerine bones. Although the record weight of the brook trout is $14^1/_2$ pounds, and the length $31^1/_2$ inches, fish of over 5 pounds may be considered exceptional.

The brook trout is native to northeastern North America from Georgia to the Arctic Circle. It has been introduced to the remainder of the United States, Canada, South America, and Europe where suited to the habitat.

In the eastern United States the brook trout has figured prominently in the development of fly-fishing, as it was the species sought before the introduction of the brown trout in the 1880s. Despite its dwindling habitat, the native is still regarded as the principal gamefish in many parts of New England, and management programs are designed to favor it over other trouts.

Brook trout spawn from September in the northernmost part of their range until early December in the southernmost regions. Egg production is determined largely by size; the number of eggs may vary from 100 in a 6-inch female to 1,200 in a 14-inch fish. As is true of salmon, this char constructs a redd in gravel in the fall, but its stream-spawning habitat requirements are more specific in that it prefers cold, spring-fed water and will enter very small brooks. In lakes, the requirements are not as rigid, for it will spawn over bark, twigs, or other material along shores or in deeper water. Incubation depends on water temperature: at 35°F, hatching requires 144 days; at 55°F, 35 days. These are mean incubating periods, as stream temperatures are rarely constant and all the eggs do not hatch at once, but sometimes continue hatching over a period of a week. Egg loss is greater at temperatures below 39°F than in the upper range (below 53°F).

Large brook trout occur in the same regions where they existed millions of years ago—with very few exceptions. Unlike the more cosmopolitan brown trout and rainbow trout, which have thrived in many parts of the world through man's distribution, the squaretail is not as adaptable. Good brook-trout water has definite chemical and physical properties, and perhaps a few characteristics with respect to size, associated species, and food supply. It is also remote.

In the eastern United States, Maine still provides some relatively inaccessible brook-trout fishing on such streams as the Allagash, Spencer, Kennebago, Moose, and upper Kennebec rivers. Official records kept at the turn of the century indicate that quite a few squaretails approaching world-record size (9–11 pounds) were caught in the Rangeley Lakes and Moosehead, but today, 2- or 3-pound trout are considered exceptional, and a 5-pounder is unusual. Elsewhere in

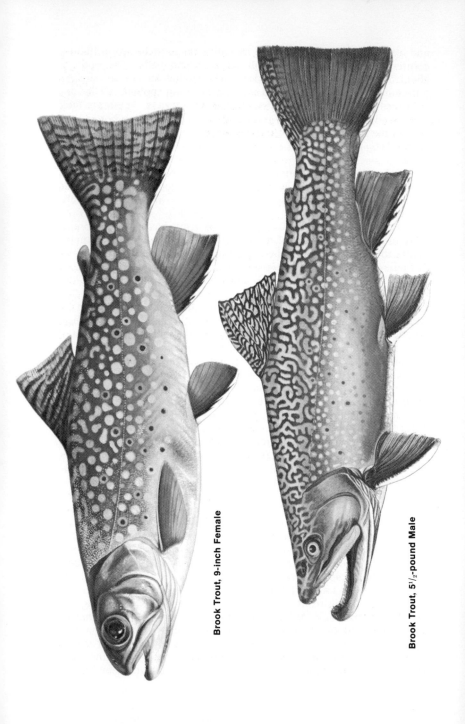

Brook Trout, 9-inch Female

Brook Trout, 5½-pound Male

the northeastern United States, brook trout become progressively smaller as one goes south; the southernmost part of the range is in the highland streams of north Georgia, where trout still exist in naturally reproducing populations. A large native here, as well as in the midwestern United States, would be a 2-pounder. The typical fishery consists of small spring-fed stream and headwater populations in the 7- to 10-inch class. There are some outstanding brook-trout fisheries in the Rocky Mountain region, but this is the stronghold of the native rainbow and cutthroat. Montana, Idaho, and Wyoming produce a 5- or 6-pound squaretail now and then, but for every such fish caught here, a score are caught in the Hudson-Ungava Bay region and in Labrador.

Several factors conspire against the widespread success of brook-trout populations. The fish require coldwater; the lethal limit is about 77°F, which is colder than the lethal limit for most other trouts, although acclimatized fish can survive for short periods at temperatures in the low 80s. However, they are never really abundant in habitats where water temperatures exceed 68°F for any prolonged period. Their preferred temperature range is 57.2°–60.8°F. In rivers having a mixed-trout population, the brookie is most often found in the headwater section and around cold tributary streams. Spring seepage in a comparatively small area is often enough to hold a number of brook trout in otherwise warm streams where brown and rainbow dominate. It has been observed that wild strains survive better at low temperatures (streams with ice cover during winter) than domestic stocks. They can also become acclimated to low oxygen concentrations, and the fingerlings at least are better adapted in this respect than the brown or rainbow. Their tolerance to both acid and alkaline waters is also greater, with a pH range of 4.0–9.8. The lumber industry, land development, poor farming practices, road building, and pollution contributed greatly to the elimination of many native trout habitats early in United States history.

Brook trout in some of the more productive Canadian watersheds, such as the Assinicca strain, are long-lived populations (up to 10 years). Elsewhere, however, 4-year-old brook trout are uncommon.

The biggest brook trout today occur in Labrador, northern Quebec, and northern Manitoba. Sea-run populations, while often larger in average size than freshwater residents, seldom attain the heavy weights of apparently nonmigratory fish. Brown trout and rainbows achieve remarkable growth in saltwater, but the sea-run brookie or salter seldom exceeds 4 pounds.

DOLLY VARDEN *Salvelinus malma*   This western char exhibits as much color variation as the degree to which its habitat varies. In saltwater it is silvery; in cold headwater mountain streams it tends to have bright orange or red spots on the sides; in lakes the spotting is often yellow and appears only on the back. Faint vermiculations on the back occur in the northern part of its range. The ventral and anal fins are whitish on the anterior border. The fish has small scales and a short vomer. Body conformation varies from slimness in residents of cold mountain streams to very fat in lake-dwelling fish whose diet is other fishes, particularly the kokanee. Weights to 32 pounds have been recorded.

The Dolly Varden is found from northern California to Alaska and around the northern Pacific to Japan and Korea. It also occurs inland in Idaho, Montana, Utah, and Nevada. Although it inhabits both fresh- and saltwater, the Dolly Varden enters marine environments only in the northern part of its range.

Named after a character (Miss Dolly Varden) in Charles Dickens's *Barnaby Rudge,* because of her pink-spotted dress, the species is sometimes confused with a similar appearing Arctic char. In the field the two can be distinguished as follows: If the spots are smaller than the iris of the eye the fish is a Dolly Varden; if the spots are larger it is an Arctic char.

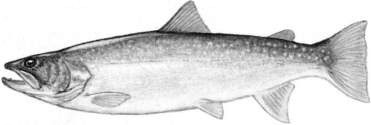

Dolly Varden

Slow-growing but long-lived (to more than 18 years), the Dolly Varden usually matures at age 6. A fall spawner, it enters streams from September to November. Like other Salmonidae, the female digs a redd in the gravel and deposits 800–3,000 eggs, depending on her body size. The eggs hatch in 30–90 days. The fry do not swim up immediately, but wiggle deeper into the gravel, where they remain for an additional 60–120 days. Young Dolly Vardens are very inactive for the first 4 years of life, after which the first seaward migration takes place if a marine environment is part of its habitat. This begins a general pattern of migrating to saltwater in the spring and returning to freshwater in the fall. The fish usually winters in lakes.

The young fish feed largely on insects, but older fish are more piscivorous.

LAKE TROUT *Salvelinus namaycush*   The lake trout, also called togue (eastern United States), mackinaw (western United States), and gray trout (Canada), is a large char. It almost always inhabits deep, clear lakes, although stream-dwelling populations sometimes occur where the rivers are connected to lakes; the latter situation is most

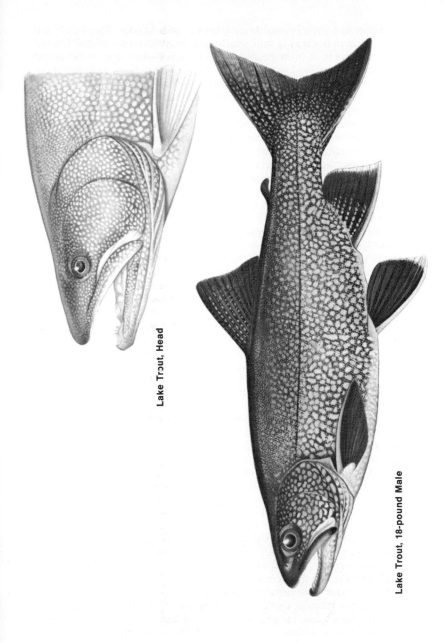

Lake Trout, Head

Lake Trout, 18-pound Male

common in Labrador, northern Quebec, and Alaska. The fish is distributed across Canada and southward in coldwaters of the United States, notably in New England, the Finger Lakes region, the Great Lakes, and scattered western lakes, where it has been introduced. In the southern portion of its range the lake trout is largely restricted to waters that exhibit thermal stratification and have an adequate supply of oxygen in their deeper areas.

The lake trout is distinguished by a raised tooth crest on the head of the vomer; the tail is strongly forked (unlike the tail of the splake hybrid, which is more nearly square). There is considerable variation in color, but the body is generally blue-gray or bronze-green, with pale spots on sides and back and on the dorsal, adipose, and caudal fins. There are 11 rays in the anal fin. The flesh color varies from almost white to red. Lake trout are known to reach a weight over 100 pounds, but they seldom exceed 40 pounds in the sport fishery.

The siscowet, a deep-bodied lake trout found in the Great Lakes region, has been given specific status (1970) as *S. siscowet*. This species, recognized by commercial fishermen as a fat (Lake Superior), is noted for its extremely oily flesh. Siscowets are ordinarily caught at depths of 300–600 feet, or deeper than the lake trout. However, their vertical distribution overlaps, as both are sometimes taken in shallow or deepwater. Presently identified as a race resembling the siscowet in its external appearance is the humper lake trout, known to commercial fishermen as the paperbelly or bank trout. The humper lake trout inhabits isolated offshore reefs (banks) surrounded by deepwater.

Lake trout breed in the fall over gravel or rocky bottoms in depths varying from 100 feet or more in the Great Lakes and Finger Lakes of New York, to shoalwater in more shallow lakes. No nest or redd is built by the female, as is the case with members of the trout group. The area is "swept" clean by the fish before spawning. Spawning time varies widely in the different lakes, occurring from September into December. The act of spawning is attended by groups of one or more females and several males, the eggs being scattered over suitable bottom. The eggs are about $1/5$ inch in diameter and settle among the interstices of rocks. Many are eaten by small lake trout, suckers, bullheads, eels, yellow perch, and other fishes. The incubation period is 166 days at 37°F and 49 days at 50°F. The young fish remain in deepwater. They tend to develop cataracts when held in shallow water in direct sunlight, as under hatchery conditions. The food of the young is made up of insects and crustaceans. Adults feed on fishes such as kokanee, whitefishes, ciscoes, burbot, and sculpins.

During the late fall, winter, and early spring when the water is cold, the lake trout may inhabit shallows, but at other times it lives in deepwater—often at depths of several hundred feet. In the northernmost portions of its range it is not so restricted by temperature, since surface waters remain cold throughout the summer.

Sunapee Trout, 12-inch Female

Sunapee Trout, 12-inch Male

SUNAPEE TROUT *Salvelinus alpinus* The Sunapee trout is very similar to the blueback trout and both are presently considered a landlocked population of Arctic chars by some taxonomists. However, at least one scientist (Dr. V. D. Vladykov, of the Fisheries Research Board of Canada), who has made an extensive investigation of the char group, showed evidence that the Sunapee trout is a distinct species, *S. aureolus*. Thus, its taxonomic position is not clear.

Originally described from Sunapee Lake, New Hampshire, it is also known to have occurred in Big Dan Hole Pond, New Hampshire; Averill Lake, Vermont; and Floods Pond, Maine. It has been unsuccessfully introduced into several other New Hampshire waters. A population of this species was once established in the Third Connecticut Lake, but disappeared when lake trout were introduced. There is an occasional Sunapee trout caught in Cornor Pond and Ossipee Pond, where this species exists in competition with brook trout. It is not known whether the Sunapee trout ever reproduced naturally in either of these ponds. Its range has been extended in Maine in recent years to include Coffee Pond and South Branch Ponds. A pure-strain Sunapee (this fish readily hybridizes with lake trout) of $3^1/_2$ pounds was taken in 1972.

During the summer months in Sunapee Lake, this species resides in depths of 60–100 feet, where the temperature is in the neighborhood of 50°F or less. In the spring it occurs in shallow water along the shores. About mid-October it may be found on a reef near the entrance to Sunapee Harbor, where it spawns. In the spring it may be found in the shallow water presumably feeding on smelts, and during the warmer months it is found in the deepest parts of the lake down to 90–100 feet. Little is known of the winter habitat except that an occasional specimen has been caught by pickerel fishermen, indicating that the trout is to be found in shallow water at that time of year.

ARTIFICIAL TROUT HYBRIDS

Splake The splake gets its name from the *sp* in speckled, the Canadian name for brook trout, and the *lake* from lake trout, indicating that this is a cross between the speckled trout and the lake trout.

The splake differs from other hybrids in that it is a fertile cross and able to produce young. In appearance, the body shape is intermediate between the two species—heavier than the lake trout but slimmer than the brook trout. The body spotting is yellow as in the lake trout, without the red spotting of the brook trout. However, when splake are placed in a natural environment, they develop the deep red ventral colors of the brook trout.

The first recorded cross of the lake trout and brook trout was made in 1878 by Seth Green, a pioneer fish culturist in New York. In 1886, a cross of these species was recorded at a state fish hatchery in Pennsylvania. The initial interest in these hybrids waned until 1946, when Warden J. E. Stenton of British Columbia experimentally planted

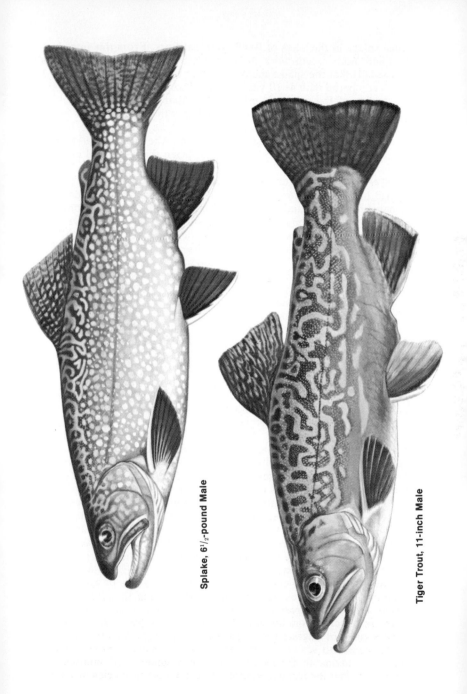

Splake, 6½-pound Male

Tiger Trout, 11-inch Male

some splake in the lakes of Banff National Park. From this introduction and more recent work in New York and Pennsylvania, it was learned (1) that the splake matures sooner than the lake trout (at 2–3 years compared with 4–10 years for the lake trout), (2) that the maximum size of the splake is greater than that of any of the present strains of brook trout, (3) that the initial growth of the splake is faster than that of the lake trout and is intermediate between the parent species, (4) that better hatchability will result when a lake trout female is crossed with a brook trout male than when the reciprocal cross is made.

Tiger Trout Tiger trout is descriptive not only of the color of this hybrid but of its disposition. The tiger trout is a cross between the female brown trout and the male brook trout. The progeny from this cross have tigerlike markings on their sides and are more aggressive than the parent species. Unfortunately, only about 35 percent of the young are able to develop because of a disease which is inherent in the sac fry. Occasionally this cross occurs in nature, notably, in the Gallatin River of Montana, but the fish are unable to reproduce because they are not fertile. Tiger trout have been produced on a small scale in private hatcheries and stocked in various club waters, where they are considered a fine gamefish.

CHINOOK SALMON *Oncorhynchus tshawytscha*   This species is the largest of the Pacific salmon, reaching 126 pounds; however, rarely does it exceed 60 pounds, and the average is about 18. The chinook salmon has irregular black spots on the back, dorsal fin, and both lobes of the caudal fin; black pigment at teeth bases and loose conical teeth characterize mature specimens. Parr marks on the young are large and well defined.

There are several races, distinguishable by the time of river entrance, which varies from January to late fall. The fish are thus termed spring, summer, or fall chinooks. The chinook salmon often travels great distances from the sea, as much as 2,000 miles in the Yukon, and seems to prefer large rivers. It spawns in June to November of each year. In the Columbia the spring race has little tendency to spawn in the main river, entering side streams from near the mouth to the headwaters. The fall fish used to spawn almost entirely in the main river system, but the advent of multiple dams has created slackwater, eliminating most of the available spawning area. The race is rapidly declining in the river system.

The chinook matures at 1 (males only) to 8 years of age. The 1-year-old mature males become ripe before going to saltwater, and some, at least, recover to reach saltwater and return. The young chinooks emerge from the gravel and may go to the sea immediately; others may not migrate for a considerable period. As a rule, the fall chinook goes to sea at 3–4 months of age, while the spring chinook usually remains in freshwater for approximately 18 months. At spawning time the fish is less emaciated than other species of Pacific

Chinook Salmon, 38-pound Female

Chum Salmon, 15-pound Male in Breeding Color

salmon, and especially is this true of the female, which may be plump and clean 500 miles from the sea. The male gets progressively blacker with the passage of time spent in the spawning area; the female may take on a rich brassy color.

While in the ocean the chinook salmon feeds on fishes, crustaceans, and squids. Anchovies, herrings, rockcod, euphausiids, and larval crabs are a dominant part of the diet. Although these salmon will strike lures, they do not feed after they enter freshwater.

The estimated ocean sport catch for Oregon, Washington, and California has reached 659,000 fish and has been close to 20 percent of total chinook landings for the three states in recent years. The chinook is the species most often caught by the sport angler, exceeding in numbers and pounds the catch of any other Pacific salmon.

CHUM SALMON *Oncorhynchus keta* This Pacific salmon is distinguished by lacking large black spots on fins and body, and by having a slender caudal peduncle, black-tinged fins (except dorsal), dark bars or streaks on the body at or near spawning time, 140–160 pyloric caeca, and 19–26 smooth gillrakers on the first arch. The green back and the slender parr marks reaching below the lateral line distinguish the young.

Runs of chums are marked by wide yearly fluctuations in numbers. The fish matures at 4–5 years of age. In part of its range it is represented by two forms, a summer and a fall fish. The summer fish enters the river earlier, reaches maturity earlier, is smaller, and does not travel up the river as far. Entrance to the river takes place from July to December.

Though the species is usually given to spawning in the lower reaches of rivers, it is found near the head of the Yukon River in Teslin Lake, which is approximately 2,000 miles from the sea. It spawns in November and December. The egg of the chum is large, approaching $5/_{16}$ inch. The chum's range is from northern California to Alaska to Korea and Japan. Its food consists largely of fishes and crustaceans. Only rarely is it taken by the sport fisherman. It is third in value of Pacific salmon, exceeded by the sockeye and pink.

The chum reaches a weight of 33 pounds, but is usually taken in sizes from 8 to 18 pounds.

Because chum salmon usually arrive at the mouths of freshwater streams late in the year (November and December), very little angling is done for this species over much of its range. However, this salmon provides good light-tackle fishing in saltwater in the Queen Charlotte Islands (British Columbia) from September until mid-October. The chum is partial to small wobbling spoons and spinners, and especially blades with some red or fluorescent red on them. First introduced in the Barents Sea in 1956 by the USSR, chum salmon have become established in Soviet streams and in northern Norway.

COHO SALMON *Oncorhynchus kisutch*   Also called silver salmon and hooknose, the coho is a popular gamefish of the Pacific Northwest and since 1967 has provided an immense fishery in the Great Lakes. In saltwater the coho is a strong quarry and often leaps when hooked. Of the Pacific salmon this species occurs in anglers' catches in numbers second only to the chinook. A good year has seen 321,000 fish taken in Oregon, Washington, and California, and the catch has exceeded 20 percent of the total landings of salmon in those states.

The coho salmon is generally silvery in color with black spots; the spotting is confined to the back and upper lobe of the caudal fin; a white gum line occurs at the teeth bases; teeth are needlelike and firm; there are 19–25 gillrakers in the first arch. Young fish have longer rays in the leading edge of the anal fin, and the parr marks are elongate. Weights up to 33 pounds 3 ounces (Little Manistee River, Michigan, 1970) have been recorded, but 6–12 pounds is usual at maturity.

The coho can spawn in gravel in the headwaters or near the sea in streams and has no outstanding requirement. It enters the rivers beginning in July and spawns from October to February. Most spawning is completed by the end of December. Most young fish migrate to the sea when a year old, but some may go earlier or wait until the third year. Maturity is usually reached at 3 years of age, but some males and a few females mature at 2 years, and a few come into the river in the fourth year. The coho's food consists of fishes, squids, and crustaceans. Large numbers of crab larvae are eaten.

The coho is found from California to Japan. The species does not travel far from the parent stream. Its chances for survival or even of enhancement in numbers are good because it spawns in largest numbers in the smaller coastal streams that do not appear to be useful in the production of hydroelectric energy or in irrigation. Unlike the chinook salmon, which undertakes long migrations, the coho salmon ranges in a more confined area with populations from one state overlapping into adjacent states. The cohos originating in northern California contribute primarily to the fisheries of that state, but also range as far north as Washington. Populations in Oregon streams range from northern Vancouver Island to northern California. Cohos from British Columbia streams mainly concentrate offshore north of Vancouver Island, but these are mixed with salmon from the rivers of Washington. Cohos from Washington rivers travel as far north as the Queen Charlotte Islands and south to northern California. Populations originating in Alaska are predominantly local in movement and contribute principally to the Alaskan fishery.

PINK SALMON *Oncorhynchus gorbuscha*   This is the smallest of the Pacific salmon, usually 3–5 pounds at maturity, reaching 10 at maximum. The size varies with the abundance of year classes. The

37

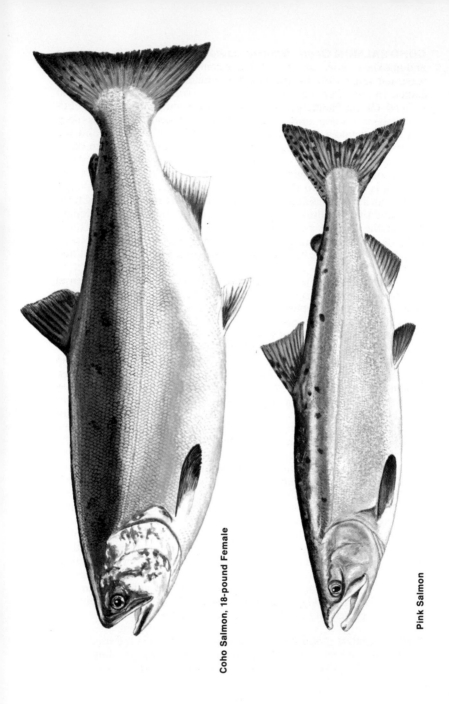

Coho Salmon, 18-pound Female

Pink Salmon

pink salmon is recognized by the large, oval black blotches on the caudal fin, the small scales (170–229 in the row above the lateral line), and the 24–35 rakers in the first gill arch. The young have no parr marks.

The fish reaches maturity in 2 years. At that time the male develops a large hump on the back in addition to a hooked snout. Spawning takes place in September and November in freshwater, usually near the sea, but a few races migrate several hundred miles. The fish enter the river as early as July. The timing of runs varies widely from odd to even years to disproportionate numbers between years or to more or less even numbers between years.

Food at sea consists largely of crustaceans but sometimes includes fishes and squids.

The ocean and Puget Sound sport fisheries take many pinks, but it is the commercial effort that accounts for the greatest harvest.

Although the pink salmon does not provide consistent angling over most of its range, this species is occasionally caught in certain rivers, particularly in British Columbia and the waters around the Queen Charlotte Islands. Planted in the Dennys River, Maine, in 1926 this species was established there for several generations.

SOCKEYE SALMON *Oncorhynchus nerka* This species is the most commercially valuable of the Pacific salmon, but it is second to the pink salmon in landings at United States ports. It is highly prized for its high oil content, excellent flavor, and color of flesh. It ranges from Korea and Japan to California, but enters rivers south of the Columbia River only as a stray. Weight at maturity is 5–7 pounds; maximum weight recorded is $15^{1}/_{2}$ pounds.

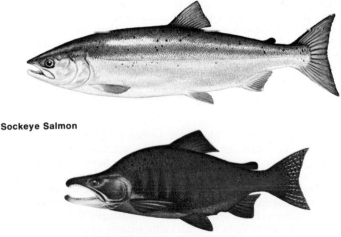

Sockeye Salmon

Sockeye Salmon, Breeding Male

The sockeye's distinguishing characteristics include a small number of gillrakers and minute spots on the back. Mature males often become bright red on the body, females dirty-olive to light red, darker on sides than the male. The young have parr marks extending to near the lateral line. Sockeye salmon enter rivers, usually those that are fed by lakes, in March to July with some variation in time. A few spawn in streams without lakes. Spawning takes place in lakes or immediately adjacent in inlet or outlet streams from August to December. Most of the adults are 4–6 years old, but some reach 8 years of age. The young spend 1–3 years in lakes, migrating to the ocean in March to May. Some fish enter the sea as fry. Vast numbers of fish utilize a relatively small area in spawning. For example, the optimal number of fish utilizing the outlet of Chilko Lake in British Columbia is 500,000 over a $3^3/_4$-mile reach of the stream, covering 269 acres or roughly 2 square yards per fish.

Food of the sockeye in the ocean consists of euphausiids and other small crustaceans.

KOKANEE *Oncorhynchus nerka* Some sockeye races are nonmigratory and are known as kokanee. Landlocked populations are popular among sportsmen. Kokanee resemble trouts, but can be distinguished from them by having more than 12 rays in the anal fin. The kokanee has a wide range in length at maturity, depending on freshwater food supplies, varying from 4 to 24 inches. Generally, kokanee mature at 8–9 inches, with the record weight about 4 pounds. In Lake Pend Oreille, Idaho, kokanee reach a length of 2–3 inches during the first year, 7–8 inches during the second year, 8–9 inches in the third year, and 10–12 inches in the fourth year. Most of the growth is from July until October, which coincides with the period of zooplankton abundance. There is little growth in winter. In Lake Granby, Colorado, females average $14^1/_2$ inches and males 15 inches. Donner Lake, California, kokanee average $18^1/_2$ inches and an average weight of 2 pounds. In northern British Columbia lakes, the usual size of the kokanee is 8–9 inches; in southern British Columbia the average is 12–15 inches. In Vermont, eggs from the same source produced kokanee up to 21 inches in one lake, while in other lakes they never exceeded 11 inches. Kokanee planted in Maine never exceed 10 inches.

CISCO *Coregonus spp.* There are 11 North American species in this group of lake-inhabiting members of the Salmonidae. The ciscoes are sometimes called gray-back, tullibee, or lake herring because they superficially resemble herrings in outward appearance. They all have large scales, usually less than 120 in the lateral line, and silvery bodies, somewhat darker on the back. The eggs are smaller than those of trouts or salmon; there are no teeth on the tongue in North American species; the snout does not markedly extend over the lower jaw. Ciscoes usually vary in length from 6 to 20 inches, but in some species a weight of 7 pounds has been recorded. All ciscoes are coldwater fishes, occurring from New England through the Great Lakes into Canada.

Little is known of the species ecology of the ciscoes. Some are schooling types with pelagic habits, staying near the surface or swimming to depths of several hundred feet. They move near shore in July and August and spawn over hard bottom in November in depths from shallow water to somewhat over 100 feet. They feed on planktonic crustaceans and bottom-dwelling insects.

The 11 species are as follows:

Arctic cisco	*C. autumnalis*
blackfin cisco	*D. nigripinnis*
bloater	*C. hoyi*
cisco	*C. artedii*
deepwater cisco	*C. johannae*
kiyi	*C. kiyi*
least cisco	*C. sardinella*
longjaw cisco	*C. alpenae*
Nipigon cisco	*C. nipigon*
shortjaw cisco	*C. zenithicus*
shortnose cisco	*C. reighardi*

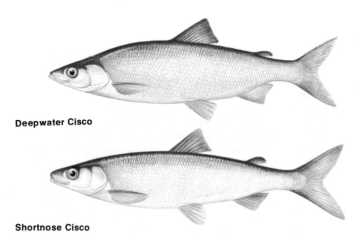

Deepwater Cisco

Shortnose Cisco

INCONNU *Stenodus leucichthys* Also called sheefish, this member of the Salmonidae departs from the usual appearance and habits of the family in having large scales, a late maturity in the female (7–12 years), a migratory habit but only to the freshwater areas in river estuaries, and an interval of 3–4 years between spawning periods. It is unique in being the only predatory member of the whitefish group in North America.

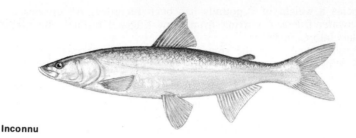

Inconnu

Migration up the rivers of Alaska and northern Canada occurs in June and July, and spawning takes place in the fall. The inconnu travels upstream as much as 1,000 miles. It is sometimes nonmigratory, living in lakes. Egg numbers per female vary from 125,000 to 325,000, and they are broadcast, coming to lie between stones on the bottom where predatory species consume large quantities. Inconnus to 21 years of age are not uncommon. The fish has been known to reach 55 pounds. The young consume plankton, becoming benthos feeders, and later in the second year of life become predatory. The inconnu feeds the year around except during spawning.

The inconnu has a limited range, but it is highly prized as a gamefish.

LAKE WHITEFISH *Coregonus clupeaformis* The lake or common whitefish is only distantly related to the familiar mountain whitefish and is more highly regarded for its game qualities. Although most frequently found in lakes, it also enters rivers and provides a considerable sport fishery in the northern part of its range.

The general coloration of the lake whitefish is silvery with a faint olive-green cast along the back. The fins are white or dusky-white, except for the caudal, which normally has a dark edge. The body is compressed, and the back in the adult is arched in front; the greatest depth is about one-fourth of the body length. The head is small, being about one-fifth of the body length. The snout is blunt and the mouth small, with the maxillary reaching a point under the pupil of the eye. There are 11 rays in the dorsal and anal fins. The scale count varies around 82–92 along the lateral line, with 11 rows above and 8

Lake Whitefish

42

below. Lake whitefish are known to attain weights of over 20 pounds, but the average is usually less than 4 pounds.

Lake whitefish spawn in the fall. Their migrations are made to shoal areas of large lakes, or they ascend tributary streams. There is considerable variation in the size of whitefish at maturity according to the racial stock. Whitefish in Lake Huron become mature at 20–21 inches in length, with a small percentage of the population reaching maturity at 17–18 inches in length. In Great Slave Lake, Northwest Territories, whitefish reach maturity at 18 inches, although 20 percent of the population is already mature at 12 inches. The smallest mature whitefish were reported from Lake Openago in Algonquin Park, Ontario; this dwarf stock matures at a length of 4–5 inches. There is no parental care of the eggs or young after spawning. Although the female whitefish deposits 10,000–12,000 eggs per pound of her body weight, only a very small percentage ever hatches. The adults spawn on gravel, where the eggs are preyed upon by yellow perch, mud puppies, crayfishes, and aquatic birds.

Lake whitefish grow slowly, and a considerable time is required for the individual to attain a weight of 1 pound in most waters.

Lake whitefish feed principally on small crustaceans and aquatic insects. They also prey on foragefishes to some extent, but this vertebrate food usually composes a very small part of the diet.

MOUNTAIN WHITEFISH *Prosopium williamsoni*   Also known as the Rocky Mountain whitefish, the mountain whitefish is endemic to lakes and streams on the western slope of the Rocky Mountains from northern California to southern British Columbia. This species has a quasi-game status in that many anglers consider it a nuisance when found in trout streams. It is not as interesting or as active as the lake whitefish. The mountain whitefish is regarded in the same way as the chub or fallfish, common to eastern trout streams. Some fisheries managers also consider the mountain whitefish a detriment in that it competes with trouts for both food and space. However, in some heavily fished western rivers where natural trout reproduction makes an insignificant contribution to the total catch, the whitefish can provide a dividend to the put-and-take type of angling.

The mountain whitefish generally resembles the lake whitefish, although the body is more cylindrical. The body coloration is brown on

Mountain Whitefish

43

the dorsal surface, shading to silver and white on the belly. The snout and lower jaw are short and blunt. The dorsal fin and the anal fin have 12–13 rays. The lateral-line scale count is usually 80–90, although there is some variation, both lower and higher. Although mountain whitefish grow to 5 pounds, the majority caught weigh less than 2 pounds, and a 3-pound fish is considered exceptional.

Mountain whitefish provide a considerable winter fishery in many parts of the West, and in regions where the steelhead is absent, such as Colorado, Utah, Montana, and Wyoming. The fish are also plentiful in Washington and on the eastern slope of the Sierras in California and Idaho. Although shore ice may extend some distance over the water, the main channels of most rivers remain open. These winter fish are taken on a variety of baits, including small midge-type flies. The natural diet of whitefish consists chiefly of caddis larvae, stonefly nymphs, and midge larvae; during the fall months they are heavy consumers of their own eggs.

ROUND WHITEFISH *Prosopium cylindraceum*   A widely distributed member of the whitefish family, also called Menominee whitefish and grayback, it differs from other whitefishes in having only a single flap between the openings of the nostrils, rather than two. Unlike the lake whitefish, which is laterally compressed, its body is cylindrical except at the head and tail, and rather uniformly tapered.

The round whitefish is silvery in color, with the dorsal surface, including the head, a bronze tinged with green. The sides are brownish and the belly light. Sexually mature individuals are more highly colored, with some red or orange on the belly; ripe fish of both sexes develop pearl organs that are more prominent on the males. It is a small species seldom exceeding 15 inches in length and a weight of 2 pounds, although fish to 4 pounds have been recorded in the Great Lakes.

Round Whitefish

The round whitefish is distributed from New Brunswick northward to Ungava Bay and westward through the Great Lakes and Canada to Alaska and the Arctic Ocean. A subspecies is found in Siberia.

This fish spawns in early winter (late November and December) in lakes on gravelly shoals at 3–20 feet in depth. The spawning whitefish do not congregate in large schools, but pair off over gravel-rubble bottom. The number of eggs per female varies between 2,500 and 10,000. The eggs usually hatch the following spring (April). The fry are heavily preyed upon by yellow perch, as well as larger gamefishes such as lake trout, landlocked salmon, and chain pickerel. Round whitefish feed on insect larvae and crustaceans.

The growth rate of round whitefish is variable, with populations in the southern limits of its distribution reaching larger sizes more rapidly and maturing earlier than populations in its northern range. Round whitefish in Lake Michigan reach a weight of 1 pound in 5 years; Lake Superior fish in 8 years; those in the Ungava Bay area in 10 years. Life span is about 12 years.

AMERICAN GRAYLING *Thymallus arcticus*   To United States anglers, the grayling is a comparatively rare freshwater gamefish, highly prized for its beauty. This is the only species of grayling found in the western hemisphere, where it is endemic to North America and Siberia. The most productive grayling fishing in the United States today exists in Alaska. Token populations occur in Montana, Wyoming, and Utah. Outside the United States, grayling are an important

American Grayling (Alaska)

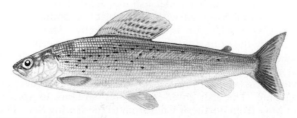

American Grayling (Montana)

45

quarry in the Yukon Territory, Northwest Territories, northern Alberta, northern Saskatchewan, and to a lesser extent in northern British Columbia. Nearly all the large oligotrophic lakes of this region, such as Great Slave, Great Bear, Athabasca, Reindeer, and Careen, also contain grayling. The species is both a lake and a river fish in North America.

The American grayling is readily distinguished from other genera of the Salmonidae by the large saillike dorsal fin, which has more than 17 rays, and a lateral-line scale count of 90–100. In coloration, grayling differ widely, not only within a region but within a single watershed; the fish may be gray, brown, purple, or silvery on the back and sides with X- or V-shaped spots on the forepart of the body and zigzag horizontal lines between the rows of scales, which, like the spots, may be vivid or indistinct. But when seen at certain angles of light, it may reflect lilac, pink, or gold, and at times the entire fish has a silvery or brassy sheen. Montana grayling are uniformly straw to silvery in color and differ considerably in appearance from the Arctic form.

The dorsal fin of the male is larger than that of the female. The female's dorsal is not only shorter, but it is high in front and low in the back. The male's dorsal is reversed, starting low and sweeping high in the rear. This disproportionate fin has irregular but distinct rows of dark spots; it is often tinged with pink or white on the upper edge. The male grayling uses its dorsal fin in a unique way; when spawning the male assumes a position side by side with the female and, tilting inward, extends and holds the saillike fin over her back. This provides orientation in accurately releasing milt as the female drops her eggs.

In the western United States, grayling seldom exceed 1 pound in size, but in Canada and Alaska fish of 4–5 pounds are recorded annually.

SMELT FAMILY Osmeridae

EULACHON *Thaleichthys pacificus* The common name of this smelt is Chinook jargon, the fish being of much importance to the Indians. The species was known as candlefish, for it was sometimes dried and fitted with a wick to give light.

In Alaska the eulachon is called hooligan, and it constitutes a small but important fishery as it is highly esteemed as a food.

The eulachon is a small, slender fish that seldom exceeds 12 inches in length. It is bluish-brown with a fine black stippling on the back shading to silvery-white on the sides and belly. The striae on the opercles follow the bone contours; pelvic fins are inserted in front of the dorsal origin. The snout is pointed, the head long, mouth large and terminal, and teeth hooked and small. There are 4–6 gillrakers on the upper half of the arch. The teeth of the eulachon are deciduous at spawning time. The fish enter freshwater streams to spawn from March to May from northern California to the Bering Sea. They mature at 2–3 years and die after spawning. The eggs, which may reach

Eulachon

25,000 in a single female, are adhesive, sticking to sand or other material and hatching in 2–3 weeks. Eulachon feed on planktonic crustaceans. Most of the commercial catch is by gillnets.

Although the eulachon has no angling value, it is a forage food for Pacific salmon and the fur seal. Eulachons are also regionally popular as a seafood. All surf smelts are too delicate and soft to stand any preserving process, although some are hard-salted and some are sold fresh. The greatest majority are smoked, however, and, having a golden-yellow color coupled with a delicate smelt flavor, they are highly esteemed by coastal Indians from California to Alaska. Sportsmen dip prodigious numbers out of rivers during the spawning runs, but the take is regulated to prevent depletion.

LONGFIN SMELT *Spirinchus thaleichthys* This smelt was first described in 1934. It is sometimes taken in shrimp trawls in 10–70 fathoms. It spawns in freshwater streams and has been taken as far up the Fraser River as Harrison Lake. It is found from central California to southeastern Alaska. Dorsal-fin origin is slightly back of pelvic origin; the anal rays are long; midlateral scales number 55–62; the pectoral fins are long; there are no striae on opercles; and the head and body have a fine black stippling.

POND SMELT *Hypomesus olidus* Though found in the North Pacific and eastern part of the Arctic Ocean from the Copper River, Alaska, to Hokkaido, Japan, as well as in the McKenzie River, Northwest Territories, Canada, the pond smelt has been introduced from Japan experimentally into a freshwater lagoon in northern California as a possible foragefish. It is almost a completely freshwater species, venturing rarely into brackish water. It spawns in the spring and its eggs are the same type as those of *Osmerus*. It is distinguished by having 0–3 pyloric caeca, an extended anal fin ray, and the attachment of the pneumatic duct behind the anterior end of the air bladder.

RAINBOW SMELT *Osmerus mordax* This species inhabits the western Atlantic, the Pacific, and the Arctic west to the White Sea, and the drainages of these oceans. It occurs as an anadromous form or is landlocked, as in the Great Lakes and many other smaller lakes in southeast Canada and northeast United States. The slender body of

Rainbow Smelt

the rainbow smelt is only about one-fifth as deep as it is long (exclusive of caudal fin) and is somewhat flattened in shape. The body color is greenish on the dorsal surface; the sides are a paler shade with a broad longitudinal silver band. The ventral surface is silvery, and the fins are flecked with tiny dusky dots. The rainbow smelt has a single large canine tooth on either side of the vomer, sometimes accompanied by smaller ones; 8–10 rays in the dorsal fin; 13 rays in the anal fin; 14–28 (rarely 13–30) pored scales in the lateral line. It grows to a maximum size of about 14 inches; however, the adults usually run 7–9 inches.

In saltwater the rainbow smelt is confined to the coastal area and is seldom found more than 1 mile from shore or at depths greater than 20 feet. The schools feed on crustaceans (chiefly shrimps), annelid worms, and other small fishes such as silversides, mummichogs, sand lances, and sticklebacks.

This smelt is taken in large quantities for both sport and commercial purposes. It is caught in harbors and estuaries in New England, as well as in tidal rivers. Sea worms (*Nereis*), shrimps, and small minnows are used as bait. The rainbow smelt is also the sole quarry of an extensive ice-fishing effort on many inland waters. It is an excellent foodfish.

SILVERSIDES FAMILY Atherinidae

ATLANTIC SILVERSIDE *Menidia menidia* This species is one of a group of small silvery fishes that inhabit both salt- and freshwater in the eastern United States and Canada. Its closest relatives are the Waccamaw silverside, key silverside, tidewater silverside, Mississippi silverside, and brook silverside. The Atlantic silverside is found along the shore and in estuaries from the southern Gulf of St. Lawrence to Cape May, often entering freshwater.

It is transparent green above, with a white belly. A silver band, edged above with a narrow black streak, runs from the upper part of the base of the pectoral fin to the base of the caudal fin. Each scale is outlined with a series of brownish or greenish dots.

Other distinguishing characteristics of the Atlantic silverside are a slender body, rounded belly; depth $7^1/_2$ in total length; caudal peduncle is slender. Head $5^1/_2$ in total length, slightly compressed; mouth is terminal, small, each jaw with a band of slender teeth. Eye 4 in head, $1^1/_4$ times its own diameter from snout. There are 2 dorsal

Atlantic Silverside

fins, first with 3−7 spines, origin slightly in front of middle of body; second with 7−10 softrays, height almost twice that of first dorsal; caudal fin is large and moderately forked; anal fin has 1 spine and 22−25 softrays, beginning under middle of first dorsal; pectorals are inserted high on sides, four-fifths length of head; pelvics are inserted on ventral edge of body under the tips of pectorals. Scales are moderate, cycloid, and covering body and head behind the eye.

Although the Atlantic silverside is a small species, seldom growing larger than 3¹/₂ inches in length, if often occurs in large schools. Silversides eat copepods, mysids, shrimps, small squids, and marine worms. In turn, they are preyed upon by larger fishes, such as the striped bass and bluefish. They spawn in shallow water in May, June, and early July. The eggs are about ¹/₂₀ inch in diameter, and each is supplied with sticky filaments for attachment to weeds or the bottom. Hatching takes place in about 10 days. The Atlantic silverside serves as an important link in the marine food chain. Easily netted in shallow water, it is occasionally used as bait and is excellent eating when fried as "whitebait."

BROOK SILVERSIDE *Labidesthes sicculus* This slender, streamlined little fish is nearly transparent when alive. It has 2 well-separated dorsal fins, the first of which contains 4−6 weak, flexible spines, and a large anal fin having 1 spine and 20−25 rays. Its color is pale olive above; it has a distinct silvery stripe along the sides. The large eyes occupy most of the small, slender head. Jaws are blunt and beaklike, and the lower jaw projects slightly beyond the upper. The larger adults attain a length of 3−4 inches.

This member of the silverside family is distributed through the central part of the United States from Minnesota to western New York in the north, and its range extends south through Florida and westward into eastern Texas. It is common in clearwater lakes and in the quieter parts of streams. Silversides often swim in schools at the surface and may skip short distances out of the water, thus earning the local name skipjack.

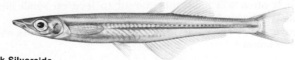

Brook Silverside

The brook silverside spawns in the spring and produces a unique egg with a sticky thread that enables the egg to float until it attaches to some object where it will remain until the larva hatches. Growth is rapid, and the fish spawn at the age of 1 year. They eat small animal food including crustaceans and insects, mainly chironomids. Few silversides live through the second winter. Thus, they have basically a 1-year life cycle.

MINNOW FAMILY   Cyprinidae

The word *minnow* has its root in the ancient Anglo-Saxon *myne*, meaning "small." While this generally describes the family Cyprinidae, there are notable exceptions, such as the carp and squawfish. Approximately 200 species are known in North America.

Most minnows are difficult for the angler to identify, as many species are superficially alike. Physical characteristics for distinguishing the various minnows, such as the number of fin rays and scale counts, may overlap. The type and number of pharyngeal teeth are also used in identification; however, the minnow must be killed and dissected to determine these.

Species are listed here by common names, alphabetically, for quick reference.

BIGEYE SHINER *Notropis boops*   This is a small olivaceous minnow with dusky sides and a very dark lateral band that passes through the eye and over the snout. The lateral line has 34–38 scales. The mouth is terminal and large, with the upper jaw about as long as the distinctively large eye. The eye is one-third to one-half as long as the head. Adults measure 2–3 inches, with the largest about $3^1/_2$ inches.

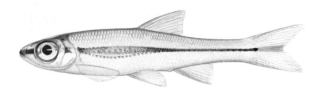

Bigeye Shiner

This shiner is found in clearwater streams of the Ohio River drainage and southwestward into Oklahoma and Arkansas. It is a sight feeder and consumes mostly animal food from the surface and at middepths. It often will jump into the air to feed on small insects hovering above the surface. Spawning occurs in midsummer.

The bigeye shiner serves as forage for large fishes and as an excellent bait minnow.

BIGMOUTH SHINER *Notropis dorsalis* This olive or greenish shiner has a large, horizontal mouth. Its scales are narrowly dark-edged, with 36–39 in the complete lateral line. The sides are silvery, and the ventral surfaces are silvery and milk-white. The length of the upper jaw is longer than the diameter of the eye. The head is flattened on its upper surface. The range of this species is from North Dakota and Missouri eastward through the Great Lakes drainage to New York.

Bigmouth Shiner

A fish of many habitats, the bigmouth shiner is reported in small streams with sandy bottoms and some current, in muddy streams, off sandy beaches, and in larger, warm tributaries. The food of this species consists of midge larvae, fragments of aquatic insects, and diatoms. The bigmouth shiner seldom exceeds 3 inches in length.

BLACKNOSE DACE *Rhinichthys atratulus* A small silvery minnow with a distinct, dark lateral band, this species has the tip of the upper lip about on a level with the lower edge of the eye. Scales in the complete lateral line number 56–70. The snout projects just beyond the oblique and subterminal mouth. The blacknose dace ranges from North Dakota to the St. Lawrence drainage and south to Nebraska and North Carolina.

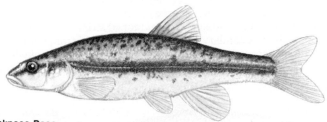

Blacknose Dace

The blacknose dace is abundant in small, rapid streams with clearwater. It can withstand the stagnant conditions of summer pools, but prefers moving water. This dace feeds on small aquatic forms including midge larvae, mayfly nymphs, and crustaceans. Little is known of the breeding habits of this fish. It apparently spawns in spring and early summer in shallow, gravelly riffles. The blacknose dace seldom reaches 4 inches in length.

BLACKNOSE SHINER *Notropis heterolepis* This silvery shiner closely resembles the blackchin shiner. The black lateral band, however, does not touch the chin. A distinctive characteristic of this species is the dark posterior borders of the scales in and immediately below the lateral band expanding to form black crescent-shaped bars. The lateral line is incomplete; there are 34–38 scales in the lateral series. The anal fin has 8 rays, seldom 7. The range of the blacknose shiner is from southern Canada to Maine and south to Iowa and the Ohio River drainage.

Blacknose Shiner

The blacknose shiner is found in clear lakes and streams in association with aquatic vegetation and over all bottom types except silt. The food of this species consists of midge larvae, other aquatic insects, and microscopic plant life. The blacknose shiner apparently spawns in early summer. A small minnow, this fish averages $2^1/_2$ inches in length.

BLEEDING SHINER *Notropis zonatus* This is one of the most beautiful minnows. As it moves, it flashes like bright silver, and when ready for spawning the male becomes bright red on the lower part of the body and head, and the fins become orange-red except on the borders. This fish has a broad black middorsal stripe and a distinct lateral stripe, with a secondary stripe above separated from both the lateral and dorsal stripes. In the young there is a pair of blackish crescents between the nostrils. The large dorsal fin is submedian; there

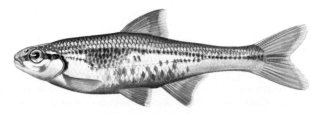

Bleeding Shiner, 4-inch Breeding Male

52

are usually 9 anal rays; the lining of the peritoneal cavity is blackish; the pharyngeal tooth count is 2,4-4,2. The eye is one-third to one-fourth as long as the head. The maxillary does not reach the eye. Mature specimens attain a length of about 5 inches.

The bleeding shiner is one of the most characteristic fishes of the Ozark region of Missouri and Arkansas and is very abundant in the clear streams of the Ozarks, where it prefers pools with moving water. It is found less frequently in fast riffles or quiet waters. It spawns from mid-April to mid-June in gravel-bottomed riffles. The unusual red and black coloration of the males at this time and the fact that large numbers spawn together make the observation of their spawning one of the most memorable activities to be seen during a spring visit to an Ozark stream.

This is a good bait species that is readily trapped or seined. Its abundance in the pools of Ozark streams makes it one of the more frequently used bait fishes.

BLUEHEAD CHUB *Hybopsis leptocephala* A large minnow reaching a total length of up to 12 inches, the bluehead chub is found from the York River in Virginia southward to the Savannah River system in South Carolina. The body of this minnow is cylindrical and only a little compressed; the mouth is rather large, almost horizontal to somewhat oblique, and subterminal. The depth of this minnow is contained 4¼ times in its total length, and the head is large and broad, one-fourth in the total length. The lower jaw is slightly shorter than the upper. The barbel is well developed. The pharyngeal teeth vary

Bluehead Chub

from 4-4 in a single row to 1,4-4,1 in 2 rows. The scales are large, and there are 40 scales in the lateral line with 10 in the transverse series and 18 before the dorsal fin. The lateral line is decurved, and the dorsal fin is located slightly posterior to the pelvic fins. Dorsal and anal fin rays number 8 and 7, respectively. This fish is similar to the river chub, *H. micropogan*, the difference being that the river chub has no caudal spot whereas the bluehead chub has a distinct, small, round caudal spot. The color of this large minnow is bluish-green above; scales are dark-ended with coppery and green reflections on the sides, and white below. The fins are pale orange. The breeding male has a red spot on each side of the head with the lower part rosy in color.

The top of the adult's head is swollen into a high crest, which is covered with breeding tubercles. Local fishermen refer to this minnow when it is breeding as the horny head. The nuptial tubercles are located on the internasal and interorbital areas, sometimes extending to the sides of the head and front of the snout, and number about 40.

The bluehead chub is the most ubiquitous nongamefish in the Piedmont watersheds. It appears in a wide variety of habitats ranging from small to medium-sized clearwater streams having sand, gravel, and rubble bottoms to large muddy rivers. The bluehead chub spawns from April to July, at which time the tubercles are the most pronounced. The average length of the fish is 5 inches, but specimens up to 12 inches have been collected.

The smaller bluehead chubs serve as forage for the largemouth bass, smallmouth bass, bluegill, redbreast sunfish, and green sunfish. The larger specimens (9–12 inches) are caught on hook and line and eaten by local fishermen.

BLUNTNOSE MINNOW *Pimephales notatus* This is a silvery minnow with a cross-hatched appearance and a dark black caudal spot. A dusky band surrounds the snout and extends to the spot on the tail. The dorsal fin has a dusky blotch on the forward portion. The back is flattened predorsally and with scales crowded. Lateral line is complete. Mouth is subterminal. The bluntnose is widespread from North Dakota through the Great Lakes and southward.

Bluntnose Minnow

The bluntnose is found in a variety of habitats. It is able to withstand high degrees of turbidity and pollution. Found in the smaller brooks and the larger lakes, it appears to prefer moderate-sized lakes and streams rich in organic matter and high in phytoplankton populations. The food of the bluntnose consists of microscopic plant and animal life along with midge larvae and other aquatic insects. It is also accused of eating eggs of other species. Spawning over an extended period from midspring to early fall, the bluntnose male develops 3 rows of sharp-pointed tubercles across the snout. The eggs are deposited on the undersides of logs, stones, or other objects. The egg masses are cleaned by the male with the spongy growth that develops on his nape. A small species, the bluntnose seldom exceeds $3^1/_2$ inches in length.

Considered an important bait species, the bluntnose contributes heavily to the diet of gamefishes and panfishes. There is some question that its spawn-eating and competitive food habits may be detrimental to other fish populations.

BONYTAIL *Gila robusta* The bonytail is a finely speckled silvery minnow with a dusky or light green back. The area around the lower fins is yellowish to orange. The body is slender and the eyes are small. Caudal fin is long, broad, and deeply forked. Ventral parts and mid-dorsal region are often incompletely scaled or naked. The origin of the dorsal fin is slightly behind the origin of the ventral fins.

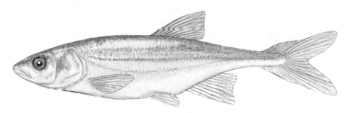

Bonytail

The bonytail is found only in rivers, streams, and lakes in the Colorado basin. It is carnivorous, feeding on insects and crustaceans. However, filamentous algae are often found in stomachs of this fish. At spawning time the sides of the head of the male become slightly reddish. The bonytail reaches a length of 15 inches, but averages about 9 inches.

Although quite bony and unsuitable for food, the bonytail is a favorite of young anglers.

BRIDLE SHINER *Notropis bifrenatus* This small straw-colored minnow has a prominent, shining, lateral black band. Body is slender; lateral line incomplete, with 13 scales before dorsal fin. This fish is similar to the blackchin shiner and blacknose shiner, but with more black pigment on the chin. It is a small but handsome species. The range of the bridle shiner is from Maine to Virginia in the Atlantic drainage.

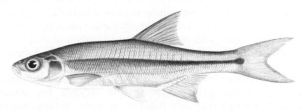

Bridle Shiner

55

The bridle shiner is found in clear, quiet water of lakes and streams, preferring shallow water with abundant vegetation over sand and mud bottom. Little is known of the food habits of this species. It apparently spawns in May and June, when gravid females can be distinguished from the males by their deeper bodies. A diminutive minnow, this fish has a maximum size of 2 inches.

Although small the bridle shiner is an attractive bait for bass and is taken greedily by yellow perch and other panfishes.

CARP *Cyprinus carpio* This Old World minnow was first successfully introduced into this country from Germany by the United States Fish Commission in 1876. Indigenous to Asia, carp were so abundant on the European continent that they were mentioned by Aristotle as early as 350 B.C.

The carp has a single serrated spinous ray in its dorsal fin along with 16–22 softrays. The lateral line contains 32–38 scales, except in the partly scaled or scaleless varieties known as mirror and leather carp. The upper jaw has 2 fleshy barbels on each side, the rearmost of which is the larger. The carp is golden-olive above, with sides becoming lighter and golden-yellow to yellowish-white below. Each scale has a dark spot at its base and is darker around its outer edge, giving the fish a cross-hatched appearance.

Since its introduction into this country, the carp has become widely distributed. Common in eastern North America, it is found from coast to coast. Although the carp is known to survive under a wide range of conditions, it prefers warm streams, lakes, and shallows with an abundance of organic matter. Carp are tolerant of all bottom types and clear or turbid waters and are not normally seen in clear, cold waters or streams of high gradient.

The carp is widely cultivated and highly regarded as a gamefish in the Old World, Historically, it was an unwise introduction to North American waters and is a textbook example of the problems encountered with exotic species. Not only is the carp a prolific breeder, but its habit of grubbing in the bottom muddies the water, thereby destroying aquatic plants and the habitat of native gamefishes. It does not hold a position of high esteem among many anglers. Nevertheless, it is a popular gamefish in some areas of the United States and is often a difficult quarry even for the skilled specialist.

Carp spawn in shallow water in the spring and summer, becoming most active at 65°–68°F. Spawning occurs both in daylight and during the night and is accompanied by considerable splashing as the females broadcast their eggs. The eggs adhere to plants and debris or sink to the bottom, where they quickly "eye," hatching within 4 days at 71°F. A 20-pound female can produce over 2 million eggs.

Carp tolerate very low oxygen levels and extreme variations in temperature. They can utilize atmospheric oxygen for considerable periods, and though they are inactive at water temperatures below

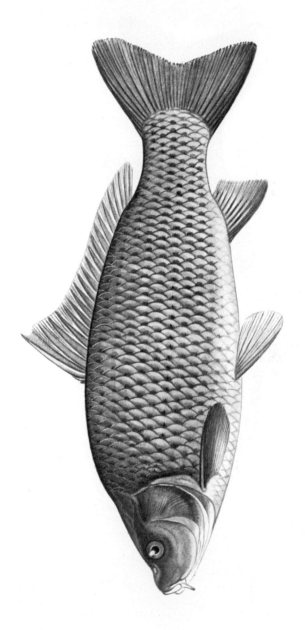

Carp

Mirror Carp

38°F, they can withstand temporary freezing. The upper lethal temperature for adult carp in a 24-hour period is about 96°F. This species attains a size in excess of 70 pounds, although the average rod-caught fish is considerably smaller. Carp have lived to 47 years in captivity, but 13–15 years is the usual life span. They are omnivorous feeders, with invertebrates such as mollusks, crustaceans, and insect larvae forming a large part of their diet; filamentous green algae and higher plants are usually consumed to a greater extent, but this varies according to season and location.

COMELY SHINER *Notropis amoenus* This is a medium-sized minnow seldom exceeding 4 inches in total length. Its geographical range is from New York southward to North Carolina on the eastern slope of the Alleghenies. The body of the comely shiner is long and compressed, the depth contained $4^7/_{10}$–$5^1/_2$ times in its total length. The head is relatively large, one-fourth the total length. The mouth is oblique, jaws equal; and the eye is equal to or greater than the length of the snout. The pharyngeal teeth are in 2 rows: 2,4-4,2. The lateral line is decurved, ending in a faint caudal spot. There are 37–39 scales in the lateral line, with 9 scale rows in a crosswise series (6

Comely Shiner

above the lateral line). The origin of the dorsal fin is well behind the insertion of the pelvic fins. The dorsal fin is about half the distance from the dorsal origin to the occiput. The number of rays in the dorsal and anal fins is 8 and 10–11, respectively. The color of this minnow is translucent green, sides silvery; there is a faint lateral band. This minnow is similar to the rosefin shiner (*N. ardens*), the difference being that the rosefin shiner has greater than 40 scales in the lateral line, whereas the comely shiner has 39 or less.

This minnow is a common inhabitant of the larger streams throughout its geographical range except for brackish-water areas. It is associated with sand- and clay-bottom streams and is tolerant of a pH range of 5.0 to 7.4. It spawns in early spring.

COMMON SHINER *Notropis cornutus* This is a large silvery shiner with a large head, mouth, and eyes. The exposed parts of the lateral scales are decidedly deeper than long; the body is slab-sided and the snout is rounded. A complete lateral line has 37–40 scales. The common shiner has a dusky dorsal band, but the lateral band is lacking. It ranges from Colorado eastward to the Appalachians. There are several subspecies.

Common Shiner

This shiner is a stream fish, preferring pools in clear, rapid water. It may also be found in lakes having tributary streams. The common shiner feeds extensively on both terrestrial and aquatic insects. Vegetable matter in the form of algae is also part of its diet. Spawning in streams in spring and early summer, the common shiner builds a depressed nest about 12 inches in diameter and 1–2 inches deep in fine gravel. Large schools of brilliantly colored spawning adults are found during breeding time. Males become bright blue with rose-colored fins. The common shiner averages 6 inches long and occasionally reaches 8 inches.

CREEK CHUB *Semotilus atromaculatus* The creek chub is a medium-sized silvery minnow with a single small barbel near the end of each jaw. This barbel may be hidden between the maxillary and premaxillary. The creek chub has a large mouth, with the upper jaw reaching to or beyond the front of the eye. This fish is bluish above and lighter below, the adult having a dark spot at the base of the dorsal fin. The creek chub is widely distributed from Montana to eastern

Creek Chub

Canada and south to the Gulf of Mexico. Within its range the ubiquitous creek chub is found in almost all streams capable of supporting fish life. It is found in small brooks or creeks throughout the spring, after which most fish move downstream to the larger waters. During the spawning season, the male acquires a rosy coloration along the sides, and tubercles form on the head. The adult creek chub is usually 3–8 inches in length, and although they have been reported in excess of 11 inches, this size is rare.

Aside from being a prized bait species and providing forage for stream-resident predator fish, the creek chub has some value as a panfish.

CUTLIPS MINNOW *Exoglossum maxillingua* This olivaceous medium-sized minnow is separated from all other minnows by its 3-lobed lower jaw with the center lobe protruding like a tongue. The upper jaw is longer than the lower. The lateral line is complete. The origin of the dorsal fin is slightly behind that of the ventral fins. The range of this species is from the St. Lawrence and Lake Ontario south into Virginia.

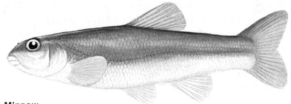

Cutlips Minnow

The cutlips is found in clear, running streams and seems to prefer clear, rocky pools but not rapids. The distinctive mouth structure of the cutlips enables it to feed on small shellfishes, which it scrapes from rocks. Although mollusks appear to be its principal food, it also eats insect larvae and diatoms. A nest builder similar to the fallfish, the cutlips male constructs a nest of stones some 18 inches across. Spawning occurs in late spring when the male apparently attempts to herd females over its nest. The cutlips minnow averages 6 inches in length.

DUSKY SHINER *Notropis cummingsae* The dusky shiner is a small minnow, seldom exceeding 2 inches in total length. The distinguishing characteristics of this trim minnow are its broad, dark lateral stripe; a decurved lateral line having a scale count of 38–40, with 6 scale rows above the lateral line and 3 below; a dorsal and anal ray count of 8 and 10–11, respectively; scales from the back of the head to the origin of the dorsal fin numbering 18–20; and a pharyngeal tooth formula of 1,4-4,1. The head of this minnow is short and flattened above. The muzzle is rounded. The standard length of the body is $4^{1}/_{3}$–$4^{2}/_{3}$ times the length of the head. The fins are large, and the fish's body is rather stout. The pelvic fins are abdominal in position. The coloration of the minnow is dark above with a light band of cop-

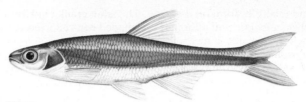

Dusky Shiner

pery-brown, bordered below by a dull steel-blue lateral stripe. The fins are slightly pigmented, and the tip of the chin is dark. The geographical range of the dusky shiner is from the Neuse River watershed in North Carolina southward to northern and western Florida and westward to eastern Alabama.

The dusky shiner is associated with blackwater acid streams. This species prefers a hard sand bottom and a moderate stream flow. The dusky shiner is a schooling fish and spawns over a sand bottom. The food of this species is small aquatic insects and zooplankton. It reaches maturity in 2 years, with its life span rarely exceeding 3 years.

EMERALD SHINER *Notropis atherinoides* This small silvery shiner has a faint lateral band that is emerald-green in color. The dorsal fin is transparent, without spots, and is positioned over or slightly behind the origin of the ventral fins. The body is slab-sided with 36–40 scales in the lateral line, fewer than 22 of which are ahead of the dorsal fin. The emerald shiner and its subspecies are widely distributed throughout Canada and south to Virginia and Texas.

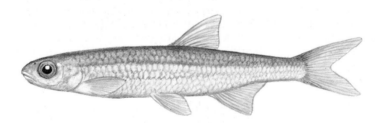

Emerald Shiner

Found in a wide variety of habitats, the emerald shiner appears to prefer clearwater over all bottom types. Remaining at middepth during the day and rising to the surface in large schools on summer nights, the emerald shiner feeds on small midges and other flying insects. Large adults are known to migrate into fast-flowing, high-gradient streams during the fall.

FALLFISH *Semotilus corporalis* A minnow similar to the creek chub in appearance and commonly called chub in eastern United States rivers, the fallfish can be distinguished from the creek chub by the absence of the dark spot on the base of the dorsal fin. The fallfish is distributed from eastern Canada into the James Bay drainage, and south on the east side of the Appalachians to Virginia. The fallfish is found in clear streams and lakes, young fish schooling in the shallows and larger adult fish inhabiting the deeper waters. The food of the fallfish consists chiefly of aquatic insects, although a variety of other aquatic forms may be consumed.

Fallfish

Spawning in the spring, this minnow, like the creek chub, takes on a rosy coloration, and tubercles form on the upper portions of the head. The fallfish builds a nest of pebbles and stones in the shoal areas of a lake or quiet pool of a stream. After the eggs are deposited, additional stones are gathered and placed on the nest by the male, the stones actually being carried in the mouth.

The fallfish grows to a somewhat larger size than the creek chub, some reaching a length of 17 inches or more. In smaller streams, however, they probably attain a maximum size of 10–15 inches.

FATHEAD MINNOW *Pimephales promelas* The fathead is a small olivaceous minnow with a more or less incomplete lateral line. A narrow, dark vertical bar is often present at the base of the caudal fin. The adult has a horizontal dark bar across the dorsal fin. The fathead, in addition to the 8 developed dorsal rays, has a stout, blunt-tipped half-ray located before the first developed ray. Together with its several subspecies, the fathead minnow is widespread from southern Canada, east of the Rocky Mountains to Maine, and southward to the Susquehanna River and to the Gulf states. In addition, it has been introduced west of the Rocky Mountains. In northern waters the fathead prefers boggy lakes, ponds, and streams; southward and westward it is found in silty lakes and streams.

The fathead feeds extensively on microscopic algae as well as other plankton. These minnows deposit their eggs beneath boards or any other flat objects that may be available in the pond or stream bottom. During the spawning season the male develops a thick, spongy

Fathead Minnow

predorsal pad on its back with which it cleans the eggs deposited by the female. In addition, the male develops golden-copper bands encircling the body just behind the head and under the dorsal fin. During this time prominent sharp tubercles also develop on the snout. A small minnow, the fathead seldom exceeds 3 inches.

The fathead is considered a valuable forage and bait species since at its maximum size it is consumed by even young predator fish. An easily propagated species, the fathead is popular with commercial hatchery operators, who raise them for bait and as forage for bass. It is reported that from 400,000 to over 1 million per acre can be raised under hatchery conditions.

FIERYBLACK SHINER *Notropis pyrrhomelas* A highly colored minnow seldom exceeding 4 inches in total length, the fieryblack shiner is found in the Santee River basin in North and South Carolina. The body of this minnow is rather deep, compressed, the depth contained $3^7/_{10}$–4 times in its total length. The head is blunt and short and is one-fourth the body length. The mouth is oblique with the jaws being equal. The eye is large, its length contained 3–$3^3/_5$ times in the length of the head. The pharyngeal teeth are in 2 rows 1,4-4,1 and are sharp, hooked, and do not have grinding surfaces. The lateral line scale count is usually 34–36, and the crosswise scale series is 9. The

Fieryblack Shiner

dorsal fin is high and longer than the head and contains 8 rays; the anal fin contains 10 rays. The color of the male is steel-blue above, milk-white below. The snout is reddish with the muzzle, upper lip, and iris scarlet. The dorsal fin is scarlet anteriorly and has a black spot posteriorly, with a milk-white tip. The base of the tail is pale, and next to it are a scarlet band and a black band. The female is duller in color.

This minnow is usually associated with sand-, gravel-, and rubble-bottom streams. It prefers waters that are relatively clear, are small to moderate in size, and have a pH range near neutral. During the breeding season the male develops 4 rows of large spines on top of its head, with a single spine on most caudal peduncle scales.

FLATHEAD CHUB *Hybopsis gracilis*   This is a light olive, slender-bodied chub. Its sides are silver and there is no lateral band. The head is broad, short, and flattened. The mouth is large, oblique, and subterminal. The lateral line is slightly decurved. This species has 8 dorsal rays and 8 anal rays. All fins have pointed rather than rounded free ends. There is a well developed barbel at the junction of the jaws. The flathead chub occupies a range from Saskatchewan south to Oklahoma.

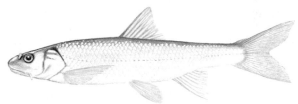

Flathead Chub

The flathead chub inhabits clear, swift streams with gravelly bottoms. Its ability to withstand turbid and silty flood conditions is notable. This chub is omnivorous, feeding on a variety of vegetation, aquatic insects, and crustaceans. It spawns in early summer and reaches a size of 12 inches.

The flathead chub is sometimes used for food, and since it will readily take the hook, it is a favorite with the small-boy fisherman. Smaller individuals are used as bait.

GOLDEN SHINER *Notemigonus crysoleucas*   This medium-sized, golden-colored minnow is known to bait dealers and sportsmen as the pond shiner. This minnow has a deep, slab-sided body with a decurved lateral line containing 44–54 scales. Like all others of the minnow family, the golden shiner has all its teeth on its pharyngeal arches, none in its mouth. The midline of the belly from ventral fins to anus is naked, the scales not crossing this strip. Young golden shiners lack the golden color, but possess a dusky lateral band that fades with age. They are often silvery in appearance, becoming dark golden as they grow older.

This minnow occupies a wide range in the eastern half of the United States from Manitoba and Quebec and southward to Florida and Mexico. The golden shiner has also been widely introduced west of the Rocky Mountains.

Golden Shiner

The golden shiner is a fish of relatively clear, weedy ponds and quiet streams. Although schools may be found in openwater, they are not often far from weed beds. The fish exhibits a definite schooling tendency throughout its life, and the young can be found in schools of considerable size. The food of the golden shiner consists largely of planktonic crustaceans. Aquatic insects, mollusks, and algae also appear in its diet.

Spawning in midsummer over an extended period, the golden shiner spreads its adhesive eggs over beds of submerged vegetation. Attended by one or two males, the female sheds her eggs while swimming, and they adhere firmly to whatever they fall upon.

Adults are usually 3–7 inches in length, with specimens seldom exceeding 10 inches.

GREENHEAD SHINER *Notropis chlorocephalus* A small highly colored minnow seldom exceeding $2^1/_2$ inches in total length, the greenhead shiner is found only in the Santee River system of North Carolina, South Carolina, and Georgia. The body of this minnow is rather stout; the caudal peduncle is deep; and the body depth is one-fifth the total length. The head is broad, one-fourth the total length. The orbit of the eye is large, more than one-third the length of the head. The interorbital region is wide, exceeding the length of the snout. The mouth is oblique, with the end of the maxilla extending beyond the margin of the orbit. The lateral line is slightly decurved, with the number of lateral-line scales numbering about 39. The transverse scale series numbers 8–9, with 16 scales before the dorsal fin. There are 8 rays each in the dorsal and anal fins. There is a distinct

Greenhead Shiner

spot at the base of the caudal peduncle, which is round or appears as an intensification of the lateral band. The pharyngeal teeth are in two rows: 2,4-4,2. The color of the male is intense during the breeding season. Most of the head and middorsal stripe of a breeding male are a metallic-green; the belly, lateral band, dorsal, and caudal bases are crimson. During the breeding season the fins are milk-white, occasionally turning light yellow.

The greenhead shiner spawns in the gravel during late spring and early summer and prefers water having near neutral pH (6.7−7.2). Its primary food is zooplankton and small invertebrates.

HIGHFIN SHINER *Notropis altipinnis* A small minnow, seldom exceeding $2^1/_2$ inches in length, the highfin is found in streams along the Atlantic coast from the Chowan River system in Virginia southward to the Santee River system in South Carolina. The body of the highfin shiner is rather short and deep, depth contained $3^1/_2$ times in its total length. The head is short, not wide, and is contained $4^1/_3$ times in the total length. The eye of this minnow is large and enters the head $2^3/_4$ times. The lateral line is decurved and contains 36 scales. Other

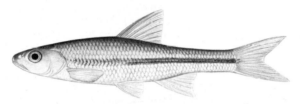

Highfin Shiner

distinguishing characteristics of the highfin shiner are: anal rays 10, very rarely 9; pharyngeal teeth in 2 rows, 2 teeth in outer row 2,4-4,2; caudal base without spot except in very young; width of eye equal to or greater than snout length; no black crescent markings between nostrils; dorsal origin nearer front of eye than base of caudal fin or about midway between these two points; height of dorsal fin more than half the distance from the dorsal origin to the occiput. The snout is marked by a dark preorbital blotch that extends onto the anterior half of the lips and is bordered above by a light streak that passes through the nostrils and around the tip of the snout.

As breeding time approaches, the male's caudal fin takes on a faint reddish color, the snout turns yellowish, and the lower lip becomes dusky. This species is usually associated with slightly to moderately turbid lower Piedmont streams having a width of 15−30 feet. The bottom strata of these shallow streams are composed of gravel, sand, rubble, and silt. The highfin shiner is a carnivorous sight feeder, eating small aquatic and terrestrial insects and larger zooplankton.

HORNYHEAD CHUB *Nocomis biguttatus* This slender, bluish-olive minnow has a black spot at the base of the caudal fin. A dusky lateral band encircles the snout and ends at the caudal spot. The sides are light olive or yellowish, ventrally pale yellow or white. The eyes are small and the mouth is almost terminal, large, and slightly oblique. A small barbel is present slightly above the angle of the jaws. The hornyhead is found from New York west to Wyoming and Colorado and south to northern Arkansas and Alabama.

Hornyhead Chub

It inhabits small and medium-sized streams having clearwater and moderate or sluggish current. It prefers a sandy, gravelly bottom with aquatic vegetation. This chub spawns in the spring, when the male develops tubercles over the whole upper part of the head, builds a nest, and guards the eggs. An omnivorous feeder, the hornyhead reaches 8 inches.

IRONCOLOR SHINER *Notropis chalybasus* This is a small minnow having a lustrous black lateral band from the snout to the caudal base and a light band above the dark band on the snout. Above the dark lateral band the fish is relatively dark; below the band the fish is

Ironcolor Shiner, 2-inch Breeding Male

pale yellow. During the breeding season the male turns bright orange on the lower half. The distinguishing characteristics of this minnow are 33 scales in the lateral line with 6 rows of scales above and 3 rows below; 16–18 scale rows anterior to the dorsal rays; a lateral line that is moderately to strongly decurved; 8 spines each in the dorsal and anal rays; pharyngeal teeth in 2 rows, usually 2,4-4,2; interior of mouth with much black pigment; and intense black pigment about anus, anal fin base, and caudal peduncle. The body is moderately elongate, the back slightly elevated, the head flat above. The head of the ironcolor shiner is contained $3^4/_5$ times in the total length of the fish. The muzzle is rather pointed and the mouth is very oblique. The lower jaw is somewhat longer than the upper jaw. The eyes are large and the caudal peduncle is slender. The ironcolor shiner is widely distributed on the coastal lowlands from New Jersey to eastern Texas and north in the Mississippi lowlands to Iowa and northern Indiana.

This minnow prefers small lowland streams and swamps, preferably with a sand bottom. The breeding season is spread over a $5^1/_2$-month period (mid-April to late September). As the breeding season approaches, the male develops tubercles on the chin and on other limited areas, and the ventral side of the fish takes on an orange appearance. This minnow is a free spawner. The male chases the female during the daylight hours during the breeding season with spawning taking place when the female stops, usually in shallow, quiet water. The eggs hatch in 54 hours at a mean temperature of 62° F. The egg sac disappears after the fifth day, and the young begin feeding on small zooplankton. The larvae swim in large aggregations until they reach a length of 12 mm. (70 days), at which time they resemble the adults and join the heterogeneous aggregations of larger ironcolor shiners. This species averages 2 inches in total length.

LAHONTAN REDSIDE *Richardsonius egregius* The Lahontan redside is a brilliantly colored minnow with a broad, deeply forked tail. The color is variable and more intense during the spawning season. The male is usually deep olive-green above, lighter on the sides, and silver beneath. Brassy and silvery metallic reflections are seen on various parts of the body. Two rather distinct brassy stripes extend from snout to tail. Brilliant iridescence is seen along the head and upper body. Below the lower stripe, the sides are strongly suffused with pink. Lateral-line scales number 52–61. The edges of the dorsal and anal fins are straight or slightly concave. This species is native to the Lahontan basin and related waters of Nevada and California.

Lahontan Redside

The Lahontan redside is a river species found in large numbers in slow ripples and quiet, shallow pools. When found in lakes, it is over submerged logs or around fallen trees or wharves. This species spawns in late spring and early summer, when it migrates up the smaller tributaries, chiefly at night. The fish attain the spawning colors described above and develop small whitish nodules over most of the body. The food of the Lahontan redside is mostly aquatic larvae and winged insects. It also has been observed consuming large numbers of sucker eggs during the spawning of this species. The Lahontan is a small minnow, the largest reaching $5^1/_2$ inches.

LAKE CHUB *Couesius plumbeus*   This bluish-silver minnow has a lead-colored lateral band. The body is moderately slender; the eyes, large. There are 8 dorsal and 7 anal rays. A small barbel is present slightly above the angle of the jaws. The lake chub ranges from southern Canada and northern United States, east of the Continental Divide to Iowa and Michigan.

This chub inhabits cold lakes and smaller streams. It is carnivorous, feeding almost entirely on insect larvae. Spawning takes place during summer in the small streams. Adults reach a size of 6 inches, but average 3 inches.

LEATHERSIDE CHUB *Gila copei*   The leatherside is a bluish-backed, silvery minnow with a dusky lateral streak. A faint orange smear may be present between the eye and the maxillary. Bright spots of the same color may be present at the bases of the pectoral and ventral fins. Scales are small; there are 80 in the lateral line. Origin of the dorsal fin is behind the origin of the ventral fins. There are 8 dorsal and 8 anal rays. The mouth is small, low, terminal, and oblique; the premaxillary is just below the level of the pupil; the maxillary reaches just beyond the front of the eye. This fish is found only in the Bonneville and Snake river drainages of Nevada, Utah, and Wyoming.

The leatherside chub inhabits clear coldwaters where it grows to a length of 6 inches. Spawning is in midsummer.

Leatherside Chub

LONGNOSE DACE *Rhinichthys cataractae*   This dark greenish-olive-backed minnow has a long snout that projects far beyond the nearly horizontal mouth. Fins are light olive or transparent. Ventral portions of the body are milky-white. The tip of the upper lip is far below the level of the lower edge of the eye. There are many dusky scales scattered over the back, giving a mottled appearance. The range of the longnose dace extends over most of the United States except the southeast coastal region.

Longnose Dace

This species thrives in swift waters. A characteristic fish of the small headwater streams of the mountain-brook type, the longnose is found in association with rushing torrents and rock pools. The food of the longnose consists of various aquatic insect larvae and some vegetable matter. Its liking for blackfly larvae contributes to its economic value. Little is known of the breeding habits of this species. It apparently spawns in early spring, and the male develops minute tubercles on the head and back. The longnose dace grows to $4^1/_2$ inches in length.

Considered of some value in the control of blackflies, this species is also an excellent baitfish. It is easily obtainable and is felt to be unsurpassed as a bait for bass. It undoubtedly provides excellent forage for trouts also.

NORTHERN SQUAWFISH *Ptychocheilus oregonensis* The squawfishes are the largest of North American minnows. Dusky-green above and silvery below, the northern squawfish has 67–75

Northern Squawfish

scales along its lateral line, 46–56 of which are before the dorsal fin. The dorsal fin contains 9–10 softrays and the anal fin, 8 rays. The range of the northern squawfish is limited to the Columbia River drainage and the coastal streams of Washington and Oregon. Three related species, the Colorado squawfish (*P. lucius*), the Umpqua squawfish (*P. umpquae*), and the Sacramento squawfish (*P. grandis*), have a minor western distribution in their respective river systems.

The squawfish are voracious minnows with pikelike habits. The adults feed on other fishes including young trouts and salmon. These fish are reported up to 80 pounds, but those taken in the Columbia River run 6–10 pounds.

Condemned by sportsmen for its predaceous habits, the squawfish is easily caught with most lures and natural baits. The young make excellent bait for trouts and other gamefishes. Though bony, large squawfish have some food value, particularly when smoked.

REDLIP SHINER *Notropis chiliticus*   A small minnow seldom exceeding 2 inches in total length, the redlip shiner is found in the Pee Dee River system of North Carolina. The body of this small minnow is elongate, the depth contained $5^1/_2$ times in its total length. The head of the minnow is broad, its length one-fourth its total length. The eye is large, one-third the length of the head. The pharyngeal teeth are in 2 rows 2,4-4,2. The lateral line is strongly decurved, complete, and has 34–37 scales in the lateral series. The anal and dorsal fin rays number 8 each. The interior of the mouth has no black pigment, nor is there

Redlip Shiner

any around the area of the vent, anal fin, and caudal peduncle. The body color of the breeding male is crimson, and there is a pale emerald stripe. The top of the head is greenish, the snout red, and the fins yellow. The dorsal and anal fins are splashed with red or orange. The lips of the redlip shiner are red. This species is similar to the saffron shiner (*N. rubricroceus*), greenhead shiner (*N. chlorocephalus*), and yellowfin shiner (*N. lutipinnis*).

Very little is known about the life history of this minnow. The redlip shiner is found in small streams, both turbid and clear. It inhabits streams having sand and gravel bottoms and prefers a pH range of 6.9–7.4.

RED SHINER *Notropis lutrensis*   This minnow is a brilliant steel-blue-backed silvery shiner. The male has an orange-red belly, a violet-colored crescent behind the shoulders, followed by a crimson cres-

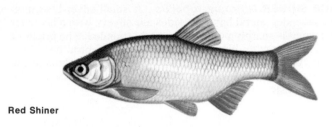

Red Shiner

cent. The fins are reddish, the anal and caudal blood-red. The female is plain greenish. The red shiner's mouth is large and quite oblique. The body is compressed, with an arched back. The lateral line is strongly decurved. Scales are large; 13 in front of dorsal. The range of the red shiner is from Wyoming to southern Minnesota and Illinois southward to Mexico.

The usual habitat of this fish is small ponds and quiet streams. Omnivorous in its food habits, this little minnow subsists on small bits of aquatic vegetation, one-celled animals, small insects, and crustaceans. Spawning in early summer, the red shiner deposits its eggs on submerged water plants. At this time the male becomes even more brilliantly colored and develops small tubercles on the head and body. A small species, the red shiner seldom exceeds 3 inches.

REDSIDE SHINER *Richardsonius balteatus* A silvery shiner with a bluish back and blackish lateral band, it has a slender and moderately compressed body. The head is short, eyes large, mouth small and oblique, scales large. There are 9 dorsal fin rays and 10–13 anal fin rays. The range of the redside shiner is in the Columbia River basin and the Salt Lake basin.

Inhabiting lakes and streams alike, the redside shiner in streams is most abundant in slow-moving pools. This species is carnivorous, and although its main diet is small aquatic insect larvae and crustaceans, it has been observed feeding on fry. Spawning time is in early summer, when the male develops a red stripe below the dorsal band and fine tubercles on the head, body, and upper sides of pectoral fins. At this time a light red stripe appears on the female. The redside attains a length of little more than 5 inches.

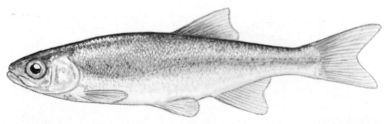

Redside Shiner

ROSYFACE SHINER *Notropis rubellus* A small silver-blue minnow with a lavender lateral band, its sides are silvery with a lavender sheen. The snout is sharply pointed; the body rounded. The origin of the dorsal fin is distinctly behind the origin of the ventral fins. Anal rays number 10–13. This species is found from North Dakota to the St. Lawrence and Hudson rivers and south to Virginia and part of the Ohio River drainage.

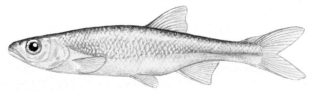

Rosyface Shiner

The rosyface shiner inhabits moderate-sized streams with clearwater, relatively high gradient, and clean bottom. It apparently winters in deeper riffles and pools. It is intolerant of turbid water and silt bottom. The food of the rosyface consists of insects and vegetable matter, including midge larvae, blackfly larvae, caddis worms, and green algae. This species spawns over sandy gravel, gravel, or bedrock in spring or early summer. The male becomes more intensely colored and develops tiny tubercles over most of the body. The rosyface seldom exceeds 3 inches.

ROSYSIDE DACE *Clinostomus funduloides* This brilliantly colored, medium-sized minnow seldom exceeds 5 inches in total length and is found in the upland streams from the Chesapeake Bay southward to Georgia. The snout of this minnow is short, and the lower limb of the pharyngeal arch is short and stout. Its distinguishing characteristics are 7–9, usually 8, dorsal rays, and 7–10, usually 9, anal rays; a sharply forked caudal fin; sides of the body pale to dark with scattered spots or mottling; a dark prominent lateral band, more pronounced on the caudal peduncle; a complete lateral band curving downward from the upper edge of the gill opening, reaching its lowest point about 7–8 scale rows from the head; a lateral-line scale

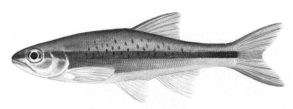

Rosyside Dace

count of usually 50; dorsal fin originating about 2–3 scale rows posterior to the base of the pelvic fins; outer margin of the dorsal fins
nearly straight; pharyngeal teeth in 2 rows, the teeth being slender
and well hooked, with the teeth in the outer row numbering 5-5 and
on the inner row usually 2-2; a short intestine with but one anterior
loop; no barbels, with the lower lip being normally formed; and the
belly between the pelvic fins and the anus being rounded. Another
significant characteristic is that the first ray of the dorsal fin is
slender and closely jointed to the second ray, there being no
membrane between them.

The rosyside dace is generally associated with small to medium-
sized, relatively shallow clearwater streams. It is most numerous in
streams having gravel and sand bottoms. During June and July the
rosyside dace reaches its highest coloration, which is rosy pink.

SAND SHINER *Notropis stramineus* The sand shiner has a
moderately stout body and large eyes. Its coloration is light olive or
straw-yellow with a silvery cast above. Sides are silvery and scales
are faintly dark-edged. The abdomen is silvery and milk-white. Fins
are transparent or tinged with white. It usually has 7 anal rays, but occasionally has 8. The front of the dorsal fin is about halfway between
the base of the tail and the tip of the snout. An irregular and some-

Northern Sand Shiner

times indistinct stripe, which expands just in front of the dorsal fin and
does not surround the base of the dorsal, also distinguishes it from
close relatives. The breeding male develops small tubercles on the
head. Most adults measure $1^1/_2$–$2^1/_2$ inches, with the largest about 3
inches.

Spawning occurs in July and August in Iowa, but has been reported
in late April through July in Missouri. The sand shiner is longer-lived
than some minnows; some fish live 3 years but most spawn at 1
year. A 1-year-old fish produces 250 eggs, a 2-year-old 1,100, a 3-
year-old 1,800.

The sand shiner is found in the Mississippi, Missouri, and Ohio
river drainages, southward into Texas and northeastward to the St.
Lawrence River. In streams it prefers sand- and gravel-bottomed

riffles and pools having considerable current; in lakes it likes exposed sand- and gravel-bottomed shores. The sand shiner is seldom found among vegetation or over silt bottoms.

SILVERY MINNOW *Hybognathus nuchalis* This olivaceous silvery minnow is from the Missouri drainage of Montana to Lake sides, and a milk-white belly. It can be distinguished from the genus *Notropis* by a small knob on the tip of the lower jaw inside the mouth. Dorsal fin is well forward. Snout slightly overhangs the horizontal mouth. Scales number 35–38 in the lateral line. The range of the silvery minnow is from the Missouri drainage of Montana to Lake Champlain and south to the Gulf of Mexico.

Silvery Minnow

The silvery minnow prefers shallow, weedy waters with little or no current. It is found over bottoms of sand or muck, but where siltation is absent. Little is known of the food habits of this species except that it prefers waters rich in phytoplankton and probably subsists primarily on microscopic plant and animal life. The silvery minnow spawns over organic debris or vegetation in early spring. A medium-sized minnow, this species averages 6 inches.

SOUTHERN REDBELLY DACE *Phoxinus erythrogaster* This is a small, fine-scaled minnow with 2 dusky longitudinal bands. It is deep greenish-olive with a series of dark blotches along the dorsal ridge and a reddish or yellowish streak between longitudinal bands. Lower sides and belly are silvery, white, or flushed with yellow, red, or crimson. Body scales are very small, 70–95 in the lateral series. Mouth is small and slightly oblique. Jaws are equal. There is no barbel. The range of this species extends from southern Minnesota to Pennsylvania and south to northern Alabama.

The southern redbelly dace inhabits permanent brooks with clearwater that are not subject to frequent flooding. It appears to require sufficient water throughout the year, as it does not migrate downstream in summer. The largest populations are found where there are undercut banks for escape cover. Primarily a vegetarian, this

Southern Redbelly Dace

dace subsists on mud-inhabiting algae. During the spawning period, this fish becomes exceedingly brilliant. Colors indicated above become more distinct, and the ventral surfaces of the head and body become a deep carmine. The fins are flushed with yellow, and a carmine spot appears on the base of the dorsal fin. Although colorful, the females are less so than the males. This species reaches a maximum length of 3 inches.

Two other species very similar in appearance are the northern redbelly dace (*P. eos*) and the mountain redbelly dace (*P. oreas*).

SPECKLED DACE *Rhinichthys osculus*   This is a grayish, speckled minnow with a faint lateral band. All fins are tinged with color. Body is slender, head short, eyes large. There are 60–64 scales in lateral line. A small barbel is usually present in a depression at the junction of the jaws. Premaxillaries are protractile.

The speckled dace and its many subspecies range west of the Rocky Mountains in coastal streams of Washington and Oregon and in the Columbia River basin south to southern California and the Colorado River drainage.

This dace is found in clear lakes and streams and is abundant in warm springs and spring flows. It seems to prefer rubble-strewn riffle areas. One subspecies is known to inhabit warm springs with temperatures of 84° F. An omnivorous feeder, the speckled dace subsists on algae and other plant material, small crustaceans, insect larvae, and small snails. Depending on water temperatures, this dace may spawn between midspring and midsummer.

Speckled Dace

SPOTTAIL SHINER *Notropis hudsonius* This is a very silvery shiner usually with a distinct caudal spot. In some large adults from turbid waters this spot is faint or absent. Usually the lower edge of the caudal fin is milk-white. The eyes are large, greater in diameter than the length of the upper jaw. The lateral line contains 36–40 scales. The range of the spottail shiner extends from North Dakota and adjacent Manitoba to the Hudson River and south to Virginia, Illinois, and Iowa. Extensions of this range into New England have undoubtedly been effected by baitfishermen.

Spottail Shiner

The spottail is a minnow of large, clear rivers and lakes. It is usually found in large schools over sand or gravel bottoms where vegetation is scant or lacking. Apparently spawning takes place in midspring in shoal areas or creek mouths. During spawning the fish attains tiny tubercles on the upper half of the head and at the base of the pectoral fins. The food of the spottail shiner consists of insects, crustaceans, and vegetation. A small minnow, the spottail seldom exceeds 5 inches.

STEELCOLOR SHINER *Notropis whipplei* A bluish-silvery shiner of moderate size, it has pronounced cross-hatching on the scales of back and sides. The lateral band is steel-blue, and a dusky blotch is found on the webbing among the last 3 dorsal rays. Anal rays number 9. The snout is pointed and the head triangular in lateral outline. Eyes are small. The body of the adult averages deeper than that of the very similar spotfin shiner. The steelcolor shiner ranges from Illinois through Ohio.

This shiner is found most commonly in rapidly flowing streams of clearwater. Its food consists of insect larvae, both aquatic and terres-

Steelcolor Shiner

trial, and small crustaceans. The steelcolor shiner spawns in late spring and early summer over gravelly riffles. This species averages 4¹/₂ inches in length.

STONEROLLER *Campostoma anomalum*   Also known as hornyhead and knottyhead, this brownish-olive minnow has a brassy luster and many dark scales scattered, usually singly or in pairs, over back and sides. Belly is whitish or yellowish. Snout overhangs mouth. Mouth has a prominent, gristly biting edge and is subterminal and almost horizontal. The stoneroller has 8 dorsal rays and 7 anal rays. This minnow and its various subspecies are found from Minnesota to Texas and eastward.

A fish essentially of riffles, in spring the stoneroller is found in small streams of moderate gradient and sandy-gravel bottoms. In summer and winter it is found in larger waters, but is virtually restricted to riffle areas. A bottom feeder, the stoneroller subsists on diatomaceous

Stoneroller

scum, mud with its insect larvae, and small mollusks and filamentous algae. The stoneroller ascends the smaller streams in spring to spawn. At this time the anal and dorsal fins of the male become brilliant orange and black, and almost the entire upper half of the body is covered with sharp tubercles. The male builds a nest by making a shallow depression in the gravel, a foot or more in diameter. A number of males may work on the same nest. The stoneroller grows to a length of 11 inches in some localities.

The stoneroller is exceptionally hardy and active on the hook, making it an attractive bait species. In Tennessee, this minnow is highly regarded as a foodfish.

SUCKERMOUTH MINNOW *Phenacobius mirabilis*   As the name implies, this is a suckermouthed minnow, yellowish or slaty-olive above and silvery below. It is distinguished from the sucker family in that suckers have more than 8 dorsal rays; the suckermouth minnow has 7. A narrow, dark stripe extends along the dorsal ridge. A dusky lateral band encircles the snout and ends in a deep-black, oblong caudal spot. Tip of upper jaw is separated from remainder of the snout

Suckermouth Minnow

by a deep groove. Lips are large and fleshy, the upper curved around the angle of the mouth. The suckermouth minnow ranges from Colorado and South Dakota to western Ohio, Louisiana, and Texas.

The suckermouth minnow prefers shallow, rapid streams rich in organic matter. It inhabits turbid waters only if the current is sufficient to prevent siltation. The suckermouth feeds on small insect larvae and snails from the stream bottom. A late spring and early summer spawner, the suckermouth male develops tiny tubercles on the upper part of the head, predorsal region of the body, and pectoral and ventral fins. This species reaches a length of 4 inches.

TAILLIGHT SHINER *Notropis maculatus*   The taillight shiner is a small, graceful, often-reddish minnow seldom exceeding 2 inches in length, with a distinct large round spot at the base of the caudal fin. A small black spot also is present above and below the large caudal spot. The distinguishing characteristics of this minnow are a poorly developed lateral line that does not extend forward on the head; a lateral line scale count of 36–38 with 5 scale rows above and 3 below; not noticeably elevated lateral-line scales; about 15 scales between back

Taillight Shiner

of head and the origin of the dorsal fin; 8 rays each in the anal and dorsal fins; and a pharyngeal tooth formula of 4-4. The head of the minnow is flattened above, and the snout is rounded. The head is contained about $4^{1}/_{2}$ times in the standard length and the eye is contained about $3^{1}/_{2}$ times in the head. The mouth is small, terminal, and oblique. The body is slender, with the depth contained about 5 times in the standard length. The pelvic fins are abdominal in position. The color of the taillight shiner is pinkish-red above, paler below. There is a fairly prominent dark stripe from the tip of the snout to the base of

80

the caudal fin, terminating in a distinct oval, dark spot about the size of the eye. The posterior interradial membranes of the dorsal fin do not contain black pigment, and the lateral-line scales have a black dot on each side of the lateral-line pores.

The geographical range of the taillight shiner is from Missouri southward in the lowlands through Arkansas and southeastern Oklahoma to eastern Texas and Mississippi. On the Atlantic coast it is found from North Carolina southward to Florida. The taillight shiner is the most common shiner in the natural lakes of Florida. This minnow appears to prefer a hard sand-bottom habitat, with the water on the acid side. In North Carolina this fish prefers the deeper areas in the swift, blackwater streams, seldom being found in the shallow-stream areas.

UTAH CHUB *Gila atraria* This large minnow can be a serious competitor of gamefishes. The original distribution of the Utah chub was in the drainage basin of Lake Bonneville and in the Snake River above Shoshone Falls. It has spread to other western waters because it is widely used as a baitfish. The coloration of the Utah chub is variable but is frequently a dark green, blue, or black on the dorsal surface, shading to a silvery or even golden color. Some individuals have bright yellow or orange ventral parts. The origin of the dorsal fin is directly over the insertion of the pelvic fins. Usually there are 9 dorsal

Utah Chub

rays and 8 anal rays. The lateral line has 45–65 scales. The oblique mouth has 2 rows of pharyngeal teeth.

The Utah chub occurs in a variety of habitats and in a broad temperature range. In Yellowstone Lake it is found where water temperatures reach 88°F. An omnivorous feeder, this chub consumes higher water plants, algae, terrestrial and aquatic insects, snails, crustaceans, and small fishes. It spawns from early to late summer and deposits its eggs at random over the bottom. It may attain a length of over 20 inches and a weight of 3 pounds, but is more frequently 5–8 inches long.

WARPAINT SHINER *Notropis coccogenis* A large colorful minnow, it sometimes reaches a total length of 5 inches. The geographical range of the warpaint shiner is from the Tennessee River uplands in

Virginia and Kentucky southward to Georgia and Alabama. It is also found in the New and Catawba-Santee river systems in North Carolina.

The body of this minnow is long, compressed, the depth a little less than one-fourth the total length. The head is pointed and the mouth is large and oblique, with the lower jaw protruding. The eye is large, contained $3^1/_2$ times in the length of head. The lateral-line scales usually number 42. The dorsal fin has 7 rays and the anal fin 9. The pharyngeal tooth formula is 2,4-4,2. The color of the warpaint shiner ranges from a light green on the back to silvery on the belly. During the breeding season the belly takes on a rosy coloration. The lateral scales have a dark edge; there is a faint lateral line and a dusky band occurs on the shoulders. A scarlet vertical bar is located between the eye and gill opening. The upper muzzle and lip are red, and a red spot occurs on the body near the base of the pectoral. The lower half of the dorsal fin is yellow and the outer half is black. The pectoral fins are white.

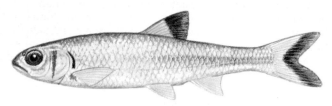

Warpaint Shiner

This highly colored minnow is found in medium to large clearwater streams having a moderately rapid current. Warpaint shiners are usually found over a rock, gravel, or sand bottom in the upper half of large deep pools. These fish are most active during daylight hours throughout the year. They mature at 2 years of age, at which time they have a mean total length of 3 inches. Spawning takes place in early June when the water temperatures are between 68° and 82°F. The warpaint shiner usually spawns over the nest of some other fish, with the male holding a territory and driving off all other fishes. During spawning the fish head toward the current with the males in the upstream position and the females to the rear. Both settle to the bottom, vibrate, and spawn. After spawning, the fish leave the nest. The food of the warpaint shiner is chiefly insects.

WEDGESPOT SHINER *Notropis greenei* This shiner receives its name from a characteristic wedge-shaped spot at the base of the tail that is detached from a lateral band; sometimes this spot may be indistinct. The fish is dusky on the back and pale below the middorsal stripe. The dorsal fin is moderately long. The lining of the peritoneal cavity is heavily speckled with black. The pharyngeal tooth count is

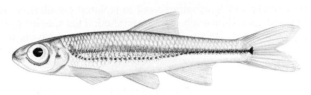

Wedgespot Shiner

2,4-4,2. The mouth extends obliquely from a point even with the center of the eye to a point below and even with the front of the eye or a little beyond.

The wedgespot is a small minnow that attains a length of about 2¹/₂ inches. Spawning takes place in July and August. It is found in the Ozarks of Missouri, Arkansas, and Oklahoma.

WHITEFIN SHINER *Notropis niveus*   A small minnow, the whitefin seldom exceeds 2¹/₂ inches in total length. Its geographical range is from southern Virginia southward to South Carolina in streams east of the Appalachian Mountains. The body of this minnow is regularly fusiform with the dorsal region more arched than the ventral. The distinguishing characteristics of the whitefin shiner are a body depth one-fifth the total standard length; a conical head, with its length contained 4¹/₂ times in the total body length; obtuse muzzle, with the mouth nearly terminal and a nonfleshy snout; an eye equal to the snout length, contained 3–3¹/₂ times in the total length of the head; 35–39 scales in the lateral line with the number of scales preceding the dorsal fin numbering 15–16; a decurved lateral line; a dorsal and anal ray count of 8 and 8–9, respectively; slightly hooked pharyngeal teeth in

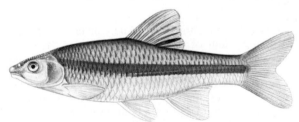

Whitefin Shiner

2 rows 1,4-4,1 with grinding surfaces. The color of this small minnow is pale, with a narrow bluish lateral band ending in a faint spot on the caudal base. There is an interradial pigmented spot located slightly anterior to the sixth principal ray on the dorsal fin. The dorsal and caudal fins are creamy to yellow in color, and the tips of these fins, as well as the entire anal fin, are charged with a milky-white pigment.

The whitefin shiner is usually found in isolated populations rather than being distributed throughout a watershed. This species prefers a pH range of 6.2–6.9. It is usually found in streams having a sand, gravel, or muck bottom. It feeds primarily on zooplankton and small aquatic insects.

WHITETAIL SHINER *Notropis galacturus* The whitetail shiner is found from the eastern slopes of the Ozarks in Missouri and Arkansas through the Tennessee Valley to South Carolina and Mississippi. This large minnow sometimes reaches a maximum length of 6 inches.

Its body is elongate, fusiform, slightly compressed, and the depth is a little less than one-fourth the total length; its mouth is large, with the lower jaw being included within the upper; the eyes are small; the somewhat decurved lateral line has 41 scales; the dorsal and anal rays number 8 each; and the pharyngeal teeth are in 2 rows 1,4-4,1. The coloration of the male is steel-blue (female olivaceous) above and silvery below. The dorsal fin has a black posterior interradial membrane, and the caudal fins are creamy-yellow at the base. During the breeding season the dorsal, anal, and caudal fins of the male are charged with a milk-white pigment, and sometimes the anal and caudal fins are reddish in color.

Whitetail Shiner

The whitetail shiners, either individually or in schools, are usually found in the upper half of small to medium-sized, fairly clearwater mountain streams having a moderate current. This fish is associated with riffle areas having a bottom of rubble, bedrock, and gravel. The species is most active during daylight hours throughout the year. The whitetail shiner reaches maturity during its second year of growth, at which time it has a total length of about 3 inches.

Spawning activity begins when the water temperature reaches 75°F. The time of day chosen for spawning is between 11:00 A.M. and 4:00 P.M. Prior to spawning, the male selects and guards a territory around a gravel nest from which he drives away all other males. Once the female is selected, the male and female turn on their sides upward and toward each other several times, each time releasing eggs and sperm. After spawning, the female leaves the nest, and the male takes over the task of guarding the eggs. Inasmuch as the eggs are sticky, they adhere to rocks, fallen tree branches, or the first object

84

they come in contact with. When the eggs hatch, the young measure about 5.5 mm. in total length. An average growth rate for this short-lived species is about 2, $2^1/_2$, and 3 inches for the years 1–3, respectively; however, few of them live to 3 years.

The whitetail shiner feeds on material that drifts along with the current, principally aquatic and terrestrial insects, depending on availability. This minnow is carnivorous. The whitetail shiner serves as forage for smallmouth bass, largemouth bass, redbreast sunfish, and others.

KILLIFISH FAMILY   Cyprinodontidae

BANDED KILLIFISH *Fundulus diaphanus*   This species superficially resembles the male of the mummichog, but is very slender, with a depressed head and an elongate snout. The tail is usually square edged or slightly concave. The scales are smaller than those of the mummichog, and the numerous light and dark bars distinguish the banded killifish from the striped killifish. The banded killifish is green to olive-green above, white below and on the lower sides. The young resemble the female in coloration, assuming the adult pattern at a length of about 2 inches. The adult reaches a length of about 4 inches.

This is a common freshwater species and also inhabits slightly brackish water. It is found from the area of the St. Lawrence River to South Carolina. A subspecies occurs to the west, extending through the Great Lakes and the Dakotas. Found generally in quiet waters, the banded killifish is common in large lakes, rivers, estuaries, and small bodies of water.

Spawning occurs in large schools from April to September. The large eggs are laid on a sand bottom, where they stick to sand or weed by adhesive threads. This killifish eats small crustaceans, mollusks, worms, and plant material. In turn, it is eaten by predatory fishes, and in this respect plays an important role in the economy of shallow-water environments.

The banded killifish is frequently used as bait. It is not as hardy on a hook as the mummichog, but nevertheless, is of some value because of its abundance and ease of capture.

Banded Killifish

BLACKSTRIPE TOPMINNOW *Fundulus notatus*   This freshwater killifish is a slim-bodied species with a dark purplish band along each side, running from the lips to the base of the tail. The dorsal and caudal fins have dark black spots. Length is up to 3 inches.

It is widely distributed from Wisconsin and Iowa to central Ohio and southward to Texas and Mississippi. It is found near the borders of lakes and streams in sluggish water. It swims on the surface and travels in large schools.

The blackstripe topminnow eats insects and small crustaceans. It is of some importance as a foragefish, but its use as a bait minnow is limited.

FLAGFISH *Jordanella floridae*   This deep-bodied little fish is olive colored, with some yellowish patches and 4–5 diffuse dark crossbars. There is 1 prominent black spot on the sides. Fins are dusky and may be speckled or barred. Scales are edged in red. The dorsal fin is long, having 16–18 rays, the first of which is a grooved spine. The flagfish is found in coastal swamps and lagoons from Florida to Yucatán.

Spawning habits are similar to those of the sunfishes. The male fans out a depression with its fins and moves larger particles and debris with his mouth. When the nest is ready, he coaxes a female onto it for spawning. The eggs are fertilized and guarded by the male. The young are protected until they can fend for themselves. Food includes both plants and animals, with algae and other plant material apparently preferred.

MUMMICHOG *Fundulus heteroclitus*   Also known as the common killifish, the mummichog is recognized by its stout body, deep caudal peduncle, short snout, large scales, and broadly rounded fins. These, in combination with the alternating dark and silvery bars and white or yellow spots on the sides, distinguish it from the striped killifish. During the breeding season the colors become more intense. The male is dark olive-green with the lateral bars distinct; the female is much paler and lacks distinct bars. The dark-barred pattern of the young disappears with age. Maximum size is 6 inches, but most are less than 4 inches; females are slightly larger.

Mummichog

86

The mummichog ranges in shallow water from Texas to the Gulf of St. Lawrence. Extremely common in coastal waters, it frequents bays, lagoons, estuaries, salt marshes, and ditches, in salt- and fresh-waters, but occurs predominantly in brackish water. It is common over mud or muddy-sand bottom, and during the winter it burrows into the mud in a torpid state.

In spring the mummichog migrates from brackish into fresher waters; it is not known if it returns to deepwater with the onset of cold weather. It is highly resistant to adverse environmental conditions, living in areas nearly devoid of oxygen, and it is moderately resistant to pollution.

Spawning occurs from April to August in only a few inches of water, following extensive courtship. The rather large eggs sink to the bottom. The young grow up in the shallow water and resemble their parents even at a small size. The mummichog is omnivorous, feeding to a large extent on plant material, detritus, worms, crustaceans, small mollusks, and small fishes.

STARHEAD TOPMINNOW *Fundulus notti* This freshwater species is easily identified by its deep, compressed body; a dark bar below each eye; and vertical bars on the sides in the male and horizontal black streaks in the female. Both sexes are olivaceous above and light on the sides and underneath; there are many small red dots on the sides of the male. In both sexes there is a bright silvery spot on the top of the head. The fish attains a length of $2^1/_2$ inches.

Starhead Topminnow

It is widely distributed in freshwater from Wisconsin and Iowa to Indiana, southward in the Mississippi River system, eastward to Florida in schools near the shores of weedy bayous and pools, and in small creeks in the South. It feeds on insects and crustaceans, catching most of them near the surface. It is of limited value as a forage- and baitfish.

SCULPIN FAMILY   Cottidae

This large family of fresh- and saltwater fishes consists mostly of small fishes. The species vary in length from 2–30 inches. A few are large enough to be used as food. They are found in waters of all depths, from very shallow to very deep.

Sculpins are distinguished by a bony support extending under the skin from the cheek to the eye. Anal fin spines are absent; pelvic fins are thoracic when present, and each has 1 spine and 2–5 softrays; the dorsal fin has fewer than 20 spines. The preopercle has 1 or more spines, variously developed, the upper sometimes antlerlike. Scales may be platelike along the lateral line; ctenoid or modified ctenoid and not covering the body below the lateral line; or absent. Pectoral fins are large. There is a greatly developed anal papilla in males of some species. The head is usually large and depressed; the eyes are high and closely set; gill membranes are connected and are often joined to isthmus. The environment has a marked effect on coloration, as does the sex in some species.

The family is most numerous in the North Pacific. There are 84 known species in the United States and Canada, excluding about 45 that occur only in Alaskan waters. Those sculpins restricted to freshwater are an important forage for gamefishes, particularly the trouts and smallmouth bass; they are widely used as bait, regionally known as bullheads or muddlers.

FOURHORN SCULPIN *Myoxocephalus quadricorni* This species and its subspecies range from the Great Lakes to the Arctic. It reaches a length of 6 inches.

MOTTLED SCULPIN *Cottus bairdi* This species ranges from southern Canada to the Appalachians, with subspecies west to the Rocky Mountains and in California. It is an important trout food everywhere it is found. This species reaches a length of 7 inches and is often used as live bait.

Mottled Sculpin

SUCKER FAMILY   Catostomidae

The sucker family, sometimes confused with some minnows, is easily distinguished by the position of the anal fin. If the distance from the anal to the tail fin is contained more than $2^1/_2$ times in the distance from the snout to the anal fin, the fish is a sucker. Excepted are carp and goldfish, which have a dorsal spine not found on suckers.

BIGMOUTH BUFFALO *Ictiobus cyprinellus*   The bigmouth buffalo is the largest member of the sucker family and the most important from an economic standpoint. However, it is seldom caught by sport fishermen. Found principally in the plains states, it ranges from North Dakota and southern Saskatchewan east to Ohio and Pennsylvania and south to the Gulf of Mexico. Large rivers and shallow lakes provide ideal habitat for the bigmouth buffalo. It often becomes extremely abundant in the shallow, fertile lakes of the Central Plains and sometimes reaches population levels of several hundred pounds per acre.

Bigmouth Buffalo

The body of the bigmouth buffalo is robust and elliptical in shape. The mouth is large, wide, oblique, and terminal, with the upper lip almost on a level with the eyes. There are no teeth in the mouth. The dorsal fin begins about midway along the back and extends nearly to the tail. There are no spines on any of the fins. The tail is moderately forked, and there are 35–43 scales along the lateral line. The color is a coppery olive-brown or slate-blue above, gradually fading to white on the belly.

The bigmouth buffalo seldom is referred to by its correct name, usually being called buffalo, buffalo-fish, common buffalo, lake buffalo, or blue buffalo.

The bigmouth buffalo taken by commercial fishermen usually weigh 3–12 pounds. Occasionally specimens reach 20–30 pounds, and one weighing over 80 pounds has been reported from Iowa.

Spawning takes place in April or May when water temperature reaches 60°–65° F. Adult buffalo school in shallow, weedy areas and scatter their eggs randomly in water up to 2–3 feet deep. A 10-pound female may spawn as many as 500,000 eggs. The eggs adhere to vegetation or debris and hatch in 10–14 days. No parental care is given the eggs or the young. The young fish remain in relatively shallow water most of the summer, feeding on small animal and plant forms of plankton. By the end of their first summer they measure 4–6 inches. In subsequent years under average conditions they measure about 11, 15, 18, 20, and 21 inches. Weight approximates 2 pounds at 15 inches, 5 pounds at 20 inches, and 10 pounds at 25 inches. Only under ideal conditions will many individuals live longer than 6–8 years and attain weights of over 20 pounds. Adulthood can be expected to occur at 3 years of age. Schooling tendencies prevail throughout life, aiding in harvest by commercial fishermen. Buffalo feed primarily on animal plankton. Entomostraca (small crustaceans) constitute about 90 percent of the diet, and the balance consists of plant material (mostly algae). Insect larvae and other bottom organisms provide only a minute portion of the diet.

Very little angling value can be associated with the bigmouth buffalo. Since its food consists primarily of plankton, it is seldom tempted by an angler's bait. Occasionally a specimen is taken on a worm or doughball or snagged by an artificial lure.

BLUEHEAD SUCKER *Pantosteus delphinus* This is a grayish-blue sucker with a large mouth, broad snout, and slender body. The upper lip is large, forming a fleshy hood over the mouth. Lips are notched at each side of the mouth. The caudal peduncle is long and slender. The scales are small and there are more than 90 in the lateral line. This species is limited to the upper Colorado River drainage.

Bluehead Sucker

The bluehead sucker is found in great abundance in mountain streams. It prefers riffle areas among the stones. The bluehead spawns in summer, when the male becomes colored with orange and pink. The food consists mostly of algae, although some aquatic insects are eaten. The maximum size of this species is about 12 inches.

The bluehead sucker is considered one of the more important foods for trouts within its range.

FLANNELMOUTH SUCKER *Catostomus latipinnis* This sucker is distinguished by its unusually large lower lip. It is a slender, fine-scaled sucker with a very long slender caudal peduncle. The snout is prominent. The sucking mouth is triangular, with very thick, greatly developed lips whose rear margins extend back to a point below the eye on each side. It has a deep cleft in the lower lip which extends two-thirds of the distance to the jaw. The eyes are small and high on the head. Its color is olive above and pale below. Fins are orange.

The flannelmouth sucker is found only in the Colorado River basin of the western United States.

Flannelmouth Sucker

This species inhabits creeks and rivers and feeds largely on vegetation. The fish spawn in the spring and reach a maximum length of $1^{1}/_{2}$–2 feet. They are used as food and can be caught on worms and similar baits.

HUMPBACK SUCKER *Xyrauchen texanus* This grotesque-appearing sucker has a prominent predorsal hump. It is grayish-silver with white or yellow underparts. The mouth is large and ventral. The lower lip is deeply cleft, separating the two lower lobes completely. Lateral-line scales number 73–95. The range of this species is limited to the lower Colorado River basin.

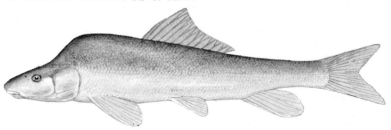

Humpback Sucker

The humpback prefers the slow-moving parts of larger streams and their backwaters. It is a spring spawner and feeds on detritus and algae. It may reach a size of 16 pounds.

LAHONTAN SUCKER *Pantosteus lahontan* This is a small brownish-olive sucker with ventral surfaces lighter to whitish. Lips are pendulous and provided with many sharp papillae. Pectoral fins are pointed and somewhat falcate. Anal fin may extend to the base of the caudal. The range of this species is confined to the Lahontan basin, Nevada.

The Lahontan sucker prefers the swift areas of streams and is not known in lakes. An upstream spawning migration takes place in early summer. There is no information on the food habits of this species. It reaches a length of 6 inches.

LAKE CHUBSUCKER *Erimyzon sucetta*   This is a small greenish sucker without a lateral line. There are usually 11–12 dorsal rays and usually 35–37 lateral scale rows. The young are often mistaken for minnows or shiners. Young chubsuckers have an intense black band from the tip of the snout to the tail. This fish has an overall bronze cast, and the dark scale edges give a cross-hatched appearance. The range of this sucker is from eastern Minnesota to New England and south to Florida and Texas.

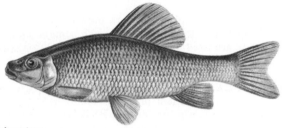

Lake Chubsucker

The lake chubsucker inhabits lakes and larger streams where turbidity and siltation are minimal. It is apparently found in association with much aquatic vegetation. Largely a bottom feeder, the chubsucker's diet consists of insect larvae, aquatic plants, and minute crustaceans. Spawning migrations occur to the smaller tributaries. The lake chubsucker rarely exceeds 10 inches in length.

LONGNOSE SUCKER *Catostomus catostomus*   As the name implies, this sucker has a bulbous snout projecting far beyond the upper lip. The fish is dark olive-slate on the back, with sides lighter and belly milky-white. Scales are sharply outlined with darker color. Lateral-line scales number more than 85. The longnose is widely distributed east of the Rocky Mountains from Alaska to Maine.

A deep-, coldwater species, the longnose ascends tributary streams to spawn in April, May, and June. At this time the male develops a rosy lateral band. Little is known of the food habits of the longnose sucker except that it apparently feeds primarily on plant material. The average size is 16 inches and 2 pounds.

Longnose Sucker

The longnose sucker has little angling value. It is caught on worms and is also taken by spearing during the spring migration period. The flesh is edible although very bony.

MOUNTAIN SUCKER *Catostomus platyrhynchus* This dark green sucker has fine black specks along the back. Ventral surfaces are white, body slender, head short. Scales are small, 90–100 in the lateral line, crowded anteriorly. Lips are full, and there is a distinct notch between upper and lower lip at the corners of the mouth. The range of this species is from the Columbia River drainage and the headwaters of the Missouri to the Bonneville basin and the Snake River drainage of Utah and Wyoming.

Mountain Sucker

The mountain sucker prefers the clear, cold mountain streams, where it is found in the rock-strewn riffle areas. This sucker spawns in late spring in the shallow tributaries. At this time the male develops an orange lateral band. The food consists mostly of algae and some aquatic insects. This species reaches a size of 12 inches.

Of little or no importance as food for man, the mountain sucker does provide excellent forage for trouts and other gamefishes.

NORTHERN HOG SUCKER *Hypentelium nigricans* This sucker is also known as hog molly or hammerhead. Identifying the northern hog sucker is relatively simple. The major features are a large head, with a depression between the eyes and a sucking-type mouth, and 4 rather broad, dark oblique bars or saddles on the body. The eyes are behind the middle of the snout. The whole body appears almost conical and is covered with large scales. The lower fins are a dull red. Some hog suckers attain a length of 2 feet, but 10–12 inches is the usual size seen.

The northern hog sucker is found from central Minnesota eastward through the Great Lakes region to New York, down the Mississippi drainage to the Gulf of Mexico. Elsewhere its southern limit extends from northern Alabama to eastern Oklahoma. It is generally present only in clear streams. Preferred habitats are riffles and adjacent areas of clear, shallow streams with gravel bottoms. It also frequents the shallow areas of lakes near the mouth of a stream.

Northern Hog Sucker

There are two very similar species of lesser distribution, the Alabama hog sucker (*H. etowanum*) and the Roanoke hog sucker (*H. roanokense*).

Spawning occurs in shallow waters or riffles in April to June, as water temperatures reach 60°F. There is some movement in larger streams to the headwaters at this time. During spawning several males crowd about a female as she takes her position over an area of sand and gravel in shallow water. Two or three usually remain at her sides as eggs are extruded. The eggs are not guarded, and there is some loss due to predation by other fishes.

A striking peculiarity of the hog sucker is its feeding habits. The large bony head, streamlined form, and well-developed pectoral fins enable it to seek its food in the more rapid parts of streams. It uses its long snout and large head to turn over rocks while it keeps its position on the riffle with the pectoral fins. Food is obtained by sucking up the ooze and slime exposed when the rocks are moved. Many insect larvae and other minute organisms are gathered in this manner. During these activities the sucker often serves as a provider for other species. As it roots a path through a riffle, it is often followed by small fishes that feed on the insects dislodged. The smallmouth bass is the game species most frequently observed enjoying this free board.

NORTHERN REDHORSE *Maxostoma macrolepidotum* The northern redhorse is one of the more colorful suckers found in the north and central states east of the Rockies and throughout central and eastern Canada. The southern extremity of its range is in Kansas and northern Arkansas; to the east it ranges through New York, Pennsylvania, and Ohio. It is a cleanwater species found in rivers, moderate-sized streams, and lakes. The northern redhorse is especially at home in swift, clear rivers and streams.

The northern redhorse is bright silvery on the sides, with a somewhat darker back. The fins, including the forked tail, are bright orange or blood-red. The rather short dorsal fin is falcate and has 12–14 rays. The typical sucker-shaped body usually has 42–44 scales along the lateral line. There are no teeth in the mouth or spines in the fins. The head is unusually short, with the suckerlike mouth positioned ventrally.

Other names often applied to the northern redhorse include redfin, redhorse, redfin sucker, and bigscale sucker.

94

The usual size of the species taken by fishermen runs 2–4 pounds; maximum weight attained is 10–12 pounds. Northern redhorses ascend small, clear streams in April or May to spawn over gravel or rubble. In lakes, they may select clean sand or gravel bars where the water is 1–2 feet deep. An adult female spawns 10,000–50,000 eggs. After spawning the parents leave the spawning grounds, and the eggs take about 2 weeks to hatch. The young feed on minute plankton until they are large enough to begin the adult diet of insect larvae and small mollusks, which are sucked from the gravel and rocky bottom. Under average conditions they attain lengths of 4, 7, 10, 13, 15, and 17 inches at ages 1–6 years, respectively. A 1-pound specimen should measure 14 inches; a 2-pounder, 17 inches; an 8- to 10-pounder, at least 24 inches. Adulthood is reached at age 3–4, and only a few individuals can be expected to live 8–9 years.

Northern Redhorse

Northern redhorses are particularly vulnerable to muddy or polluted water. They are found only rarely in such waters, and when normally cleanwaters are occasionally subjected to these conditions, heavy mortality among the redhorse population can be expected. This inability to withstand silt and pollution has greatly decreased the distribution of the species as modern civilization has systematically dirtied most of the major rivers and streams.

Northern redhorses are viewed with favor by anglers in some localities. They are most readily caught during and just after their spring spawning runs and may be taken on worms, grubs, and crickets. They are one of the best eating species of the sucker family.

QUILLBACK *Carpiodes cyprinus*   The quillback is 1 of 4 species of carpsuckers (*Carpiodes* spp.), all of which have very similar characteristics. They are so difficult to distinguish that ichthyologists have been confused over the natural range of each species owing to obvious misidentifications reported in the literature. The other 3 species are the river carpsucker (*C. carpio*), the plains carpsucker (*C. forbesi*), and the highfin carpsucker (*C. velifer*).

The 4 species of the genus *Carpiodes* are silvery, deep-bodied fish, with the anterior rays of the dorsal fin much longer than the rest of the fin rays, especially in the quillback. The color is light olive above with silvery sides and white belly. The scales give off silvery, greenish, and bluish reflections. The mouth is toothless, small, and subterminal, with rather thin lips that are flesh or white in color. The number of lateral-line scales runs 33−41. The tail is deeply forked, and there are no spines on the fins. The flesh is exceedingly bony.

The primary range of the carpsuckers includes the Missouri, Mississippi, and Ohio river drainages and eastward to the Atlantic drainage with the exception of the northern New England and southeastern coastal states. They are primarily large-river fishes, though the quillback may be found in most of the Great Lakes.

Carpsuckers often are referred to as white carp, silver carp, highfin, white sucker, quillback, or river sucker.

Maximum weights vary from about 3 pounds for the highfin carpsucker to 10−12 pounds for the river carpsucker.

Spawning of carpsuckers takes place in April or May when water temperature is about 60° F. The tiny eggs are scattered randomly in

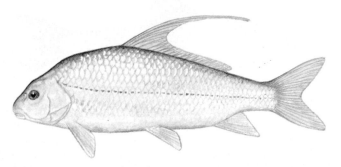

Quillback

shallow water, and no parental care is given before or after they hatch. The number of eggs per female may approach several hundred thousand. Incubation takes place in 8−12 days. The tiny fry feed on minute plankton and reach a length of 2−4 inches by the end of the year. Averaging 3 inches in growth the first year, they measure about 6, 9, 11, 13, and 15 inches at ages 2−6, respectively. Weight is about 1 pound at 13 inches, 2 pounds at 16 inches, and 3 pounds at 19 inches. Adulthood is attained at 3−4 years of age. Few live longer than 8 years.

As adults, carpsuckers tend to travel in schools. They usually remain close to the bottom, where they apparently browse on minute plant and animal organisms (periphyton) associated with rocks and debris.

Annual mortality is high, especially when the carpsuckers are 6 inches or shorter and ideal forage for predatory fishes. Even for adults, mortality probably runs 60−70 percent annually.

The carpsuckers are not of particular importance to anglers. Though occasionally taken on worms, doughballs, bread, or snag hooks, they usually are caught by fishermen in quest of other species.

SHORTHEAD REDHORSE *Moxostoma breviceps*   A red- or pink-tailed sucker with dark spots at the base of each scale, the shorthead resembles the common redhorse except that its head is smaller and more pointed. Its dorsal fin is falcate. The range of the shorthead redhorse is the Ohio River drainage in Ohio, Pennsylvania, and Kentucky.

This sucker is found in small and large streams and in lakes. It avoids clearwater and appears to prefer warmer temperatures. Its food consists mostly of animal matter, including mollusks and insect larvae.

The shorthead redhorse apparently enjoys some popularity with anglers, as it is often seen on anglers' strings along with the common redhorse. Where it is abundant, it is taken commercially in pound nets.

SILVER REDHORSE *Moxostoma anisurum*   This is a silvery sucker with the rear edge of the dorsal convex. The length of the largest dorsal ray is usually as long as the distance from the space between the eyes to the origin of the dorsal fin. The lower lips of this sucker are very full. The body is silvery and white with dark-edged scales without dark spotting at their bases. The tail is light slate-colored. The range is from Manitoba to the St. Lawrence drainage and south to northern Alabama and Missouri.

The silver redhorse is an inhabitant of large streams, where it prefers long, deep pools with slow currents. It is tolerant of turbidity and siltation. The food of this redhorse is primarily immature aquatic insects. Spawning takes place over gravel bars. The usual size of this sucker is 11–22 inches, and specimens have been reported to 8 pounds.

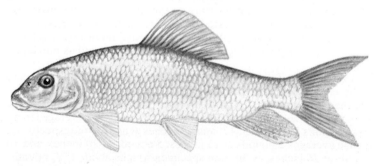

Silver Redhorse

97

SMALLMOUTH BUFFALO *Ictiobus bubalus* The smallmouth buffalo is second only to the bigmouth buffalo in size attained by species of the sucker family and in economic importance. Though seldom caught by anglers, it contributes significantly to the commercial harvest of fish in the central states. Its range is similar to that of the bigmouth buffalo, being found from North Dakota east to Pennsylvania and south to the Gulf of Mexico. Found principally in large rivers and warm lakes of the plains states, it requires somewhat cleaner and deeper waters than its close relative, the bigmouth. This requirement has caused a general decrease in abundance and restriction of range as civilization in the central states has gradually silted and polluted many major rivers and lakes.

The body of the smallmouth buffalo is more compressed and the back more elevated (humpbacked) than in the bigmouth buffalo. The mouth is small, subterminal, almost horizontal, and protracts downward. Lateral-line scales number 37–39. The color generally is lighter than that of the other buffalo, being a slaty-bronze or olive above and fading to white or yellowish on the belly. Other characteristics are similar to those described for the bigmouth buffalo.

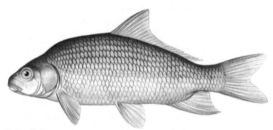

Smallmouth Buffalo

Other names often given the smallmouth buffalo are razorback buffalo, roachback, and thicklipped buffalo.

Average size of the species runs smaller than that of the bigmouth buffalo. Commercially harvested specimens run 2–10 pounds, but an occasional fish weighs 15–20 pounds. One smallmouth buffalo taken in Tennessee weighed $28^{1}/_{2}$ pounds; 40 pounds is listed as maximum weight.

Most aspects of the smallmouth buffalo's life history are similar to or the same as those of the bigmouth buffalo. Primary differences are that the smallmouth relies more on insects and bottom organisms for food, requires cleaner waters, and grows more slowly. Average length approximates 5, 9, 12, 15, 17, and 19 inches at ages 1–6, respectively. Weight averages 2 pounds at 15 inches, 5 pounds at 20 inches, and 10 pounds at 26 inches. A 30-inch specimen weighs about $17^{1}/_{2}$ pounds.

The smallmouth buffalo is not considered of value to the angler, since only an occasional, accidental catch is made by sport fishermen.

SPOTTED SUCKER *Minytrema melanops* The presence of dark spots on the base of each scale distinguishes this species from others of the sucker family. Color is silvery with a dark olive back. Spots on the scales form prominent longitudinal stripes. Lateral line is indistinct or absent. Outer margin of dorsal fin is concave. Scales in lateral series number 43–45. Lips are thin and striated. The range of this species is from southern Minnesota to Pennsylvania and south to Texas and Florida.

Spotted Sucker

An inhabitant of larger streams and lakes with sand, gravel, or hard clay bottoms, the spotted sucker is intolerant of turbid waters and industrial pollutants. Little is known of the breeding habits of this species. It apparently spawns in early spring, when the male develops 3 lateral bands: the lower chocolate-gray, the middle grayish-pink, and the upper dark lavender. The food of this sucker consists of mollusks and insect larvae. It reaches 18 inches in length.

STRIPED JUMPROCK *Moxostoma rupiscartes* The striped jumprock is a small sucker rarely exceeding 10 inches in total length. Its geographical distribution is the Piedmont and mountain portions of the Santee, Savannah, Altamaha, and Chattahoochee river systems of North Carolina, South Carolina, and Georgia. The distinguishing characteristics of this species, which separate it from other *Moxostoma,* are as follows. Its head is wider than deep and the lips are semipapillose; the lowermost caudal ray is dusky in color; it has 10, but occasionally 11, dorsal rays; the head depth, at occiput, goes into

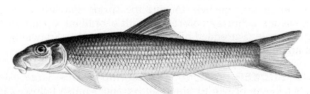

Striped Jumprock

99

the predorsal distance 3 or more times; the scales on the middle part of the lateral line are smaller than the eye; a lateral-line scale count is usually 44; a dusky-colored edging appears on the dorsal fin; the anterior edge of the eye lies decidedly behind the lower lip; the occipital line is curved forward; the last dorsal ray is shorter, more than $1^1/_2$ times in the dorsal base; there are 12 or less, rarely 13, dorsal rays; the margin of the dorsal fin is falcate; and the scales around the caudal peduncle number 16.

This sucker is essentially a small-stream fish found in the Piedmont and the mountains. In most cases it can be associated with fairly fast water or riffles, and it prefers a sand, gravel, or rubble bottom. The striped jumprock spawns when the water temperature approaches 56°F. At this time the male has minute white tubercles scattered over the head, snout, anterior scales, and on the anal and caudal fins. This pattern is also noticeable in females, but there are fewer tubercles and they are much smaller. This fish received its name jumprock because of its peculiar habit of leaping from the water.

TAHOE SUCKER *Catostomus tahoensis* This is a large, dark-colored sucker with a large head. The body is dark and the fins dusky. The mouth is large; the lips are moderate in size, upper pendant, the lower rather full. Scales are small and crowded forward; 85–90 in the lateral line. Dorsal fin is short and low with 10 rays. This species is native to the Lahontan system of Nevada and California.

Tahoe Sucker

The Tahoe sucker is both lake and stream dwelling and appears to be the most abundant sucker within its range. Little is known of the food habits of this species. During the spring spawning season the male develops a brassy coloration with a brilliant vermilion lateral stripe. A female is attended by as many as 25 males. Spawning occurs over a gravel nest amid much thrashing and churning.

WEBUG SUCKER *Catostomus fecundus* This large, slender-bodied sucker is brown to black above and whitish below. Fins are dark. Dorsal fin is long and low with 12–13 rays. Lateral-line scales number 64–75. The range of this sucker is confined to the Bonneville and the upper Snake rivers in Utah and Wyoming.

Abundant in the lakes and rivers within its range, the webug sucker in some areas is at home in waters well above 80°F. Spawning in June, this species is observed in large numbers in the tributary streams. It spawns in a manner similar to that of others of the sucker family in that 2 males attend each female, and eggs are spread among the sand and gravel of the creek bed. The webug sucker is an omnivorous feeder and is said to consume large numbers of trout eggs. The webug reaches a length of 25 inches and a weight of 12 pounds.

WHITE SUCKER *Catostomus commersoni* This olive-brown, cylindrical sucker has 55–85 scales along the lateral line. The rounded snout projects only slightly or not at all beyond the tip of the upper lip. The dorsal fin contains 10–13 rays. The commonest of all suckers, the white sucker, ranges from northern Canada south to Florida and west to Montana.

White Sucker

The white sucker is quite tolerant of a great variety of conditions. It apparently prefers large streams and the deeper water of impoundments. It is found in fastwaters and sluggish streams and in association with dense weed beds. It is tolerant of large amounts of pollution, siltation, and turbidity and is able to survive in waters low in oxygen.

White suckers feed on a variety of foods, including aquatic insect larvae, crustaceans, mollusks, and algae, particularly those forms found in bottom ooze.

Normally migrating into streams of all gradients and all sizes to spawn at night, the white sucker deposits its slightly adhesive eggs in shallow water. The vigorous spawning act serves to cover the eggs lightly. These suckers are also known to spawn in the shoal areas of lakes. Radical changes in color of these fish, especially the male, take place during the spawning act. The back becomes olive-colored with a bright lavender sheen, and there is a lateral band of pink or red along the side.

The white sucker usually runs 10–20 inches in length, and commercial fishermen have reported weights as high as 8 pounds.

A soft and bony fish, the white sucker is not highly valued for food, but during the spring spawning run, the flesh is firm and palatable.

CATFISH FAMILY   Ictaluridae

In the field, bullheads can be quickly separated from other catfishes on the basis of caudal-fin shape. All bullheads have emarginate or rounded tails. The only major catfish with a rounded tail is the flathead, but it also has an extremely large free-moving adipose fin, which differs from the small adipose of the bullhead. The miniature madtoms can be separated from both catfishes and bullheads by their adnate adipose fins, which give the impression of a continuous fin with a slight notch on the upper posterior half of the body.

BLACK BULLHEAD *Ictalurus melas*   The black bullhead, similar in appearance to the yellow and brown bullheads, is distinguished by its dark-colored or spotted chin barbels and its pectoral spines without serrations. Color dorsally is black, dark green, or yellowish-green; sides yellower or whiter; underparts bright yellow, yellow, or milk-white. Body is chubby and deep at dorsal origin; angle steep from dorsal to snout. Adipose fin is prominent, with free lobe. The range of the black bullhead is from New York and North Dakota to Texas. It has been widely introduced elsewhere.

This catfish seems to prefer silty water with a soft mud bottom. It is highly tolerant of many types of industrial and domestic pollutants and of warm water.

Spawning takes place in spring; eggs are laid in nests or depressions or sometimes attached to plants and debris. As is the habit of others of the catfish family, the black bullhead guards the nest and young for some time. A mostly carnivorous species, it subsists on insects, small fishes, and mollusks. The black bullhead is a smaller member of the catfish family and seldom reaches more than 2 pounds, but has been recorded to 8 pounds.

The horned pout of the central states, the black bullhead, is a commonly stocked farm-pond species that is well adapted to most water conditions, easily raised, and an excellent table fish.

Black Bullhead

BLACK MADTOM   *Noturus funebris*   Found along the Gulf coast from western Florida to Louisiana, the black madtom is distinguished by its anal fin with 20–25 rays. It is an inhabitant of springs and small

Black Madtom

creeks with a moderate current and some aquatic vegetation. Maximum length is about 4 inches. It is seldom used as bait, but has some value as a foragefish for basses.

BLUE CATFISH *Ictalurus furcatus*   A pale blue catfish with a deeply forked tail, its anal fin contains 30–36 rays and is straight on its rear edge. The eyes appear to be located in the lower half of the head. The color is silvery-pale blue above, lighter on the sides, and silvery or milk-white below. The blue catfish is distributed in large rivers from Minnesota and Ohio southward into Mexico, and has been introduced into Atlantic coast streams.

Blue Catfish

Less fond of turbid waters than the other catfishes, the blue catfish prefers the clearer, swifter streams. In its natural range it was apparently more abundant prior to extensive impoundment of streams. It is found over stream bottoms of bedrock, boulders, gravel, or sand. Feeding in swiftly flowing rapids or chutes, the blue catfish prefers fishes and crayfishes in its diet. Spawning in the manner of others of its family, the blue catfish builds its nest in a sheltered area under a rock or log; both male and female assist in rearing the young. The blue catfish is the largest of the catfish family, sometimes reaching over 100 pounds, although the average is less than 50 pounds.

BRINDLED MADTOM *Noturus miurus*   This small, mottled catfish has poisonous pectoral spines. Color is grayish with dorsal blotches. Pectoral spine has 4–8 sharp teeth on the rear edge. Tail is rounded.

Adipose fin has no free lobe and is separated from caudal by a slight notch. Upper jaw is longer than lower jaw. Eyes are rather large. The brindled madtom ranges from Illinois to southern Ontario and to Mississippi and Oklahoma.

This species appears to prefer quiet, clear streams over sand bottoms and organic debris. A secretive fish, it hides by day under stones, roots, or logs. Little is known of its breeding habits, but it appears to spawn much in the manner of others of its genus. An omnivorous feeder, the brindled madtom subsists on various aquatic organisms found in the organic debris in which it lives. This species is quite small, averaging less than 4 inches in length.

BROWN BULLHEAD *Ictalurus nebulosus* This is a medium-sized, slender-bodied catfish with dark chin barbels. The anal fin has 20–24 rays, and the tail is slightly emarginate. Rear edges of the pectoral spines are endowed with many sharp teeth. The color is yellow-brown to light chocolate-brown with vague darker mottlings above, lighter sides, and yellow or milk-white below. The natural range of the brown bullhead is from Maine and the Great Lakes south to Florida and Mexico. It has been widely introduced elsewhere. The brown bullhead prefers weedy, deeper waters of lakes and sluggish streams. Although not commonly found in turbid waters, it is associated with mud or deep muck as well as sand and gravel bottom.

An omnivorous feeder, the bullhead may consume anything from plant material to fish. Owing to its bottom-feeding habits, however, insect larvae and mollusks form a major portion of its diet. The bullhead feeds mostly at night, feeling for its prey with its sensitive barbels.

The brown bullhead spawns in a nest consisting of a shallow depression or cleared spot usually sheltered by logs, rocks, or vegetation. Adhesive eggs are laid in cream-colored clusters. One or both parents guard the nest and young and have been observed cleaning eggs and fry by taking them into their mouths and then blowing them gently back into the nest. The adults stay with the young until they are swimming freely, sometimes until they are 1 inch in length. The brown bullhead adult is commonly 6–16 inches in length and seldom exceeds 3 pounds.

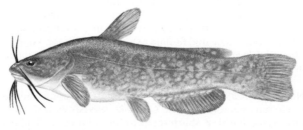

Brown Bullhead

CHANNEL CATFISH *Ictalurus punctatus* This is the only spotted catfish with a deeply forked tail. Like all members of the North American catfish family, the channel catfish possesses long barbels about the mouth, 4 under the jaw, 2 above, and 1 on the tip of each maxillary. The anal fin contains 24–30 rays. This species is most easily separated from the blue catfish and white catfish by the number of anal rays and the presence of black spots.

This catfish varies in color from bluish or olivaceous-silvery above and silver-white below in young individuals to dark blue or black above and whitish below in older specimens. The black spots are small and irregular, and may be few or many in different individuals.

The range of the channel catfish extends from the Great Lakes and Saskatchewan River southward to the Gulf of Mexico and into Mexico. The fish has been introduced with varied success both east and west of its natural range.

Channel Catfish, 2 Pounds

The channel catfish inhabits lakes and larger rivers that have clean bottoms of sand, gravel, or boulders. It is not often found in association with dense weed beds. The adults are highly migratory, ascending small streams to spawn. Yearlings and subadults apparently are more tolerant of fast currents than are adults. This catfish feeds, as do others of its family, on nearly all aquatic forms including fishes, insects, and crustaceans. It feeds chiefly at night, sometimes in rather swiftly flowing water.

The channel catfish male attains a darker blue-black coloration during the spawning season. The eggs are deposited in a nest below an undercut stream bank or under a log or stone. The nest is guarded by the male for some time after the fry have hatched.

Channel Catfish, 57 Pounds

105

Among the larger species of the catfish family, the channel catfish is most commonly taken at 11–30 inches in length and up to 15 pounds in weight. Commercial fishermen have reported the maximum weight to be about 60 pounds.

The channel catfish is considered by some to be superior to other members of its family because of its excellent food and sport-fishing value.

FLAT BULLHEAD *Ictalurus platycephalus*   Found from the Roanoke River in Virginia southward to the Altamaha River in Georgia, this species has 21–24 anal rays, an emarginate or slightly forked tail, a flattened head, and a narrow black margin on all median fins. In some watersheds the body may have a strong yellowish coloration, and the fish is sometimes confused with the yellow bullhead. Howev-

Flat Bullhead

er, the lower third of its dorsal fin has a prominent black band or blotch. The flat bullhead occurs in streams, lakes, and ponds with soft muck, mud, or sand bottoms. It feeds principally on vegetation, snails, and mussels. Only a small poundage of this species is taken commercially, but its flesh is comparable to that of the channel catfish. Maximum size is about 2 pounds.

FLATHEAD CATFISH *Pylodictis olivaris*   This large, square-tailed catfish has a wide, distinctly flattened head and a short anal fin with usually 14–17 rays. Its lower jaw is always longer than the upper. Its general coloration is brown, mottled with darker brown. The upper and lower edges of the caudal fin are white or lighter than the rest of the fin. The flathead catfish is distributed in large rivers in the Mississippi valley south into Mexico.

Preferring long, deep, sluggish pools of larger rivers, the flathead catfish is normally found over hard bottoms. Omnivorous in its food habits, this catfish appears to prefer a fish diet. It has been observed to lie quietly in shallow water with its large mouth wide open. Frightened fish have been seen darting into the open mouth, to be quickly swallowed.

Like most of its family, the flathead is popular with anglers because of its excellent flavor and large size. Although 3- to 4-pound fish are

Flathead Catfish

considered average, this species may attain weights up to 100 pounds. Handlines and trotlines are popular methods, using crayfish or whole or cut fish as bait.

GREEN BULLHEAD *Ictalurus brunneus* Found from Cape Fear, North Carolina, to the St. Johns River in Florida, this species has 17–20 anal rays, an emarginate caudal fin, an inferior mouth with decurved snout, and a flattened head. Although the body coloration is generally uniform, it is sometimes spotted and occasionally mottled. The green bullhead occurs in streams and rivers with a moderate to swift current over gravel or rock bottoms. It is usually caught in pools below riffles and dams or in deep channels. Gravid females have been found from February to July, and the species is believed to spawn throughout the year. Nocturnal and omnivorous, the green bullhead consumes principally vegetation, insects, minnows, and snails.

Green Bullhead

Good eating, it is of little commercial value owing to its small size. Maximum weight is about $1^1/_2$ pounds, but the average is $^1/_4$ pound. This fish is readily caught on scent and natural baits.

HEADWATER CATFISH *Ictalurus lupus* This species is found from northeastern Mexico to the Pecos River drainage of Texas, but little is known of its life history, as it is rarely identified by commercial or sport anglers. The headwater catfish greatly resembles a small channel catfish. However, the body lacks spots (present in a channel catfish of comparable size) and the caudal fin is not deeply forked. The base of the anal fin is longer than the head length.

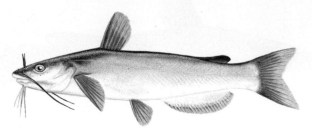

Headwater Catfish

SPECKLED MADTOM *Noturus leptacanthus*   This catfish is found from eastern Louisiana to Florida and north to South Carolina. Its anal fin has 18 rays or less. An inhabitant of small- to moderate-sized creeks with a coarse sand or gravel bottom and moderately swift currents, the speckled madtom reaches a maximum length of about 3 inches.

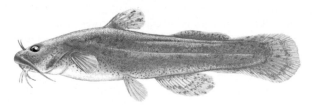

Speckled Madtom

SPOTTED BULLHEAD *Ictalurus serracanthus*   Found from northern Florida to southern Georgia and westward to southeastern Alabama, the spotted bullhead has a very limited range. This species has 20–23 anal rays, a flattened head, and is readily distinguished by its spotted body and the strong serrations on its pectoral fins. This bullhead occurs in large streams and rivers with moderate currents and in impounded lakes within its range. Little is known of its life history. Ripe fish are found from December to July. Relatively abundant in limited areas, it may outnumber the white and channel catfishes in certain locations. A mollusk feeder, it is often called snailcat.

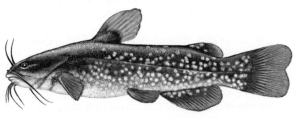

Spotted Bullhead

108

It is rarely taken with nets, but commonly in commercial slat traps and on hook and line. Edible but small, its maximum weight is probably about 1 pound, with the average in the Suwannee, Ochlockonee, and Apalachicola rivers running $^1/_4$ pound.

STONECAT *Noturus flavus* A yellowish catfish with rounded or square tail and an inconspicuous adipose fin, the stonecat is yellow-olive to blue-black above, with lighter sides, and yellowish or milk-white underparts. The caudal fin has a light border. The adipose fin is bound to the body over its entire length. The upper jaw is much longer than lower jaw, and there are no teeth or serrations on the rear edge

Stonecat

of the pectoral spine, but there is a poison gland at its base. The body is slender. The range of the stonecat is from Montana to the Great Lakes and south to Texas.

Primarily a riffle species, the stonecat, as its name implies, is found in rocky streams and rocky, windblown lake shallows. Spawning in early summer in much the same manner as other catfish, the stonecat deposits its eggs on rocks and logs, and the adults guard the eggs and young for some time. An omnivorous feeder, the stonecat consumes a variety of aquatic animals and plant material. The stonecat is a small species, seldom reaching 12 inches in length.

In some areas the stonecat is said to be of extreme importance as food for the smallmouth bass.

TADPOLE MADTOM *Noturus gyrinus* This is a small, yellowish-brown madtom with a tadpole-shaped body. There are no barbs on the posterior edge of the pectoral spine, but a poison gland at its base. The

Tadpole Madtom

lower jaw is as long or nearly as long as the upper. The caudal fin is very rounded and the eyes are small. The adipose fin is high but with no free lobe. The range of this madtom is from North Dakota to Quebec and south to Florida and Texas. Introduced into the Columbia River drainage.

The habitat of the tadpole madtom is stillwater of streams, lakes, marshes, and even springs. It is found hiding under stones and logs. Apparently mostly carnivorous, the tadpole madtom feeds on crustaceans, aquatic insect larvae, and some fishes. This species spawns in early summer in the manner of others of the catfish family. The tadpole madtom seldom reaches a length of more than 4 inches.

WHITE CATFISH *Ictalurus catus*   A bluish and silvery fish, with a moderately forked tail, the white catfish has 19–23 rays in the anal fin. Lacking distinct spots, this catfish may give a bicolor appearance, as there may be a sharp demarcation line between the darker color of the lower sides and whitish ventral areas. Some specimens appear mottled with colors ranging from milky-gray to dark blue.

White Catfish

The natural distribution of the white catfish extends from the Chesapeake Bay region in coastal streams southward to Texas. It has been introduced widely on the West Coast and into the Northeast.

The white catfish, in its native range, inhabits the fresh- and slightly brackish water of streams, ponds, and bayous. Although it is tolerant of rather swiftly flowing streams, it prefers a more sluggish current than does the channel catfish. It appears to occupy a habitat rather intermediate between that of the channel cat and the bullheads. The white catfish is somewhat migratory in its spawning habit, although it is less so than the channel catfish.

An omnivorous feeder, the white catfish subsists on nearly all aquatic forms, including fishes and aquatic insects. Smaller than the channel catfish, this species runs 10–18 inches long and seldom exceeds 3 pounds.

YAQUI CATFISH *Ictalurus pricei*   Found from northern Mexico into southern Arizona, little is known of its life history, as the species is seldom identified by commercial or sport anglers. It is easily con-

Yaqui Catfish

fused with a channel catfish. However, the body lacks spots and the caudal fin is not deeply forked. The base of the anal fin is shorter than the head length. The anterior part of its dorsal fin is conspicuously higher than the posterior part.

YELLOW BULLHEAD *Ictalurus natalis*   This yellowish catfish has a rounded tail and light barbels. Dorsally it is yellow-olive to slaty-black, depending on habitat. The sides are lighter and more yellowish. The lower surface of head and body is bright yellow, yellow-white, or milk-white. Anal fin has 23–27 rays. Rear edges of pectoral spines have sharp teeth or serrations. The yellow bullhead is separated from the brown and black bullheads by white or light barbels, the absence of spots on the body, and more anal rays; it is distinguished from the blue, white, and channel catfishes by the rounded or square tail. The range of the yellow bullhead is from North Dakota to the Hudson River and southward to Florida.

Yellow Bullhead

The yellow bullhead appears to be most abundant in sluggish streams and shallow portions of lakes and of streams and ponds over soft bottoms. Spawning in a manner similar to others of its family, the yellow bullhead deposits its eggs in a nest or burrow in May and June. The nest may be under a stone or log, or it may be an excavated burrow a little larger than the fish itself. Both sexes participate in the nest building. The male guards the yellowish-white, adhesive eggs and the young fish for some time after they leave the nest.

The yellow bullhead is a scavenger and consumes almost anything found in the water—minnows, crayfishes, insect larvae, and snails by preference. Plant material is also found in the diet.

This catfish attains a length of 18 inches and weight of 3 pounds.

Because few anglers distinguish the yellow from the brown bullhead, it is difficult to ascertain its value. Cyclic in abundance, the yellow bullhead enters the southern United States commercial fishery to some extent when populations are at a peak. The cream-colored flesh has good food value, but this bullhead should be iced soon after capture or it is inclined to have a mushy texture.

ARMORED CATFISH FAMILY   Loricariidae

This large family of catfishes is indigenous to northern and central South America. There are many genera: some have bony plates covering the body, including the ventral surface; others are naked on the lower side. The first group also has an adipose fin; the second does not.

Armored Catfish

The armored catfish was accidentally introduced into Florida, and its present range is unknown. Numerous specimens have been caught in creeks, rock pits, and canals north of the Miami area and in the Tampa Bay area, notably Six-Mile Creek; these locations coincide with major tropical fish farms. There are many armored catfishes weighing up to 100 pounds, but the genus present in the United States (*Plecostomus*) is apparently one of the smaller members of the family. Like the walking catfish, its distribution has been limited by water temperature. Armored catfishes have powerful pectoral spines that serve for locomotion when the fish is working forward along the bottom against swift currents. Caught on all the usual catfish baits, it is edible but virtually impossible to clean. Amazonian Indians toss the fish in the fire whole and crack the "shell" to pry loose the meat.

WALKING CATFISH FAMILY   Clariidae

There are numerous species of clarid catfishes distributed from Africa and Madagascar over the whole of southern Asia to the Philippines and the Malay Archipelago. They are all elongate (sometimes

Walking Catfish

eellike) catfishes with broad, flat head and 4 pairs of long barbels. Characteristic of the entire family is an accessory air-breathing organ in the form of either paired tubular blind sacs extending backward from the gill chamber or of an aborescent accessory organ projecting into the gill chamber. These air-breathing organs permit clarids to live in poorly oxygenated water and to exist out of water for prolonged periods.

One species, *Clarias batrachus*, is known to occur in the United States. It was accidentally introduced into Florida from Bangkok in 1966 and is now found in a discontiguous range in the Tampa Bay area and from Lake Okeechobee south to Miami. Because the walking catfish can migrate overland (it walks on its sharply pointed pectoral fins while sculling with its tail) and thrives in brackish water, its ultimate range is unknown. Only the lethal temperature zone (41°–48°F) has kept the species from invading other states; this may change on the genetic basis of thermal history. Exposed to low temperatures for brief periods, the survivors could become adapted. Known predators are snook, basses, and gars. They have also been found in the stomachs of bluefish. The walking catfish is often seen on Florida roads after a rain. Nocturnal in habits and readily caught on scent baits, particularly cheese, it is edible, but the foul-smelling skin is difficult to remove. Use extreme caution in handling, as pectoral spines cause severe pain.

CHARACIN FAMILY   Characidae

PIRANHAS Also known as *caribe* (Spanish), these freshwater fishes are native to South America. However, individual specimens have been recovered in United States waters (Florida and Ohio) during recent years, evidently dispersed by tropical-fish collectors.

Piranhas are generally flattened from side to side and have a high body; all have a fleshy adipose fin on the back between the dorsal and caudal fins. The head is blunt, with short, powerful jaws containing many sharp cutting teeth. Of the many characins in South America, only a few are piranhas, and of approximately 25 piranhas only about 4 species are dangerous to man. One species grows to 2 feet, but the others are smaller. Piranhas have a wide distribution throughout the rivers of Colombia, Venezuela, the Guianas, Brazil, Paraguay, and south to central Argentina. They occur in swarms, at which time they pose the greatest danger, especially in muddy waters; they are repor-

113

tedly less dangerous in clearwaters. Small fishes are their usual diet, but injured or dead animals are readily and eagerly devoured. Their ability to detect blood in the water is legendary, but more likely they are able to perceive the vibrations of the injured or struggling animal.

There are many tales about the danger of the piranha, but some authorities feel that, while the piranha is indeed a potential danger and undoubtedly has taken its toll of humans and other animals, many of the stories may be traceable to a relatively few, but spectacular, instances that have been repeated and embellished over the centuries, making it appear that the piranha does nothing but actively seek out human blood and devour hapless beings. Nevertheless, these tales are remarkable. One authenticated report tells of a 100-pound capybara (a large rodent) from which the flesh was stripped in less than a minute; another, no less authentic, documents a man and his horse falling into the water and both being picked clean except for the man's clothes, which were undamaged. Thus, because of its sharp teeth, its speed, the large numbers in which it travels, and its at least alleged danger, the piranha should certainly be treated with caution.

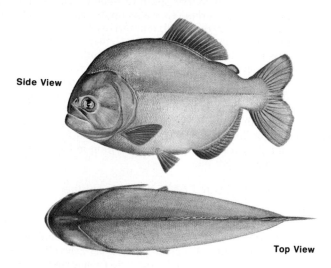

Side View

Top View

Red Piranha, 14-inch Female

In past years piranhas were brought in alive to the United States as special "pets" for aquarists, and there were some reports that these were accidentally or deliberately being released into local waters. Because there is always the possibility that these might successfully reproduce and become established in warm waters, federal injunctions have been levied against importing piranhas for sale.

CICHLID FAMILY Cichlidae

This large family of fishes is native to Africa and South America. Only one species, the Rio Grande perch (*Cichlasoma cyanoguttatum*), is indigenous to United States waters. In recent years numerous exotic cichlids have been taken in Florida, notably the banded cichlid (*C. severum*), convict cichlid (*C. nigrofasciatum*), firemouth

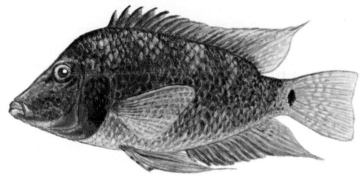

Firemouth Cichlid

cichlid (*C. meeki*), oscar (*Astronotus ocellatus*), black acara (*Aequidens port alegrensis*), and blackchin mouthbrooder (*Tilapia melanotheron*). These introductions, accidental or intentional, are attributed to tropical-fish farms and collectors. A few species have also been recorded in warm springs of Nevada, Wyoming, Montana, and Texas. Only the Mozambique mouthbrooder (*T. mossombica*) and the peacock pavón have been introduced into the United States on a supervised experimental basis.

PEACOCK PAVÓN *Cichla orinocensis* This is one of the most widely distributed cichlids found in the freshwaters of tropical South America. A first-class gamefish, the pavón has been the subject of management programs in both Florida and Texas and has been successfully introduced into Puerto Rico, Panama, and Hawaii.

This fish is generally basslike in appearance, with a prominent hump developing on the posterior region of the head in the breeding male. The adult body coloration is a gray-green or purplish-green on the dorsal surface, shading to golden-yellow or bronze on the sides. The belly coloration varies from snow-white to dusky-yellow and is often bordered by bright orange. The peacock pavón has 3 black to dusky bars on its sides. All pavóns possess a prominent ocellated black spot on the base of the caudal fin that suggests the vivid eye of a

115

peacock tail plume; hence the popular American name, peacock bass. The pelvic, anal, and lower half of the caudal fins are yellowish-green to brick-red in color. The dorsal fin and upper half of the caudal fin are a translucent blue-green sometimes with white spots. Some pavóns are characterized by an interrupted lateral-line canal; others have a continuous lateral line. The caudal fin is slightly rounded and completely scaled; the anal and pelvic fins are partially scaled. The peacock pavón attains weights of 28 pounds or more, with the average in some Venezuelan streams running 5–6 pounds.

SUNFISH FAMILY Centrarchidae

The sunfish family consists of 30 recognized freshwater species native only to North America and ranging in size from the inch-long pygmy sunfish to the 20-pound largemouth bass. The structure of the dorsal fin is characteristic for this family: the fin consists of two parts, a spinous portion and a softrayed portion, united in a single structure instead of divided into separate fins.

Owing to the similarity in spawning behavior, natural hybridization is not uncommon among sunfishes, although crosses are mainly confined within tribes or congeneric species, such as a bluegill with a pumpkinseed (*Lepomis*) or a black crappie with a white crappie (*Pomoxis*). More than 20 different crosses have been identified among wild hybrids. The largemouth bass has been successfully crossed artificially with the smallmouth bass.

For field identification purposes, the sunfish family can be separated into three groups: sunfishes (*Elassoma, Enneacanthus, Lepomis, Centrarchus, Acantharchus, Ambloplites, Archoplites*), crappies (*Pomoxis*), and black basses (*Micropterus*). In the discussion that follows, species of sunfishes, crappies, and the 6 species and 5 subspecies of black basses are each arranged in alphabetical order, by common name.

BANDED PYGMY SUNFISH *Elassoma zonatum* This tiny perchlike fish has an olive-greenish color and about 10 vertical dark bars on each side. There is a dark spot on each side below the origin of the dorsal fin. The lateral line is absent, the dorsal fin is shallowly notched, and the tail fin is rounded. The maximum length is about $1^1/_2$ inches.

This little fish is distributed from southern Illinois to Texas and east to western Florida. It is considered a swampwater fish, living in these waters and bayous under mats of heavy surface vegetation.

The pygmy sunfish starts breeding in the middle of March when water temperatures reach 62°–68°F. Spawning continues to the first part of May. It is believed that the fish do not build a nest. The spawning takes place 1 foot or less from the bottom, and the eggs are

Peacock Pavón, 17-pound Male

dropped 40–60 at a time in submerged vegetation for protection. One female less than 1¹/₂ inches produced 970 eggs. Maturity in these fish may be reached before they are 1 year old. One male in its third summer was ¹/₃ inch long.

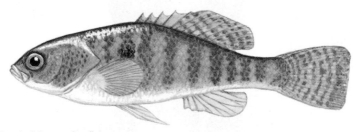

Banded Pygmy Sunfish

BANDED SUNFISH *Enneacanthus obesus*   A small, chubby fish with a rounded tail, the banded sunfish has 5–8 dark vertical bars (which may be indistinct) on its sides. It has a dark opercular spot on

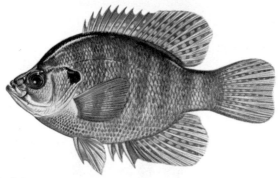

Banded Sunfish

the gill flap (more than one-half the size of the eye), which is usually velvet-black in color bordered with purple.

The banded sunfish is most often found in sluggish streams of the Atlantic drainage from southeastern New Hampshire to central Florida.

The banded sunfish seldom reaches 3 inches in length and has no angling value. It is utilized as forage by larger gamefishes.

BANTAM SUNFISH *Lepomis symmetricus* This small sunfish with a rounded, deep body is characterized by its extremely large scales along the incomplete lateral line. Many of the lateral-line scales lack pores. The gill flap has a light margin, and the pectoral fins are rounded. Maximum length does not exceed 3 inches.

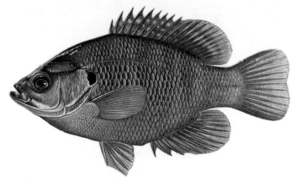

Bantam Sunfish

The bantam sunfish is found in the Mississippi drainage from southern Illinois to Louisiana.

It feeds mostly on insect larvae, such as dragonfly nymphs and midge larvae.

Because of its small size, the bantam sunfish has no value to the angler.

BLACKBANDED SUNFISH *Enneacanthus chaetodon* This diminutive sunfish has 6–8 sharply defined black bars across the straw-colored body and fins, the shoulder bar passing through the dorsal fin. The mouth is very small, the fins are high, the scales are very large, and the tail fin is rounded. This is considered one of the handsomest of sunfish, and the Latin name means literally the "butterfly" fish.

It ranges in coastal streams from New Jersey to Florida. In New Jersey, this sunfish lives in strongly acid waters of the pine barrens at a pH of 4–5. Experiments have shown that it fails to thrive in aquaria at pH values higher than 6.5.

Blackbanded sunfish build disk-shaped nests in sand in 1 foot of water or less. Spawning takes place in May. One pair spawned in an aquarium, and in 2 days the eggs hatched. Spawning again took place

Blackbanded Sunfish

the following day. As is true of most other sunfish species, the male guards the nest. The maximum length of this fish rarely exceeds $2^1/_2$ inches, and 4 years of age seems to be about maximum in the wild, although aquarium fish have lived up to 6 years. This secretive fish apparently feeds at night in weedy environments on bottom insect larvae and plants.

BLUEGILL *Lepomis macrochirus* The most popular panfishes in United States waters, the bluegill is regionally known as bream (Southeast), sun perch, blue sunfish, and copperbelly.

The bluegill varies in color probably more than any other sunfish. The basic body color ranges from yellow to dark blue, and those coming from sterile quarry holes often appear almost colorless. The sides are usually marked by 6–8 vertical, irregular bars. The distinguishing features of the adult are a broad, black gill flap with no trim, a black blotch on the posterior of the dorsal fin, and a long pointed pectoral fin. The mouth does not extend beyond the eye. The maximum size is about 15 inches, and rare specimens may weigh up to $4^1/_2$ pounds.

The original distribution was from Minnesota through the Great Lakes region to Lake Champlain in the East, south to Georgia, and west to Arkansas. Because of its use in farm ponds, the bluegill thrives in most states.

Bluegills prefer quiet, weedy waters where they can hide and feed. In the daytime the smaller fish are close to shore in coves under an overhanging limb or under a dock. The larger fish prefer the adjacent deeper waters in the daytime but move into shallow areas in the morning and evening to feed.

Bluegill, Female

Bluegill, Male

This sunfish spawns in late May when the water temperature reaches about 67°F. Spawning may continue until early August. Shallow saucerlike nests are excavated in the sand and gravel and are vigorously guarded by the male. One female may deposit as many as 38,000 eggs, which, under normal weather conditions, hatch in 2–5 days. The young are protected by the male for a few days and then must fend for themselves.

In the North, the young grow a little over 1 inch a year and reach 4–6 inches in 3 years if the competition with others of its kind is not too heavy. A 9-inch specimen may be 6–8 years old. In the southern part of their range growth is much faster. Sizes of over 4 inches in the first summer have been recorded.

The food of the bluegill consists of insects and some vegetation. As they grow bluegills take the larger forms of insects and crustaceans. Mayflies, damselflies, and crustaceans make up a large part of their diet. In the summer when aquatic animal life is scarce, they consume more plant food.

BLUESPOTTED SUNFISH *Enneacanthus gloriosus* This attractive little sunfish has a basic body coloration ranging from light olive to almost black. The light green to dark blue spots on the body are ar-

Bluespotted Sunfish

ranged to form a definite lateral pattern. The gill flap is short and black; the unpaired fins are heavily spotted; and the tail is rounded.

The bluespotted sunfish is found in the Atlantic drainage from southern New York to Florida. It lives in shallow, weedy acid waters and often in situations where the oxygen concentration is too low for survival of companion species.

122

The 5- to 12-inch circular nest is built among the aquatic plants, but is not necessarily excavated through to the bottom algae. The eggs adhere to plant particles and rootlets.

This sunfish is too small (maximum length about 4 inches) to be considered an angler's quarry. It does serve as forage for larger gamefishes, however, and has ecological value in mosquito control.

DOLLAR SUNFISH *Lepomis marginatus* The dollar sunfish is a dwarf relative of the longear sunfish and was once regarded as a southeastern subspecies of that form. It differs from the longear in having a shorter gill flap with a broader, light margin and larger scales.

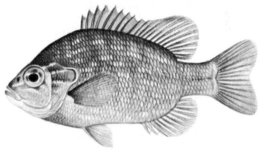

Dollar Sunfish

The lateral-line scales are usually 40 or less, and the rows on the cheek number 4. The longear has 40–45 lateral-line scales, and the cheek scales number 6. The dollar sunfish is olive with orange spots and many streaks of emerald on the sides and cheeks. The pectoral fin is rounded. Maximum length is about 6 inches.

EVERGLADES PYGMY SUNFISH *Elassoma evergladei* This tiny perchlike sunfish is an inhabitant of the swampy areas of southern Georgia and Florida. It has a rounded tail and large eyes. The color ranges from brown to green, and is often blotched with brilliant blue. The lateral line is obsolete, and there are usually 27–30 scales along each side of the body.

The Everglades pygmy sunfish builds a simple nest from bits of plants into which the eggs are placed. The nest is guarded by the male.

This sunfish seldom reaches more than $1^{1}/_{2}$ inches. It is utilized as forage by larger gamefishes.

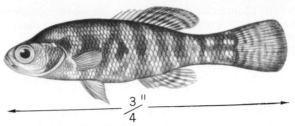

Everglades Pygmy Sunfish

FLIER *Centrarchus macropterus*　The flier is a short-bodied sunfish that appears almost round in profile. Its distinguishing characteristic is the anal fin, which is almost as long as the dorsal fin. The flier is greenish in color with dark spots on each scale below the lateral line forming longitudinal lines. There is a black spot below each eye, and a black spot on the posterior portion of the dorsal fin.

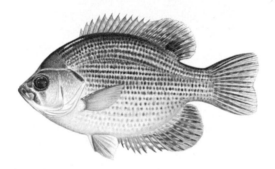

Flier

The flier is a southern species, ranging from Virginia to Florida and northward in the Mississippi valley from Louisiana to southern Illinois. It inhabits lowland streams, bayous, and swamps, often in areas of highly acid waters where other sunfish species are restricted. The flier feeds on insect larvae, particularly mosquito larvae, and other small organisms.

Spawning takes place in late spring or early summer. One flier female, 5 inches long, contained 5,600 eggs. The early growth is equivalent to that of other sunfishes. At the end of the first year (Virginia) the flier reaches 3 inches in length, $4^1/_4$ inches by the second year, and $6^1/_2$ inches by the end of the fourth year.

GREEN SUNFISH *Lepomis cyanellus*　This short, stocky sunfish, usually an olive-green color with a brassy tint on the lower sides and belly, is sometimes called green perch, sunfish, sand bass, rubber tail, or bluespotted sunfish. Its distinguishing characteristics are the

Green Sunfish

heavy lips and large mouth extending beyond the front of the eye, 3 spines in the anal fin, and a black blotch on the posterior of the dorsal and anal fins. The gill flap is edged with a light color. The maximum size is about 9 inches.

The original distribution of this fish was west of the Alleghenies through the Great Lakes region and south throughout the Mississippi Valley and west into Colorado and New Mexico. Depending on the area, the green sunfish can be found in large and small lakes, rivers, streams, or artificial impoundments. It is also tolerant of siltation and lives where few other species can exist.

The breeding habits of the green sunfish are similar to those of the bluegill. They spawn in colonies in shallow water. The saucer-shaped nests are built and guarded by the males. Spawning takes place from May through August with the peak, in the northern states, in June. The number of eggs varies with the size of the fish, but 2,000–10,000 may be deposited from one female. The young grow 1–3 inches the first year. They reach maturity and spawn at 2 years of age at a length of about 3 inches.

The green sunfish feeds on insects, small crustaceans, and small fishes.

LONGEAR SUNFISH *Lepomis megalotis* The longear, a highly colored sunfish, can be distinguished from other sunfishes by its exceptionally long, flexible gill flap, which is narrowly bordered with scarlet. Its sides are flecked with blue or yellow, and the cheeks have irregular lines of blue or green. The head profile is sharp, the pectoral fin is short and rounded, and the mouth is moderately large, ending under the eye. The northern longear grows to a maximum length of about $4^1/_2$ inches; the central longear reaches 9 inches in length and 10 ounces in weight.

The longear and its subspecies are found from the Dakotas east to the upper St. Lawrence River and south to Florida and Texas. It prefers clear, weedy streams, ponds, and bogs.

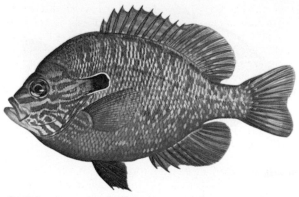

Longear Sunfish

This sunfish builds a nest like most of the other sunfishes and spawns in the North in late June until early August. It reaches sexual maturity in the third summer. It takes 5 years for the northern longear to reach 4 inches. It grows to about 8 inches. The food is principally aquatic insects, crustaceans, and small fishes.

MUD SUNFISH *Acantharchus pomotis* This little-known and secretive panfish is small and heavyset, with 5–8 indistinct, dark longitudinal bands along the sides. It has a rounded tail, and the mouth is large, extending beyond the middle of the eye; the body is a dark green color. It seldom reaches 6 inches in length.

The mud sunfish ranges from southeastern New York to Florida in the lowland streams and sluggish waters of the coastal plain.

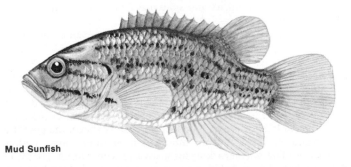

Mud Sunfish

OKEFENOKEE PYGMY SUNFISH *Elassoma okefenokee* This pygmy sunfish was first recognized in 1956 by tropical-fish hobbyists. Specimens were sent to the Academy of Natural Sciences of Philadelphia and, there, were confirmed as a new species. The

Okefenokee differs from the Everglades pygmy sunfish by having the top of the head scaleless and the male dorsal fin darker throughout. The color pattern of the female is rather contrasting, consisting of dark brown bars or blotches on a light background. The body colors of the male are blue and brown with an iridescent blue crescent on all fins except the pectorals. Its background color is velvet brown. The name of this pygmy sunfish is taken from the locality where it is found, the Okefenokee Swamp of southern Georgia. It seldom reaches 2 inches in length.

This fish is found in very soft, acid waters. It prefers hiding under plants overhanging clear deepwater.

ORANGESPOTTED SUNFISH *Lepomis humilis* The outstanding feature of this little sunfish is the 20—30 bright red or orange spots scattered irregularly on the sides of the male. The female has the same color pattern, but has brown spots. The black gill flap of this species is margined with white, and the sides of the head are often streaked with brown or red. It is called redspotted sunfish, dwarf sunfish, and, erroneously, pygmy sunfish.

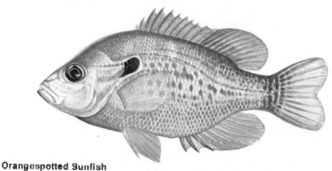

Orangespotted Sunfish

This species is widely distributed in the Mississippi Valley from western Pennsylvania to North Dakota and south to Texas, Mississippi, and northern Alabama. The orangespotted sunfish usually spawns in colonies in water less than 3 feet deep. Sometimes the water is just deep enough to cover their bodies. The main spawning period is late April or early May, but some may straggle into early August. A female lays 25—300 eggs at a time. This species grows to about 4 inches.

The food consists of insect larvae, crustaceans, and occasionally small fishes.

PUMPKINSEED *Lepomis gibbosus* The pumpkinseed, or common sunfish, is a popular freshwater quarry among children. Undoubtedly more fishermen in the northern United States have started

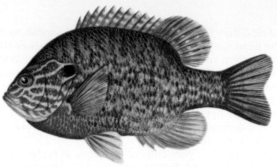

Pumpkinseed, 6-inch Male

their angling careers on this species than on any of the other panfishes. It is easily caught, stays within angling reach of shore, and it is
a colorful and scrappy individual. It is easily identified by the rigid
black gill cover with a bright red or orange spot on the tip. The body is
light olive with a sprinkling of various-colored spots on the sides.
Emerald-blue lines radiate backward from the snout and eye region.
The mouth is small and does not extend beyond the front of the eye.
The pectoral fins are long and pointed. The young of the pumpkinseed
have a yellow belly, which aids in distinguishing them from young
bluegills. Maximum length is about 9 inches.

The pumpkinseed is distributed from the Dakotas east to the Maritime Provinces of Canada, south along the Atlantic coast to northern
Georgia, and in the Mississippi River system from western Pennsylvania to Iowa.

The pumpkinseed inhabits standing water with soft bottom covered
with sunken plant material. It prefers weed patches, docks, and logs
for cover, and is most often found in these localities. The larger fish
are less likely than bluegills to be found in the openwater.

The pumpkinseed feeds on small mollusks, insects, and fishes.
Some biologists feel that the diet consists more of small fishes than
does that of the bluegill. Therefore, pumpkinseeds are less likely to
become stunted since they help to decrease the number of their own
young.

The pumpkinseed spawns in the same manner as the bluegill and at
the same time. Saucer-shaped nests are excavated in colonies some-
time between late May and early July. The height of the nesting
usually occurs in June. Each nest usually contains several thousand
eggs deposited by one or more females depending on how enticing the
guardian male was. The eggs incubate for 5–10 days, depending on
the temperature. The young grow $^1/_2$–3 inches the first year. In many
waters it takes 3 years to reach 4 inches and 6 years before growth
exceeds 6 inches. Maturity is usually reached at 2 years, and in
stunted populations the spawning fish may be no longer than $2^1/_2$
inches.

REDBREAST SUNFISH *Lepomis auritus* Regionally known as the yellowbelly sunfish, longear sunfish, sun perch, or redbreast bream, it is one of the brightest colored and most game of the medium-sized sunfishes. It is usually yellow on the sides and crimson on the ventral surface, particularly in the breeding season. The distinguishing character of this sunfish is the long, black gill flap, which is narrower than the eye and has no yellow or red trim. The mouth is small and does not extend beyond the eye. The pectoral fins are short and round. The maximum size is about 11–12 inches and $1^1/_2$ pounds.

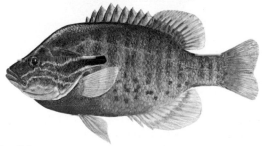

Redbreast Sunfish

Although this fish is sometimes found in lakes and ponds, it reaches its greatest abundance in the rivers of the Atlantic drainage in association with smallmouth bass and rock bass. The redbreast sunfish ranges from New Brunswick east of the Alleghenies to Florida.

The food consists of crustaceans, insects, and small fishes. On this varied fare it grows to 1–2 inches the first year, 2–$3^1/_2$ inches the second year, and by the fourth year it may reach 6 inches.

The spawning habits of the redbreast are very similar to those of the bluegill. When the water temperature reaches 68°F, a shallow nest about 12 inches in diameter is fanned out in the gravel by the male. He guards the nest and protects the young for a short period after they hatch.

REDEAR SUNFISH *Lepomis microlophus* A popular panfish in the southern United States, it is regionally known there as the shellcracker, stumpknocker, and yellow bream. The redear can be distinguished from the pumpkinseed, which it most closely resembles, by the lack of spots on the dorsal fin and of bluish bands on the sides of the head. The gill flap of the redear is semiflexible, bending to right angles; that of the pumpkinseed is rigid.

The body color is variable, from bronze to blue-green with darker spots. There are 5–10 dusky vertical bars on the sides. The gill flap has a whitish border, with the tip accented with a bright red spot on

Redear Sunfish

the male and orange on the female. The mouth is small, but not extending beyond the front of the eye, and the pectoral fins are long and pointed. Redear sunfish of over 4 pounds have been caught in Florida, North Carolina, and Virginia. The record is $4^1/_2$ pounds (1970).

The original range of the redear was south of the range of the pumpkinseed from southern Illinois south to Florida and Texas. In recent years it has been stocked in many states just north of its natural area, and in some western states, notably New Mexico. The redear has a definite preference for large, quiet waters and has a tendency to congregate around stumps, roots, and logs. It frequents openwaters and seems to require less vegetation than the pumpkinseed.

The redear has been widely introduced into farm ponds because it is believed to be less prolific than the bluegill and therefore less likely to cause an overpopulation of stunted fish. It depends largely on mollusks for food and does not compete severely with insect-eating fish. The redear has highly developed grinding teeth or "shell-crackers" located in its throat, which are capable of crushing snails—its favorite item of diet.

ROANOKE BASS *Ambloplites cavifrons* This freshwater panfish closely resembles the rock bass. It differs in having a concave cranium profile, whereas the profile of the rock bass is straight or slightly convex in older fish. The cheeks of the Roanoke bass are scaleless or have only a few deeply embedded scales, compared with the completely scaled cheeks of the rock bass. The Roanoke has 3 spines in the anal fin; the rock bass has 6.

First described from the Roanoke River in Virginia and presumed to be confined to that drainage, it remained unrecognized in the Tar and Neuse river watersheds of North Carolina until 1963. It prefers moderately large streams with a hard substrate, usually rock or gravel. It feeds principally on fishes and crayfishes. The Roanoke bass attains a larger size than the rock bass, with 1-pound fish not uncommon. Specimens weighing 4 pounds have reportedly been taken.

ROCK BASS *Ambloplites rupestris* This robust sunfish is aptly named. The more stone rubble and large stones in an area, the more likely one will find a good concentration of these fish. The Latin species name literally means "of the rocks." Regionally, it is sometimes called black perch, goggle-eye, red-eye, and rock sunfish. There is at least one subspecies in the southern United States.

The rock bass is a rugged-appearing sunfish of dark olive coloration. The sides are mottled with brownish and brassy blotches. The scales have a basal spot forming interrupted lateral streaks. The eyes are red, the mouth extends beyond the eye, and the dark blotch on the gill flap is typically margined with white or gold. There are 6 spines in the anal fin and 11–12 in the dorsal fin.

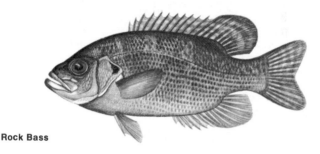

Rock Bass

The rock bass is distributed from Vermont to lower Lake Winnipeg in Manitoba and south to the Gulf states. It has been widely introduced into other states.

It usually takes 5–7 years to reach 8–9 inches. The record is 3 pounds (1974).

SACRAMENTO PERCH *Archoplites interruptus* This is the only member of the sunfish family native west of the Rockies. It is blackish over the back, with mottled black-brown and white sides, and usually marked with 7 vertical black bars. The anal fin has 6–7 anterior spines, and there are 12–13 dorsal spines. The dorsal-fin base is much longer than the base of the anal fin.

The Sacramento perch was indigenous to the Sacramento–San Joaquin drainage and the smaller Pajaro River systems. It since has been introduced into Nevada and western Utah. This is one of the largest sunfishes, reaching 20–24 inches in length and a weight of nearly 10 pounds.

Spawning takes place in May or June in waters 1–2 feet deep. The females produce a large number of eggs; one female of $10^1/_2$ inches contained 84,000 ova. Spawning takes place over boulders with heavy algae cover. No nest building is evident; rather, the adhesive eggs are attached directly to heavy growths of algae on rocks or to

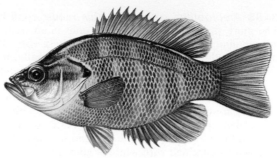

Sacramento Perch

plants in an area 18 inches in diameter. This "perch," which is actually a sunfish, differs from the other members of its family because it does not make a nest in a sandy or gravel depression; the eggs do not need constant care, and the eggs and young are left unguarded. This trait of abandoning the nest was not originally detrimental to the survival of the Sacramento perch, but the introduction, by man, of competing species has had an adverse effect on its numbers.

The food of the Sacramento perch is similar to that of many other sunfishes. It consists of insects when young and foragefish in later life. The young leave the shallows at about 2 inches in length. The growth is generally to 6–7 inches in the first year, 8–9 inches in the second year, 8–10 inches in the third year, and 9–11 inches by the fourth year.

SPOTTED SUNFISH *Lepomis punctatus* The spotted sunfish is one of the least known of the small sunfishes. Like the warmouth, it is regionally known as a stumpknocker. Its olivaceous body is heavily spotted with black or brown. It has a plain spot on the gill flap and no blotch on the dorsal fin. Each scale is pigmented at the base, and the pectoral fins are rounded. The form that occurs from southern Illinois to Texas is prominently lined with horizontal rows of red spots with a few diffuse, dusky spots on the head. The maximum length is about 6 inches.

Spotted Sunfish

132

Its range is from South Carolina to Florida and from southern Illinois to Mississippi and west to Texas.

WARMOUTH *Lepomis gulosus* This freshwater panfish of minor importance is sometimes called the goggle-eye or goggle-eyed perch. The thick-bodied warmouth superficially resembles the rock bass, but can be distinguished from the latter species by the 3 spines on the anal fin, teeth on the tongue, and the small spots on dorsal and anal fins. The color varies from olive to gray, with mottled markings on sides and back. The mouth is large, extending beyond the eye, and the eyes are reddish. Maximum length is about 11 inches.

This species is found from Minnesota east through the Great Lakes region to western Pennsylvania and south to Texas and Florida. It has also been introduced in California, Washington, and Idaho.

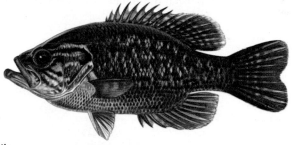

Warmouth

The warmouth prefers dense weed beds and soft bottoms, but failing these conditions, the fish is found around stumps, hence the name stumpknocker. It has more tolerance for muddy water than most species.

The food of this sunfish is crayfishes, aquatic insect larvae, and fishes. Most of the feeding is done early in the morning. By afternoon the feeding ceases.

The warmouth reaches sexual maturity at about $3-3^1/_2$ inches. In Illinois it spawns from mid-May to mid-August. The male builds the nest in water from 6 inches to 5 feet deep, usually near some projecting object and on a bottom of loose stones containing silt and detritus. Ovaries of the females may contain as many as approximately 126,000 eggs. The year the young are hatched they may grow to $1^1/_2$ inches. At the end of the seventh year the fish may be $8^1/_2$ inches long. It grows to about 10 inches.

BLACK CRAPPIE *Pomoxis nigromaculatus* A popular freshwater panfish in the United States, like the closely related white crappie, it may grow to 4–5 pounds in suitable environments. The black crap-

133

pie is flattened in appearance, with silvery sides grading to dark olive or black on the back. Spots or blotches are scattered irregularly on the sides and on the dorsal, anal, and caudal fins. There are 6 anal spines and 7–8 dorsal spines. It differs from the white crappie in this respect, since the white crappie has only 6 dorsal spines.

The range is from southern Manitoba to the upper St. Lawrence River in Quebec and then south through eastern Nebraska and western Pennsylvania to northern Texas and southern Florida, then north along the Atlantic coast to North Carolina. It has been introduced farther north along the Atlantic drainage and in the West and as far north as British Columbia.

The black crappie likes quiet waters and seeks more vegetated areas than the white crappie. It also prefers less turbid waters than the white crappie. It is gregarious and often travels in schools. This species does not seem to reach the abundance so characteristic of the white crappie.

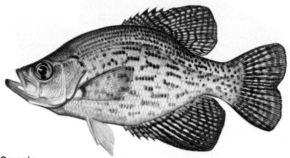

Black Crappie

The black crappie is strictly carnivorous, feeding on small fishes, aquatic insects, and crustaceans.

Spawning takes place in late spring or early summer in saucer-shaped nests excavated amid aquatic vegetation. The nests are crowded in colonies in 3–6 feet of water. A $1/_2$-pound female will produce 20,000–50,000 eggs, and one large female contained 158,000 eggs. Maturity is reached at 2 years. The average growth rate is 1–$3^1/_2$ inches the first year and $3^1/_2$–8 inches the second year. It usually requires 4 years to reach 12 inches. The maximum length is about 20 inches.

The best fishing for the black crappie is in the spring in the pre-spawning periods when the fish are congregated in large schools.

WHITE CRAPPIE *Pomoxis annularis* A popular freshwater pan-fish in the United States, the white crappie may grow to a fairly large size in suitable environments. It is the only member of the sunfish family having 6 spines in the dorsal fin and 6 spines in the anal fin.

White Crappie

This is one feature distinguishing it from the related black crappie, which has 7–8 dorsal spines. Also, the spots on the sides of the white crappie are arranged in 7–9 vertical bars, while those of the black crappie are scattered. The sides of the white crappie are silvery-olive, shading to an olive-green on the back. The paired fins are plain, and the median fins are mottled. The white is more elongate, and the black has a high, arched back in comparison. Both species range from silvery to yellowish, but while the white has 8–9 dark vertical bands on its side, the black crappie has irregular dark mottlings that suggest an old calico print. For this reason it is sometimes called calico bass. Because both have tender mouths, they are also called papermouths, and because the male guards the nest at spawning time, they are also called bachelor perch. Although the usual white crappie is 6–12 inches in length and weighs less than 1 pound, 2- to 3-pound fish are not uncommon, and individuals of over 5 pounds have been recorded.

The white crappie was originally distributed from Nebraska eastward to Lake Ontario, and southward through the Ohio and Mississippi rivers to Texas and Alabama, and northward from there along the coastal plain to North Carolina. It prefers silty rivers and lakes to clearwater and is common in southern impoundments. The first introduction of crappies to western waters was made in Lake Cuyamaca in southern California in 1891. These fish were later planted in other parts of the state, but the white crappie survived only in the San Diego area and in the Colorado River drainage. The white crappie is not a bottom dweller and consequently can be found over both hard or soft bottom. It can tolerate more turbidity than the black crappie and does not need the cool clearwater required by the latter species.

When small, this crappie feeds on aquatic insects and plankton, but when it grows larger, the major portion of its diet is fishes.

Crappies are noticeably cyclic in their populations. They may be caught readily for 2–3 seasons, then practically disappear for the same length of time. One factor advanced is that abundance is affected by a dominant year class. In a good year, when spawning and food conditions are right, the crappies produce a large brood, which survives. This is known as a dominant brood, and in subsequent years the dominant brood devours its own young as well as other fishes. This periodic elimination of young continues until the original dominant is so reduced in number that the surviving members can no longer remove all the young spawned during that period. Then the cycle repeats. During part of the cycle the great majority of fish may be of catchable size, and this is followed by a period in which only 1–2 percent of the crappies are large fish. As with all pan species, overcrowding also affects the size of fish caught. Usually, in the early history of a lake, the crappies grow very large (2–4 pounds is not uncommon), and unless they are cropped, they become so dense that subsequent young gradually settle into a slower rate of growth. The crappie is short-lived, seldom reaching the age of 6.

The spawning habits of the white crappie are typical of the nest-building sunfishes, except that the nests are in deeper water, sometimes up to 8 feet deep. Their food consists of all kinds of fishes, mollusks, shrimps, plankton, crayfishes, and insects. Fishes, especially gizzard shad, form well over 50 percent of their diet in the South; a larger amount of insects is eaten in northerly areas such as Iowa, Illinois, and Wisconsin.

GUADALUPE BASS *Micropterus treculi* A distinct species of black bass, the Guadalupe is found in the Colorado, San Antonio, and Guadalupe river systems of south-central Texas.

It has a striped lateral band, as does the spotted bass, but the stripes are broader and darker and extend up over the midsides. The mouth does not extend beyond the eye and, as in the spotted bass, it contains glossohyal teeth on the tongue. The Guadalupe also differs from related forms in the number of dorsal spines, anal spines, and soft-rays of the dorsal, pectoral, and anal fins. This is a small species, rarely exceeding 12 inches in length.

The Guadalupe bass is most common in clear-flowing streams, where it feeds chiefly on aquatic insects. Despite its small size the fish provides good sport in fastwater environments.

LARGEMOUTH BASS *Micropterus salmoides* One of the most important freshwater gamefishes in North America, the largemouth bass is regionally known as green bass, green trout, Oswego bass, and black bass.

Largemouth bass are found in almost every state, but originally they were indigenous to southeastern Canada through the Great Lakes, and south in the Mississippi Valley to Mexico and Florida, and up the Atlantic coast as far north as Maryland. This range gradually extended west of the Rockies about 1887, when largemouths were introduced to the Columbia River system, then east into New England.

The largemouth thrives best in shallow, weedy lakes or in river backwaters. It prefers weedy habitats, not only because a food supply is available in these areas, but also because aquatic plants and sunken debris furnish protection. The fish is usually found in water less than

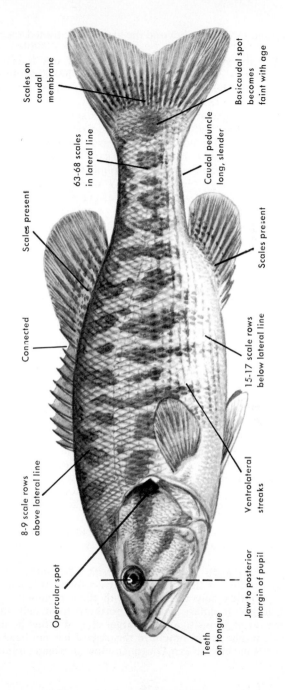

Scales on caudal membrane

Basicaudal spot becomes faint with age

63-68 scales in lateral line

Caudal peduncle long, slender

Scales present

Scales present

Connected

15-17 scale rows below lateral line

8-9 scale rows above lateral line

Ventrolateral streaks

Opercular spot

Jaw to posterior margin of pupil

Teeth on tongue

Guadalupe Bass

20 feet deep and rarely goes beyond the area where rooted vegetation will grow.

The food of the young largemouth consists of tiny crustaceans; larger fish eat insects, crayfishes, frogs, and fishes. Feeding drops off in late fall and winter, but when the water temperatures warm in the spring, heavy feeding resumes.

Largemouth bass spawn in the North in the spring when the water temperatures reach 62°–65° F. This can be from early May to late June depending on the latitude. The male bass cleans out a nest about 20 inches in diameter and 6 inches deep in sand or gravel, if it is available. If not, the male fans out the nest in most any type of bottom, including silt and clay. Nesting usually occurs within 7–8 feet offshore in 12–36 inches of water. The nests are never close together, but are separated by a distance of 20 feet or more. When the nest is completed, the male bass entices a female to spawn. A female largemouth usually lays only a few hundred eggs at a time, which are fertilized by the male. The eggs are adhesive and fasten to the bottom of the nest. The female bass departs, but may return to spawn with the same male or spawn in the nest of one or more other males. Often several females spawn in a single nest. The number of eggs per nest is dependent upon the number of females utilizing it and may vary from a few hundred to several thousand eggs. Female bass usually contain 2,000–7,000 eggs per pound of body weight.

The male largemouth guards the nest during incubation and for a short time after the young emerge from the eggs. The eggs usually hatch in 7–10 days depending upon water temperature. At a temperature of 65° F, hatching takes place in about 10 days; at a temperature of 80° F, within only 5 days. Bass fry remain on the nest until the yolk sac has been absorbed, after which they school, frequenting the shallow water, which is rich in microscopic food (plankton). They may remain in schools until over 1 inch in length, a characteristic that distinguishes them from the smallmouth species, the fry of which scatter when only $1/2$ inch in length. At this stage the largemouth fry are a yellowish, transparent color with a very pronounced black stripe down the body. They feed on Entomostraca but, as they grow, seek increasingly larger food items, feeding on smaller fishes when less than 2 inches long.

The largemouth bass is one of the most popular gamefishes in the United States. It is caught on a wide variety of live baits and artificial lures.

Florida Largemouth Bass *Micropterus salmoides floridanus* This subspecies of the largemouth bass found throughout the peninsula of Florida may intergrade with the largemouth bass of southern Georgia. It differs from the northern form only in scale counts; however, it grows to a much larger size. Whether heredity is more important than environment in this regard has not been determined. In 1959 the city of San Diego, California, began an intensive

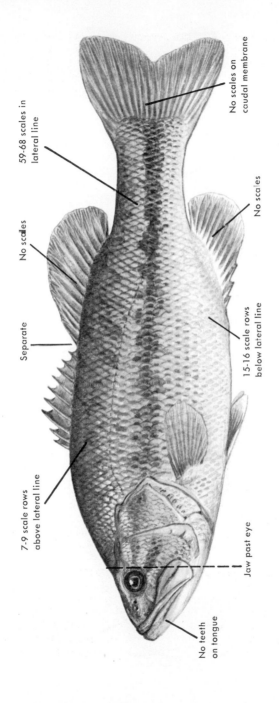

No scales on caudal membrane

59-68 scales in lateral line

No scales

No scales

Separate

15-16 scale rows below lateral line

7-9 scale rows above lateral line

Jaw past eye

No teeth on tongue

Northern Largemouth Bass

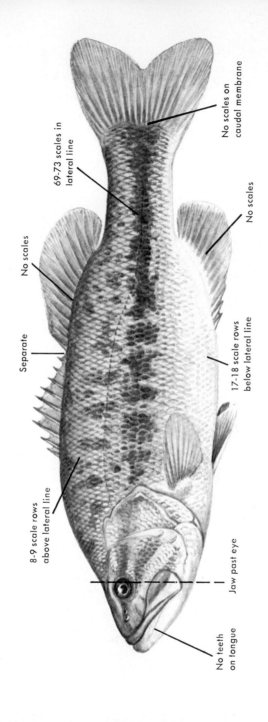

No scales on caudal membrane

69-73 scales in lateral line

No scales

Separate

No scales

17-18 scale rows below lateral line

8-9 scale rows above lateral line

Jaw past eye

No teeth on tongue

Florida Largemouth Bass

program to stock a chain of lakes with the Florida subspecies; this has resulted in doubling the weight of the average bass caught (record 20 pounds 15 ounces, 1973) as compared with the northern form, which was long established in these same waters. The world's record largemouth of 22 pounds 4 ounces was taken in Montgomery Lake, Georgia, an area where intergrades are common.

REDEYE BASS *Micropterus coosae* This black bass greatly resembles the smallmouth. When young, the distinctive color pattern of the redeye consists of dark vertical bars (which become obscure with age) and brick-red dorsal, caudal, and anal fins. The red color of eyes and fins easily separates this species from other basses.

The redeye bass was first identified from the upland tributaries of the Alabama and Chattahoochee river systems in Alabama, and the Savannah River drainage in Georgia. In more recent years it has been found in the Conasauga drainage in southeastern Tennessee and the Chipola River system in Florida. The redeye usually inhabits the upland drainage areas, being present in small streams and ponds built upon these watersheds.

The spawning habits of the redeye bass are similar to those of the smallmouth bass, except that the redeye will not spawn in ponds or lakes. In the northern part of its range it spawns in late May, June, or early July. Some 3-year-old fish as small as 4 $7/10$ inches have been found to be mature. One 5 $7/10$-inch female contained 2,084 eggs.

In Tennessee the growth rate of the redeye bass is slow compared with that of other warmwater fishes. Growth is fast the first year, but decreases as the fish becomes older. On the average a 10-year-old fish grows about 1 inch a year. In Alabama the average size is about 12 ounces.

Shoal Bass *Micropterus* sp. cf. *M. coosae* The redeye bass occurs in two forms or races: the Apalachicola form, or shoal bass, which has prominent basicaudal and opercular spots but superficially resembles a smallmouth bass (erroneously called the Flint River smallmouth), and the Alabama form, which is usually much brighter in color but whose basicaudal spot is faint or absent.

The status of the shoal bass is not clear in present taxonomy. However, it differs in scale counts, color, and number of pyloric caeca; it also grows to at least 6 pounds in size.

SMALLMOUTH BASS *Micropterus dolomieui* This is one of the most important freshwater gamefishes in North America. Its robust body has a brownish or bronze cast with vertical dark olivaceous bars. In contrast to the largemouth bass, the upper jaw does not extend beyond the eye, and the dorsal fin has a very shallow notch. The young can be distinguished by the tricolored tail, which has the outermost portion edged in white, the middle portion with a black band,

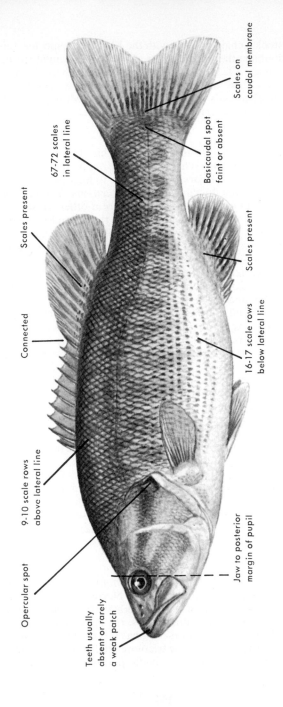

Scales on caudal membrane

67-72 scales in lateral line

Basicaudal spot faint or absent

Scales present

Scales present

Connected

16-17 scale rows below lateral line

9-10 scale rows above lateral line

Opercular spot

Jaw to posterior margin of pupil

Teeth usually absent or rarely a weak patch

Redeye Bass

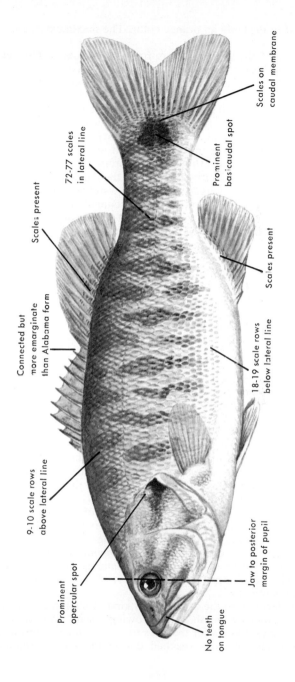

Scales on caudal membrane

72-77 scales in lateral line

Prominent basicaudal spot

Scales present

Scales present

Scales present

18-19 scale rows below lateral line

Connected but more emarginate than Alabama form

9-10 scale rows above lateral line

Prominent opercular spot

Jaw to posterior margin of pupil

No teeth on tongue

Shoal Bass

and closest to the body an orange color. The maximum size is about 12 pounds.

The range of the smallmouth is from Minnesota to Quebec and south to northern Alabama, then west to eastern Kansas and Oklahoma. It has been introduced in many other states from coast to coast.

The geography of the smallmouth bass can be traced by the growth of American railroads. Until 1869, its range was largely confined to the Lake Ontario and Ohio River drainage systems, but as the wood-burning diamond stackers rolled south and west, the bass became a commuter. The original brood of the Potomac basin, for example, came from the Ohio River by riding over the Alleghenies on the Baltimore and Ohio in buckets hanging in the water tender. This resulted in some widely scattered plantings, and eventually the smallmouth arrived in California from Lake Ontario via New York.

The smallmouth is usually found in rocky locations in lakes and streams. It prefers clear, rocky lakes with a minimum depth of 25–30 feet and with temperatures in the summer no less than 60° F and no more than 80° F. In streams, this bass prefers a good percentage of riffles flowing over gravel, boulders, or bedrock.

The first food of this species consists of minute crustaceans; later it graduates into insect larvae, crayfishes, and fishes.

The smallmouth bass matures at different ages depending on its growth and the latitude of its environment. In the North males mature at 3 years of age and about 9 inches in length. In more southerly locations, both sexes are mature at 2 years. Smallmouths often move into small and large tributaries to spawn. Spawning normally takes place when the water temperature reaches 60°–70° F. This may occur from late April to early June, depending on the season and location. The male builds the nest by fanning out the gravel, coarse sand, or stones with his tail. The nest is built in 3–22 feet of water, depending on its clarity. The nests, which are 14–30 inches in diameter, are deeper in clearwater than in turbid water. After the nest is completed, the male selects a ripe female and drives her to the nest. After she has spawned, she is driven from the nest and another ripe female selected. Often as many as three females lay their eggs in one nest. Although a female produces 2,000–7,000 eggs per pound of body weight, all the eggs do not ripen simultaneously. A nest may contain from 200 to several thousand eggs with the average being about 2,000. The eggs incubate in 2–9 days, depending on the temperature. After hatching, the fry leave the nest a few hours after swimming up. There is little or no parental care. Except for the gold iris of the eye, young smallmouths are pitch-black.

Growth depends on the amount and kind of feed, the temperature of the water, and the length of the growing season. In some infertile streams, it takes 4 years for the bass to reach 9 inches. In the larger fertile rivers, 9 inches is reached during the second summer; it

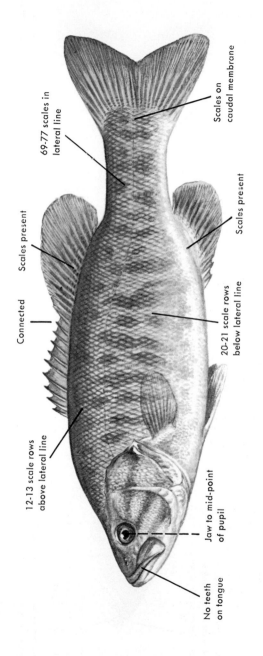

69-77 scales in lateral line

Scales on caudal membrane

Scales present

Scales present

Connected

20-21 scale rows below lateral line

12-13 scale rows above lateral line

Jaw to mid-point of pupil

No teeth on tongue

Northern Smallmouth Bass

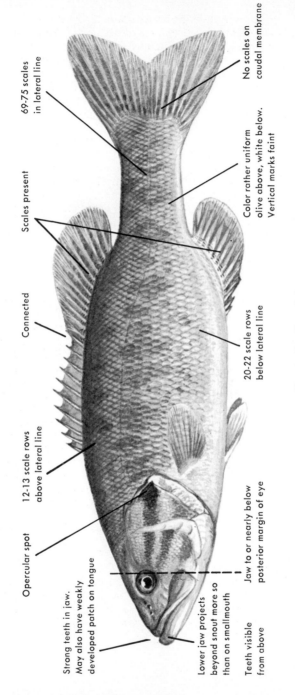

69-75 scales
in lateral line

No scales on
caudal membrane

Scales present

Color rather uniform
olive above, white below.
Vertical marks faint

Connected

12-13 scale rows
above lateral line

20-22 scale rows
below lateral line

Opercular spot

Neosho Smallmouth Bass

Strong teeth in jaw.
May also have weakly
developed patch on tongue

Lower jaw projects
beyond snout more so
than on smallmouth

Jaw to or nearly below
posterior margin of eye

Teeth visible
from above

requires 7–10 years in these rivers to attain 18–20 inches.

Neosho Smallmouth Bass *Micropterus dolomieui velox* This subspecies of the smallmouth bass occurs in the Neosho River and adjacent tributaries of the Arkansas River in Oklahoma, Arkansas, and Missouri. Owing to the construction of large impoundments on the Neosho River, the natural habitat of this subspecies has been greatly reduced to the upper reaches of some of its tributaries, and this distinctive local form of smallmouth has become quite rare.

The Neosho smallmouth is more slender than the northern form and is easily distinguished by its lower jaw, which projects beyond the snout to the extent that its teeth are visible from above. The upper mandible extends to or nearly below the posterior margin of the eye. The coloration is rather uniform, being dark olive above and fading to white below with only faint vertical markings.

The subspecific name *velox* ("swift") refers to its characteristic as a gamefish. Found in fastwater habitats, the Neosho smallmouth probably made the reputation of many Ozark bass rivers in years past. To what extent the original stock has been modified by interbreeding with the northern form of smallmouth is not known, but the typical Neosho subspecies is prized for its rarity.

SPOTTED BASS *Micropterus punctulatus* A popular freshwater gamefish, sometimes called Kentucky bass or Kentucky spotted bass, the spotted bass was not properly identified by fishery taxonomists until 1927, although a naturalist, Rafinesque, and fishermen on the Ohio River recognized it as a separate species long before then. A cursory examination of this species would wrongly suggest that it is a hybrid between the largemouth and smallmouth basses because it has some characteristics that are similar to one species or the other or are intermediate between the two. The spotted bass is olive-green on the back with many dark blotches that are usually diamond-shaped. The lateral band is a series of short blotches. Below the lateral line the scales have dark bases that give rise to the lengthwise rows of small spots responsible for the common name. Often confused with the largemouth, the spotted bass differs in having a mouth that does not extend beyond the eye and spotting below the lateral line. It differs from the smallmouth in having spotting below the lateral line and lacking vertical bars on the sides.

A young spotted bass resembles a young largemouth, but the juvenile spotted bass has spots along the belly and a prominent black spot at the base of the tail. The tricolored tail is marked like the smallmouth's in orange, black, and white.

The spotted bass does not grow as large as either the largemouth or the smallmouth. The maximum size attained is about 5 pounds. This black bass occurs in the Ohio-Mississippi drainage from Ohio south to the Gulf states and west to Texas, Oklahoma, and Kansas. Eastward its range extends to western Florida.

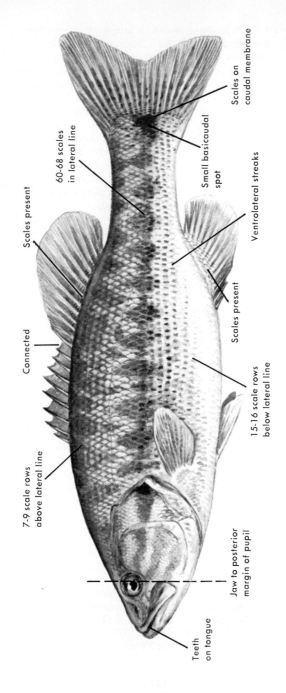

Scales on caudal membrane

Small basicaudal spot

60-68 scales in lateral line

Scales present

Ventrolateral streaks

Connected

Scales present

7-9 scale rows above lateral line

15-16 scale rows below lateral line

Jaw to posterior margin of pupil

Teeth on tongue

Northern Spotted Bass

In the North, the habitat of the spotted bass in streams might be called intermediate between those of the largemouth and smallmouth basses. In streams the smallmouth inhabits the riffle area, the largemouth the weeded coves, but the spotted bass prefers long, deep, silted pools in sluggish waters. In the South the habitat of the spotted bass is entirely different; it occurs primarily in cool, gravel-bottom streams and clear, spring-fed lakes. In a lake in the TVA system in Tennessee, spotted bass were taken at a depth of 100 feet, while smallmouths were caught no deeper than 60 feet and largemouths were found close to the surface.

The food of the young spotted bass is small crustaceans and midge larvae, but larger fish eat larger insects, fishes, crayfishes, frogs, worms, and grubs. Breeding follows migration upstream into shallow waters, where nests much like those of the other two black basses are constructed. The spawning habits are similar to those of the largemouth, but the nests are small, not over 15 inches in diameter. The young grow to $1^1/_2$–4 inches the first summer. Maturity is reached at about 7 inches.

Two subspecies (the Alabama and the Wichita spotted basses) occur in limited areas.

Alabama Spotted Bass *Micropterus punctulatus henshalli* This subspecies of the spotted bass is found in the Alabama River system in Mississippi, Alabama, and Georgia. The Alabama form has been authenticated to 8 pounds in weight and 24 inches in length (Smith Lake, Alabama, 1966).

Wichita Spotted Bass *Micropterus punctulatus wichitae* This subspecies of the spotted bass occurs in the Wichita Mountains of Oklahoma.

SUWANNEE BASS *Micropterus notius* This species was first distinguished by biologists from the University of Florida in 1941 at Ichtucknee Springs in Columbia County, Florida. Since that time it has been located by other workers in Florida in the Santa Fe River, the Withlacoochee River (in Madison County), and the main body of the Suwannee River to its mouth. Essentially a stream bass, the species is unique in tolerating the high-acid and low-fertility habitat of the Suwannee River.

It has markings similar to the redeye and spotted basses and other characteristics more like the smallmouth bass. The sublateral dark streaks of the redeye and spotted basses are imperfectly developed and only regularly aligned in the region of the tail. The shallow, notched dorsal fin, the deep body, and the vertical elongation of the lateral blotches are similar to those of the redeye-smallmouth complex. The spot at the base of the tail fin and the broadened lateral blotches can be likened to the markings of the spotted bass. The one unique marking of this species is the bright blue on the lower anterior parts.

149

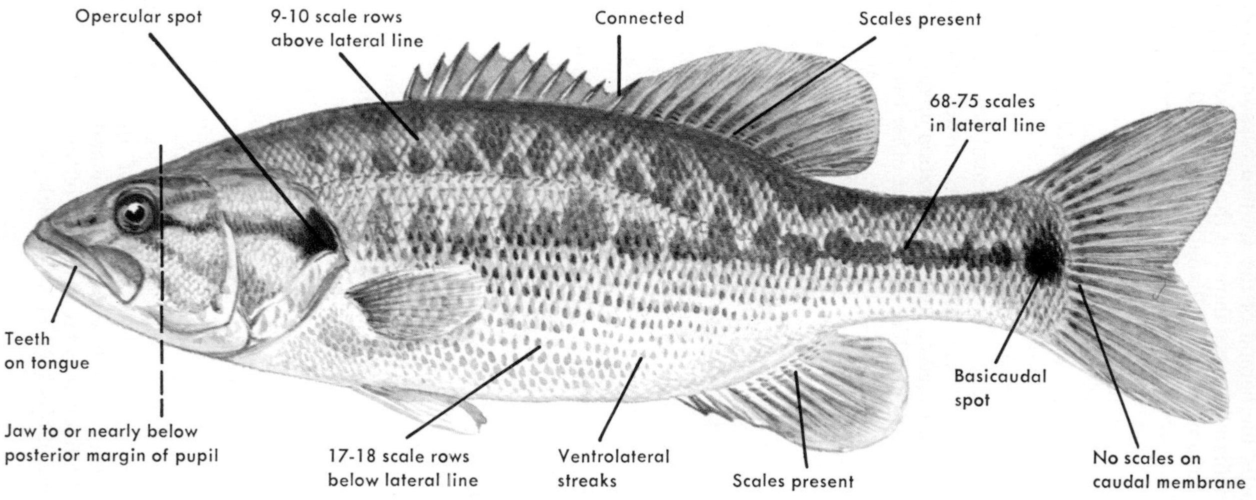

No scales on caudal membrane

68-75 scales in lateral line

Scales present

Basicaudal spot

Connected

Scales present

9-10 scale rows above lateral line

Ventrolateral streaks

Opercular spot

17-18 scale rows below lateral line

Teeth on tongue

Jaw to or nearly below posterior margin of pupil

Alabama Spotted Bass

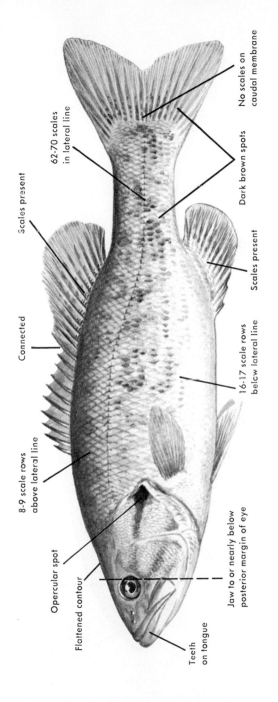

No scales on caudal membrane

62-70 scales in lateral line

Scales present

Dark brown spots

Connected

Scales present

8-9 scale rows above lateral line

16-17 scale rows below lateral line

Opercular spot

Flattened contour

Jaw to or nearly below posterior margin of eye

Teeth on tongue

Wichita Spotted Bass

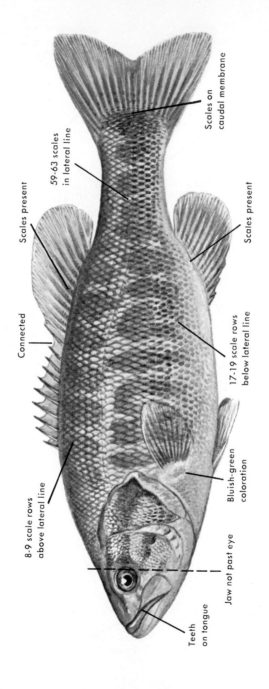

Scales on caudal membrane

59-63 scales in lateral line

Scales present

Scales present

17-19 scale rows below lateral line

Connected

8-9 scale rows above lateral line

Bluish-green coloration

Jaw not past eye

Teeth on tongue

Suwannee Bass

The Suwannee bass seldom attains a length of 10 inches or a weight of 12 ounces. However, individuals up to $2^1/_2$ pounds have been taken. Unlike other bass species, which tend to lie and feed along the deeper edges of a river around brush and undercuts, the Suwannee bass always remains in midstream. Subject to extreme fluctuation, often 20–30 feet below its banks in dry periods, the Suwannee provides its best fishing when the water is low and the fish are concentrated.

PERCH FAMILY Percidae

DARTERS The darters, all members of the perch family, are of the subfamily Etheostominae. There are 95 species of darters in the United States and Canada. In range they occur only east of the Rockies and into southern Canada and northern Mexico.

To most fishermen the darters are those colorful little "minnows" occasionally included in their bait buckets. Only close observation will reveal them in their natural habitat, since they are usually only a few inches long and stay hidden among rocks and debris on the bottom. Their name, darters, is derived from the fact that they do not swim in the ordinary fashion, but dart from place to place. These movements are so rapid the eye can scarcely follow them. One second a darter will be seen lying motionless on the bottom, and the next second it has disappeared, only to reappear a foot or so away. They never suspend themselves in the water and have only a rudimentary swim bladder.

Iowa Darter

Johnny Darter

Most of the darters do not exceed 3–4 inches in length, and some are even smaller. Only one, the log perch, reaches a length of about 8 inches. They all have the perch family characteristics of 2 separate dorsal fins, with spines in the first dorsal and anal fins. Their tails, however, are not forked. Their bodies are slender and heads or snouts usually pointed. The pectoral fins are highly developed and are disproportionately large. These fins are used both to propel the fish in their darting movements and to stabilize them as they rest on the bottom. Coloration varies greatly among species, but the one common characteristic is that they all are brilliantly colored. During spawning season the males display the most vivid colors of any freshwater fishes. Pinks, reds, and yellows contrast with the darker colors.

The darters generally are found in relatively clear coolwaters. Some species live only in cold streams, while others inhabit the larger rivers, and some are found in lakes. Spawning takes place in late spring or early summer. The male selects and guards a nesting area, usually in the gravel, and the female digs a shallow depression into which a few hundred eggs are deposited and fertilized immediately by the male. The eggs are sticky and adhere to the gravel. The male guards the nest until the eggs are hatched.

The darters are primarily carnivorous, eating such foods as small insects and zooplankton.

SAUGER *Stizostedion canadense*   The sauger is closely related to the walleye and is similar to the walleye in nearly all respects. Everything that can be said about the walleye can be said about the sauger with either more or less emphasis. For example, the walleye is known to inhabit only large bodies of water, but the sauger inhabits only the *largest* bodies of water. The sauger is found primarily in the Great Lakes, the very large lakes in the northern states and Canada, and in the Mississippi, Missouri, Ohio, and Tennessee rivers and some of their major tributaries. Persistent artificial stocking of adult sauger in smaller lakes has always ended in failure. Why the sauger will not thrive in smaller lakes or rivers remains a biological mystery. The species is known to travel great distances, but there is no explanation of why movement is vital to its existence.

Only in recent years has the sauger attained a position of prominence among anglers in the United States. This increasing recognition is due to the huge dams constructed across the major rivers of the nation, especially the Tennessee River and its tributaries and the Missouri River. The huge reservoirs formed by these dams make ideal habitats for the sauger. And, perhaps of equal importance, these dams block their upstream migrations and provide concentration points and excellent angling in the tailwaters immediately below the dams.

The sauger, like the walleye, has a round and elongate body, forked tail, spines on the first dorsal fin and the anal fin, sharp canine teeth on the jaws and palatine (roof of the mouth), and large, glassy-colored eyes. The white belly blends into an olive-gray on the sides and back, sometimes with a brassy tinge. The back is crossed with 3–4 dark saddles that extend down the sides. The dorsal fins are marked with small dark spots, which are arranged in the form of definite longitudinal rows. The white color of the belly extends to the tip of the tail, but this coloration does not spread out at the end of the tail and form a definite white tip as it does in the walleye. Internally, the sauger has 3–9 (usually 5) pyloric caeca each of which is much shorter than the stomach. The second dorsal fin of the sauger has 18–22 rays, usually 19–20; anal fin with 2 spiny and 11–12 softrays; 85–91 scales along the lateral line; and cheeks usually, but not always, well scaled.

The name sauger is becoming more widely used and accepted as the species gains prominence with anglers. However, the name sand pike continues to be used in many localities. Other commonly used names include river pike, spotfin pike, jackfish, and jack salmon.

The sauger attains a maximum weight of about 8 pounds in the Missouri River, but only 3–5 pounds elsewhere. The reason for this size discrepancy is not definitely known, but probably reflects a racial or perhaps even a subspecific difference. Sauger weighing 4–6 pounds are rather common in the catches of anglers fishing in the reservoirs and tailwaters of the huge Missouri River dams. The average catch weighs from 1 to 3 pounds. Elsewhere, sauger run from $^3/_4$ to $1^1/_2$ pounds, with a 3- or 4-pounder a rarity.

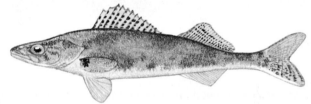

Sauger

Maximum age attained by sauger in the Missouri River and the southern states is 5–7 years; individuals in the northern states and in Canada may live 10–14 years. Growth of the Missouri River sauger averages 6 inches during each of the first 2 years of life, and 3 inches each year thereafter. Sauger from the southern states grow 6–8 inches during each of their first 2 years of life, but only $1^1/_2$ inches each year thereafter. In the Far North, sauger grow about 4 inches the first year, 3 inches the second, 2 inches the third, and about 1 inch each year thereafter. Sauger from the Missouri River and the southern states generally attain adulthood in the third year of life; those from northern waters may be 5–6 years old before reaching maturity.

Sauger weigh 1 pound at a length of about 14–15 inches, 2 pounds at 18 inches, 3 pounds at 20 inches, and add an additional pound for each $1^1/_2$ inches in length thereafter.

155

WALLEYE *Stizostedion vitreum vitreum*   The walleye is the largest member of the perch family, attaining a weight of over 20 pounds. Its size, sporting qualities, and savory flesh make it one of the most important game species in North America. Though originally found primarily in the northern states and Canada, widespread stocking has extended its range throughout the East and to all but a few of the states in the Far West and South. It is common in large bodies of water, seldom being found in streams or in lakes smaller than 50–100 acres. Its predaceous habits and its popularity with anglers make it a favored species for purposes of stocking and management by conservation officials in most states. The walleye is also relatively easy to hatch and rear artificially. Its habitat requirements include coolwater (summer temperatures preferably less than 85°F), clear or unmuddied water, adequate food in the form of foragefishes, extensive gravel or rubble areas on which to spawn, and plenty of lake area deeper than 10 feet.

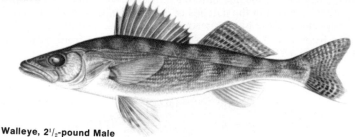

Walleye, 2¹/₂-pound Male

The walleye has a round and elongate body, forked tail, spines on the first dorsal fin and the anal fin, sharp canine teeth on the jaws and palatine bones (roof of the mouth), and large eyes with a glassy cast, which shine under light at night. The belly is light-colored, blending into olive-green or brassy-olive-buff on the sides and back. The back is crossed with 6–7 narrow dark bands. Markings on the tail and spinous dorsal fin serve to distinguish the walleye from its close relative, the sauger. The tail of the walleye has a silver or milk-white tip on the lower lobe, which is absent in the sauger. Often, this silvery tip affords the first sighting of the fish when it is being brought in close to the boat or shore. The spinous dorsal fin of the walleye usually is streaked or blotched with dark pigment, but there are no regular or clearly defined rows of spots such as are found in the sauger. One large dark spot or blotch is present near the base of the last 2–3 spines of the walleye, but is absent in the sauger.

The walleye is known by this name throughout most of North America. The term walleyed pike is sometimes used, although this truly is a misnomer as the fish is not a member of the pike family. In areas of Canada it may be called a number of names, including pike, jack, jackfish, and pickerel.

156

The size of the walleyes that end up on the stringer usually runs 1–3 pounds, depending upon where they are caught. A 6- to 8-pounder is a walleye to be proud of, and anything over that is a trophy. In most states where walleyes are abundant, yearly records run 12–16 pounds. It has been recorded to 25 pounds.

In the spring, when the water temperature reaches 45°–50° F, the adult female moves to a spawning area, where her arrival is awaited by the males. The spawning area may be a tributary stream, a shallow area of a river, or a desirable shoal area of a lake. In any case, it should be and usually is an area with clearwater 1–5 feet deep and with the bottom covered with rubble or gravel. The area also is likely to have current, the result of either flowing water or the action of waves. If such conditions do not exist, the adult fish may spawn in other areas, but survival of the eggs and young will suffer.

Upon hatching, the walleye is about $1/2$ inch long and paper-thin, making it difficult to spot with the naked eye. For several days it drifts about, absorbing the yolk sac and gaining strength. When the yolk sac is absorbed, the fry begins feeding on microscopic animals (zooplankton), first the smallest of these and later the larger ones. When it has attained a length of several inches, fishes become its primary diet. Adults spend most of the time in deeper waters by day, and at night they may move into shore to feed.

By the end of summer the walleye has attained a length of 4–12 inches. If it is a fast-growing individual living in a fertile lake in the central or southern states, it may attain a length of 15–16 inches by the end of its second year. In this case it will reach adulthood and spawn during its third year of life. If it is living in the northern states or Canada, it may take 4 or even 5 years to reach a length of 12–15 inches and take on the role of a parent. However, the fast-growing southern fish seldom live longer than 6–7 years, while the slow-growing northern populations often live 12–15 years.

Blue Pike *Stizostedion vitreum glaucum* This subspecies of the walleye is found only in Lake Erie. Within this lake it frequents deeper and cooler waters than does the walleye. There are other so-called blue pikes in Lake Ontario, the Lake Huron and St. Lawrence River drainages in Ontario, and Lake Winnipeg in Manitoba. However, it is not certain whether these can be properly identified as the same subspecies.

Blue pike can be distinguished by their grayish-blue cast and the absence of the brassy yellow mottlings of the walleye. The pectoral and pelvic fins are bluish-white rather than clear or yellowish as in the walleye. The blue pike's eyes are larger and set closer together than are those of the walleye.

YELLOW PERCH *Perca flavescens* This is the most widely distributed member of the Percidae. It is regionally known as ringed perch, striped perch, coon perch, and jack perch. The yellow perch is generally classified as a panfish, and though lacking the sporting qualities of its larger relatives, the walleye and sauger, it provides fine fishing for the multitude of anglers seeking fast action and good eating. The yellow perch is found in the southern portions of west-central and eastern Canada, south to Kansas, Missouri, Illinois, Indiana, and Ohio. In the Atlantic drainage it is present from Nova Scotia to South Carolina. Its natural range has been greatly enlarged through widespread stocking, and it is now present in many of the far western states. The perch is at home in small and large lakes alike, and though found in rivers it is considered primarily a lake fish. Cool clean water with ample amounts of sandy or rocky bottom make the better perch lakes.

The perch has a moderately elongate body that is slightly compressed, giving it a somewhat humpbacked appearance. The 2 dorsal fins are separated, and the tail is moderately forked. Spines are present on the first dorsal fin, the anal fin, and the pectoral fins. The mouth contains many tiny teeth but no canine teeth. The opercle or gill cover is strongly serrated and contains 1 or more sharp spines. Coloration may vary but usually is olivaceous on the back blending into a golden-yellow on the sides and white on the belly. From 6 to 8 dark bands extend from the back to below the lateral line. It has 12–13 softrays in the dorsal fin and 7–8 in the anal fin, 57–62 scales along the lateral line, and 8–10 rows of scales on each cheek.

The angler's catch of perch usually consists of fish weighing $^1/_4$–$^3/_4$ pound. However, some lakes occasionally produce a crop of jumbos weighing 1–2 pounds. Such lakes are sure to attract an army of anglers. Maximum size attained is about 4 pounds.

Embedded in a sticky, gelatinous mass strung over weeds or brush, a perch begins its life as one egg among 10,000–75,000 spawned in a ribbonlike string by an adult female. The gelatinous mass absorbs water rapidly as it is emitted by the female, and may swell to the size of 2 handfuls. The eggs are fertilized by one or more males who are at the side of the female as she emits the spawn. The spawning act usually occurs at night in weedy or brushy areas several feet deep when the water temperature is about 45°–50° F. In relative terms, this is about a week after walleye spawning.

Fertility of the eggs is ordinarily very high, and under good conditions one-fourth to one-half of the eggs will hatch into minute fry in 2–3 weeks. No protection is provided by the parents, and after hatching, the life of a perch is extremely hazardous. Being a slow swimmer and traveling in large schools, it affords excellent food for predaceous fishes, especially the walleye. The young perch seek the protection of weeds and brush and feed on small zooplankton and insect larvae. The slow growth of the perch, usually 2–4 inches the first year, keeps it within the size range of prime forage for practically all gamefishes throughout its first year of life and even into its later years. Thus the

Yellow Perch, 3½-inch Juvenile

Yellow Perch, 13-inch Male

odds for survival are very low (perhaps 1 in 5,000) during this first year.

Growth of a perch under normal conditions averages 3 inches the first year, 3 inches the second, 2 inches the third, and about 1 inch each year thereafter. These growth rates vary with latitude and with habitat conditions. Maximum age in the Far North is about 11 years, while in the southern end of its range 5–6 years is maximum. A $^1/_4$-pound perch measures about 8 inches, a $^1/_2$-pounder 10 inches, a $^3/_4$-pounder 12 inches, and a 1-pound perch 13–14 inches.

In its second and third years of life the yellow perch continues to provide good forage for other fishes, since it ranges in size from 3 to 6 inches during its second year and from 5 to 8 inches during its third year. During these years the hazards of life account for as high as 60–80 percent of the population each year. Thereafter, the usual annual loss may be in the range of 50–70 percent. Adulthood usually is attained at the age of 3–4 years, at which time the hardiest and most fortunate few survivors take on the task of filling the void created by death from disease, parasites, and predaceous fishes.

The food of the yellow perch after it has reached a size of several inches gradually changes to larger zooplankton, insects, young crayfishes, snails, and other small fishes, including the young of its own species. Continuing to travel in schools throughout its life, it roams throughout the lake, often staying in the deeper areas during the day and moving closer to the shallows toward evening. There is some evidence that at times the males and females travel in separate schools. Schools also may consist primarily of perch of the same age class and size.

It is unlikely that one can overestimate the angling value of the yellow perch. Wherever the perch is found it provides hours of fun and pounds of delicious food for fishermen of all types and angling proficiency in all seasons of the year.

PIKE FAMILY Esocidae

CHAIN PICKEREL *Esox niger* This popular gamefish in the eastern and southern portions of the United States is elongate and bears black chainlike, vermiculate markings on the sides. The body color varies from green to bronze. The chain pickerel can be distinguished from its nearest relatives, the grass pickerel and the redfin pickerel, by the number of branchiostegals, which in the chain pickerel are 14–16. The chain pickerel also has a slimmer snout, with the length of the snout being longer than the distance between the back edge of the eye and the edge of the opercle.

The natural distribution of chain pickerel is in regions where the larger pikes are either rare or absent. This range extends from Maine to east Texas and north to the Great Lakes. The center of abundance is east of the Alleghenies in New Jersey, southern New York, Connecticut, Rhode Island, Massachusetts, and southern Maine. These

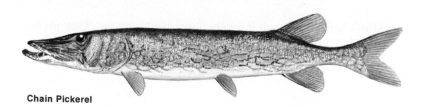

Chain Pickerel

Atlantic states produce some big pickerel, particularly in coastal ponds and brackish creeks. Although not too common in most of the South, chain pickerel grow to large sizes in Georgia and Florida. They are easy to catch and grow to sporty lengths rather quickly. The chain pickerel reaches 14 inches in 3 years; it takes about 6 years to attain a stout 20 inches, and if it survives to the probable maximum of 10 years, it should be 36 inches long and weigh approximately 9 pounds.

MUSKELLUNGE *Esox masquinongy* The largest members of the pike family, muskellunge are prize freshwater gamefish. They are big (15–30 pounds is not unusual) and are sometimes caught in the 50–60 pound class. Although muskellunge is the accepted common name in the United States, this fish is officially designated in the laws and publications of Canada as maskinonge.

The muskellunge is a fish with an elongated body about 6 times as long as it is deep. The front of the head is shaped like a duck's bill, and the head is scaled. The dorsal and anal fins are set well back on the body. The muskellunge can be distinguished from other pikes by the lack of scales on the lower half of the cheeks and gill covers. Also it can be further differentiated from the northern pike by the number of sensory pores on the lower jaw or mandible. The northern pike usually has 5, while the muskellunge has 6–9 mandibular sensory pores on each side. The markings on the sides of the muskellunge may be barred, dark-spotted, or plain; adult northern pike almost always have light-colored, bean-shaped spots on the sides.

There are 3 recognized subspecies of muskellunge. Since the descriptions overlap, the subspecies are best separated by geographic distribution. The Great Lakes muskellunge (*Esox m. masquinongy*) is generally considered to inhabit the Great Lakes basin. The Ohio or Chautauqua muskellunge (*Esox m. ohioensis*) is found in Chautauqua Lake, New York, and southward through the Ohio drainage. The tiger or northern muskellunge (*Esox m. immaculatus*) is indigenous to Minnesota, Wisconsin, and the portion of Michigan close to the Wisconsin border. The range of the muskellunge, in general, is north to Lake Abitibi in the James Bay drainage, west to the Lake of the Woods in the Hudson Bay drainage, in Minnesota and Wisconsin in the Upper Mississippi drainage, the Ohio drainage from New York through Pennsylvania to Tennessee, North Carolina, and Georgia in the TVA system, and east in the Great Lakes basin to the St. Lawrence drainage.

Muskellunge are found in rivers, lakes, and streams. They prefer the quiet waters normally in an area of submerged weed beds. They are usually associated with clearwaters, but in West Virginia the muskellunge inhabit the muddier streams. This fish usually remains in less than 15 feet of water, but is sometimes found in waters to depths of 40–50 feet and in waters that have little vegetation.

Little preference is shown by adult muskellunge for food. They take what is most available. In Canada, depending on the region surveyed, 51–71 percent of their diet consisted of yellow perch. It has been stated that they prefer softrayed fishes rather than basses, bluegills, and perches, but this again probably depends on availability. Other food items found in the stomachs of large muskellunge include snakes, muskrats, ducks, crayfishes, walleyes, suckers, minnows, and salamanders. Muskellunge feed best at 68° F. When the water temperature reaches 90° F they stop feeding. Below 68° F feeding slows.

The muskellunge is considered to be one of the fastest growing of the freshwater fishes. At 6 years it is twice as long as a largemouth bass and almost twice as long as a walleye of the same age.

The greatest growth occurs in early summer and early fall when temperatures are optimum. Growth is more rapid during the first 3 years; after the second year, growth decreases until about the thirteenth summer, when it is hardly more than 1 inch per year. Females tend to grow faster than males, and at 5 years of age the female is 3–6 inches longer than the male. However, the females weigh the same as males in proportion to their length. The average Canadian muskellunge reaches the legal length (30 inches) by the fifth summer, but this may vary between 4 and 7 years. In Tennessee, in the extreme southern range of the muskellunge, few fish are taken over 5 pounds or over 30 inches. The legal limit in this southern state is 25 inches. Farther to the north, the Wisconsin muskellunge reaches the legal size of 30 inches in the fourth summer.

The usual age of most creeled muskies is 3–6 years. There are several records of 18- and 19-year-old fish, but the oldest fish ever recorded was a specimen of $69^7/_{10}$ pounds, whose age was determined by scales and vertebrae to be 30 years.

NORTHERN PIKE *Esox lucius* A freshwater gamefish of circumpolar distribution, in the United States the pike is most common from New York through the Great Lakes regions to Nebraska. However, the species has been widely introduced in many states of the South and West. The northern pike caught by anglers are often large (up to 20 pounds in many areas), and owing to their size and activity when hooked, are highly desirable gamefish.

The northern pike is a very elongated, somewhat laterally compressed fish. The head is large and has a flat dorsal surface. The duck-bill jaws have large, sharp pointed teeth. The roof of the mouth has short, backward-pointing teeth. The entire cheek is covered with

Muskellunge, Chautauqua or Barred

Northern Pike

small scales, but only the upper half of the gill cover has larger scales. This scalation pattern is one of the most distinguishing characteristics of the northern pike. Five sensory mandibular pores are found on each side of the lower jaw. The back is dark green shading to lighter green on the sides and to white on the ventral surface. On the sides are many bean-shaped yellow spots, but the fins are heavily dark spotted. The young up to 6–7 inches have light vertical bars.

Northern pike in the southern portion of their range spawn occasionally at 1 year of age, but most spawn initially at 2 years of age. In Minnesota 84 percent of the spawners were 3–5 years old. Only 1 percent were 2 years old, and 15 percent were older than 5 years. It has been observed that the size range and composition of spawning-run catches are indicative of the length and composition of fish that anglers will catch later in the season.

Northern pike usually spawn in the early spring as soon as the ice goes out of the spawning areas. The dates vary yearly according to the lateness of the spring. In Iowa they may spawn in the third and fourth week in March; in Minnesota and Pennsylvania they may spawn in the first few weeks of April. In Saskatchewan, they usually do not

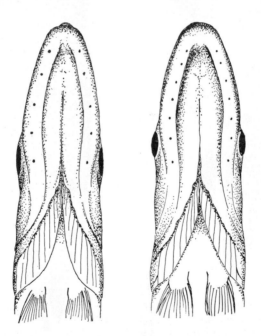

One feature that distinguishes northern pike and muskellunge is the number of mandibular pores, which appear as tiny holes along the ventral margin of the lower jaw. The pike has 5 or less mandibular pores; the muskellunge, 6 or more.

spawn until May. In Alaska they are reported to spawn in July.

Most spawners run from 6:00 P.M. to 9:00 A.M., with the peak between 9:00 P.M. and midnight. Even though they may run at night, there is no spawning until the daylight hours. The height of the spawning usually takes place in the afternoon. The most intense spawning activity has been noticed on sunny days when there was very little wind.

In Minnesota and Canada a mutant form of northern pike occurs. This is apparently a true-breeding variety called the silver pike. Superficially it differs from the northern pike only in the markings. The body is usually a dark silver or gray, and each scale is flecked with gold. This mutant form breeds with others of its kind rather than with the muskellunge and typical northern pike. Specimens rarely exceed 10 pounds.

An Asian species, the amur or black-spotted pike (*E. reicherti*) was introduced on an experimental basis in the United States (Pennsylvania, 1968) with no apparent success.

Northern pike feed largely on other fishes, principally yellow perch and suckers where abundant. Part of their nonfish diet consists of frogs, insects, freshwater shrimps, crayfishes, mice, and aquatic birds. Feeding is done entirely during daylight hours.

Northern pike are one of the fastest-growing of freshwater fishes, but their rate of growth varies according to latitude. In Great Bear Lake, which is located on the Arctic Circle in Canada, it takes about 7 years for pike to reach 20 inches and 12 years to reach 30 inches. In Pennsylvania, on the extreme southern edge of their range, they reach 20 inches between the second and third years and 30 inches between the fifth and sixth years of life. In Minnesota in the southern, more fertile lakes, growth is 12–18 inches the first year; in the northern part of the state it is 6–14 inches. Males rarely exceed 24 inches. The largest male reported in Saskatchewan was $30^1/_2$ inches, weighed 6 pounds, and was 10 years old.

As the fish grow larger the range in weights is more extreme. A 45-inch fish may weigh 15–30 pounds. Also as the fish grow larger, they become proportionately heavier. A 16-inch fish weighs about 1 pound; a 32-inch fish weighs 7–10 pounds. It has been recorded to 46 pounds.

REDFIN PICKEREL *Esox americanus americanus* The redfin pickerel and the grass pickerel (*Esox a. vermiculatus*) are the smallest members of the pike family, seldom exceeding 14–15 inches in length. Collectively, they are known as little pickerel. They can be distinguished from the young of the muskellunge (*E. masquinongy*) and the northern pike (*E. lucius*) by the scales on the cheeks and opercles. Like the chain pickerel (*E. niger*), the little pickerel have fully scaled cheeks and opercles. They differ from the chain pickerel in branchiostegal count. The little pickerel have 11–13 branchio-

Redfin Pickerel

stegals, and the chain pickerel has 14–16 branchiostegals. The adult chain pickerel has chainlike vermiculate markings on the sides, while the adult redfin or grass pickerel has vertical bars on the sides. Also the little pickerel have short, broad snouts. The distance from the tip of the snout to the front of the eye is shorter than the distance from the back of the eye to the posterior margin of the opercle. The chain pickerel has a slimmer snout, with the length of the snout being longer than the distance from the back edge of the eye to the edge of the opercle.

The redfin is confined to the Atlantic drainage and extends south through the coastal plains from Maryland to Georgia. It is widely distributed in Florida, but diminishes in numbers south of Lake Okeechobee. It extends west in the Gulf states through Georgia and Alabama. In Alabama it is reported to intergrade with the grass pickerel.

The grass pickerel is considered the western subspecies of *E. americanus*. The eastern border of its range extends from the St. Lawrence River near Montreal southwest in the tributaries of Lake Ontario and Lake Erie to the western slope of the Appalachian drainage in Pennsylvania, eastern Kentucky, Tennessee, and into Alabama, where it intergrades with the redfin pickerel. Its northern range in Canada is limited to the drainage of the St. Lawrence, Lake Ontario, and Lake Erie.

TEMPERATE BASS FAMILY   Percichthyidae

STRIPED BASS *Morone saxatilis*   The striped bass on the Atlantic coast has an extreme range from the Gulf of St. Lawrence to the St. Johns River in northern Florida and in the Gulf of Mexico from western Florida to Louisiana. The center of abundance appears to be from South Carolina to Massachusetts. On the Pacific coast, where it was introduced in 1886, the extreme range is from the Columbia River in Washington to Los Angeles, California. The present center of abundance on the Pacific coast is in the San Francisco Bay region. The fish are coastwise in distribution and are rarely taken more than a few miles offshore. The striped bass is anadromous and is found in fresh- and brackish water, with preference shown for bays, deltas, and estuarine areas. It exists as a landlocked form also, notably in the southern United States.

The trunk of the striped bass is $3^1/_2$–4 times as long (to the base of the caudal fin) as it is deep. The fish has a long head, a moderately pointed snout, and a projecting lower jaw. The 2 dorsal fins are of about equal length, and both are triangular in outline; these fins are separated. Although the color may vary, as a rule the striped bass is dark olive-green (hence the name greenhead) to steel-blue or almost black above, becoming silvery on the sides and white on the belly. The sides have 7–8 longitudinal dark stripes that follow the scale rows; 3–4 stripes are above the lateral line, 1 on it, and 3 below it. The upper stripes are the longest and may reach to the caudal fin. The stripes are often interrupted or broken and are usually absent on young fish of less than 6 inches.

Striped bass females reach sexual maturity beginning at the fourth year at a length of 18–24 inches and a weight of 4–6 pounds. By the sixth year all females are mature. Males begin to mature at 2 years, and nearly all are ready for spawning at 3 years. Stripers in the Chesapeake region continue to breed to the age of 14 years. Elsewhere, spawning is somewhat curtailed after the fish reach 10 years. A 4-year-old female produces about 65,000 eggs; a female about 13 years old produces nearly 5 million eggs.

During the spawning period striped bass ascend rivers from brackish or saltwater. The season usually begins in April in southern waters and extends into July in the St. Lawrence River area. Water temperature is an important factor, and actual spawning may vary as much as a month from one year to the next. Spawning begins at 55°–65°F with a peak at 60°–67°F. Probably the most famous breeding grounds are on the Roanoke River at Weldon, North Carolina, about 100 miles above tidewater. Here, spawning takes place in the rapids in an area of boulders and rocks. New York investigators found eggs and young striped bass in the Hudson River at locations with a pronounced current and sand or gravel bottom. In California the delta areas of the Sacramento and San Joaquin rivers are the principal spawning grounds. In the Chesapeake region spawning occurs in relatively quiet, upper tidal areas in fresh- or brackish-water streams.

During the spawning act a single, large female bass is surrounded by a number of smaller males. These so-called rock fights are frequently observed but are really courtship and spawning antics. Each of the greenish-colored eggs is 1.1–1.35 mm. in diameter. One hour after extrusion, the egg absorbs water creating a protective perivitelline space, and its size increases to an average of 3.63 mm. There is no parental care, and the semibuoyant eggs drift downstream for some distance. Hatching takes place in 3 days at 58°–60° F and in less than 48 hours at 71°–72° F. The yolk sac is absorbed in about 6$^1/_2$ days. Because freely spawned striped bass eggs must remain suspended in a current until hatching, most landlocked environments, such as reservoirs, are physically deficient for natural reproduction. Freshwater populations have been maintained by stocking young striped bass, and, despite initial difficulties in hatchery procedures for obtaining females with freely flowing eggs, a modern technique of inducing ovulation with the use of a hormone (chorionic gonadotropin) has proved very successful.

The striped bass grows to moderately large size. The heaviest recorded weighed 125 pounds (Edenton, North Carolina, 1891). This fish was probably at least 6 feet long.

Striped bass weigh about $^3/_4$ pound when 12–13 inches long or 2 years old; $2^3/_4$–3 pounds at 18–20 inches; 5 pounds at 24 inches; 10–15 pounds at 30–32 inches; and 18–20 pounds at 33–36 inches. A 20-pound bass averages 36 inches and 7 years old, a 30-pound bass is about 38 inches and 10–11 years old, a 40-pound bass is about 40–42 inches and 14 years old, a 50-pound bass is about 50 inches and 17–18 years old. A 23-year-old striped bass has been recorded. This length-weight relationship is about the same on both the Atlantic and Pacific coasts. The striped bass female grows larger than the male and weighs more than the male at any given length. Despite the lake environment, in fertile waters landlocked striped bass in excess of 50 pounds have been caught.

Studies have been made to determine the racial structure of Atlantic coast striped bass populations. These investigations, together with tagging experiments, proved that definite races do exist. Among the distinguishing features are fin-ray and lateral-line scale counts. The term "race" is used in the sense that it implies a lower level of differentiation other than a subspecies. Evidence shows that races exist in the Nova Scotia–New Brunswick area, the Hudson River area, the Chesapeake area, the Albemarle Sound area in North Carolina, the Santee-Cooper area in South Carolina, and the St. Johns River area of Florida. The Hudson River race showed 70–80 percent separation from Chesapeake stocks. In addition, differences were noted in upriver and downriver fish from the Hudson. Subraces were also noted in the Chesapeake area, and the landlocked freshwater population appears to be different from the downriver brackish-water population in the Santee-Cooper area.

ARTIFICIAL HYBRID

Sunshine Bass This hybrid was originally a cross between the male striped bass and the female white bass (Tennessee and South Carolina), but now includes female striped bass × male white bass (Florida). The body is silver in color; the stripes above the lateral line are continuous, those below are interrupted. The fish has been recorded to 20 pounds in Georgia (1977).

WHITE BASS *Morone chrysops* The white bass is one of the most popular gamefishes in the United States today. At the turn of the century it was found scattered from the Great Lakes south to Arkansas, Kansas, and Missouri, and from the western slope of the Allegheny Mountains west to the Mississippi River system. Continual transplanting has consolidated its distribution and has extended

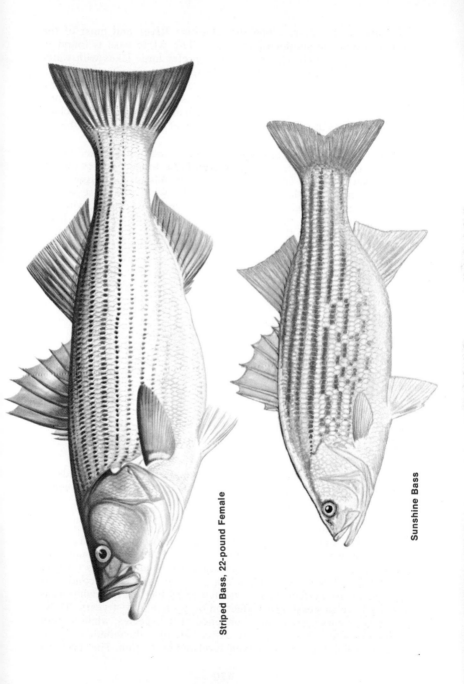

Striped Bass, 22-pound Female

Sunshine Bass

its range to the states along the Missouri River and most of the southern and the southwestern states. The white bass is found in large streams and rivers, but seems to prefer large lakes with water that is relatively clear. Rarely will the species maintain a population in a lake of less than 300 acres. Extensive construction of reservoirs, especially in the South and Southwest, has greatly favored the white bass. In addition to expansive waters, habitat preferences include extensive areas of waters deeper than 10 feet and gravel or rubble on which to spawn.

The white bass has a moderately compressed body, forked tail, 2 separate dorsal fins, teeth on the base of the tongue, spines on the first dorsal fin, and 3 spines on the anal fin. About 10 narrow, dark lines or stripes run the length of the body, with 5 of these stripes lying above the lateral line. The mouth is typically basslike, with the lower jaw projecting beyond the upper jaw. To distinguish it from the yellow bass, note the silvery color, unbroken stripes, protruding lower jaw, 11–12 soft anal-fin rays, and teeth on the base of the tongue. The separated dorsal fins and the stripes along the sides serve adequately to distinguish it from all members of the sunfish family.

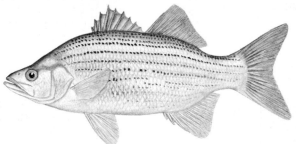

White Bass

The usual size of white bass caught by anglers runs $^1/_2$–2 pounds. A 3- to 4-pounder is a trophy, and anything over that approaches record size. Maximum size attained is about 6 pounds.

White bass spawn from late April to early June, depending on the latitude. The female may deposit from about 25,000 to 1 million eggs. Fertilized by a male as it leaves the female, the egg settles to a gravel- or rock-strewn bottom in 6–7 feet of water. Favorable conditions, including current or wave action and steady temperatures (usually 58°–64°F), allow the egg to hatch in 2–3 days. However, conditions must be nearly perfect; this is attested to by the fact that white bass usually have successful reproduction only once in 3–4 years. These successful years produce an abundance of the species, while in poor years only a few, if any, survive. After hatching, the minute fry joins its kind in massive schools seeking food and protection. The survivors

170

at this stage represent only a small percentage of the eggs spawned. Food in the form of minute zooplankton is taken at first, and as the weeks pass larger crustaceans and insects are eaten. Small fishes, if available, also contribute heavily to the diet later in the summer.

At summer's end the white bass measures about 5 inches in northern waters and $7^1/_2$ inches in southern waters. Growth for the year terminates in September or October, when water temperatures drop below 55°–60°F. From then until the water warms again the following spring, only enough food will be taken to maintain a slow rate of metabolism.

White bass often retire to deeper waters during the day and invade the shallows at twilight. When feeding on small fishes, they often present a startling and spectacular sight. Their schools are so compact and their feeding so voracious that they sometimes cause the smaller fishes to break the surface or swim up on shore.

The life expectancy of a white bass is short. Few live more than 3–4 years in the South or 4–5 years in the North. Even in the North maximum age is 7–9 years, while in the South it is 6–7 years. Adulthood usually is attained during the third year of life but may be delayed a year in northern waters or where growth conditions are poor. Average length attained in the North is about $5^1/_2$, 10, 13, 14, 15, and $15^1/_2$ inches at ages 1–6, respectively. In the South comparable lengths are about $7^1/_2$, 12, $14^1/_2$, 16, 17, and 18 inches.

A white bass weighs $^1/_2$ pound at $10^1/_2$ inches, 1 pound at 13 inches, 2 pounds at 16 inches, and 3 pounds at $17^1/_2$ inches. It has been recorded to 5 pounds.

WHITE PERCH *Morone americana*   This popular panfish is caught in fresh-, brackish, and saltwater from Nova Scotia to North Carolina and occurs inland as far as the Great Lakes. It is not a true perch, but a member of the Percichthyidae, and in small sizes there is a general similarity between it and the striped bass. The perch is about $2^1/_2$–3 times as long as it is deep (not counting the tail) and is more flattened, which gives it a chunky appearance. There is no space between its 2 dorsal fins, although they are separated by a notch. The white perch has about 48 rows of scales between the gill cover and the base of its tail, whereas there are 60 or more in the striped bass. The first dorsal fin of the white perch has 9 spines and the second dorsal fin has 1 spine and 12 rays. The anal fin originates under the second dorsal, and the ventrals, which are armed with 1 stout spine on the forward margin, are located slightly behind the pectorals.

The most apparent difference between the two species is coloration. When very small, a white perch may have pale longitudinal stripes similar to those of the striped bass, but ordinarily, and at the size perch are usually caught, no stripes are present. Its back or dorsal surface varies from olive to a dark blackish-green, shading to paler silvery-green on the sides and silvery-white on the belly. White perch

White Perch

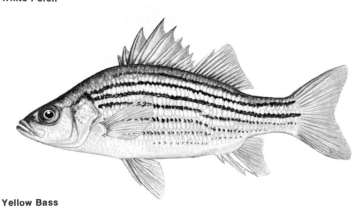

Yellow Bass

taken in saltwater or brackish-water ponds are apt to be lighter in color.

The average white perch is 8–10 inches long and weighs 1 pound or less. In the more fertile New England ponds fish up to 15 inches in length weighing about 2 pounds are not uncommon. Perch of over $2^1/_2$ pounds are rare, although it has been recorded to $4^3/_4$ pounds. But the fish is active for its size, and wherever it occurs the white perch is numerically abundant.

The white perch has a long life span. Fish 12 years old are common, and Maine has recorded at least one in its seventeenth year.

Although perch are caught in pure saltwater at various locations, they are more plentiful in ponds connected to the sea and in brackish bays and estuaries. Even though schools of perch in saltwater wander about in the search of food, they are resident populations in any area they inhabit. During the winter the fish congregate in the deeper parts of bays and creeks, where they either hibernate or endure the cold weather in a dormant state. In the spring and early summer the saltwater perch that migrate into rivers from Massachusetts south to Chesapeake Bay constitute an important sport fishery. However, the strictly landlocked perch populations are becoming more numerous.

YELLOW BASS *Morone mississippiensis* Regionally known as barfish, brassy bass, stripe, striped bass (erroneously), and streaker, the species is a temperate bass, found only in freshwater, as is its close relative, the white bass. The two species exhibit rather similar life-history characteristics, and both are eagerly sought by fishermen. The yellow bass has a very restricted range, however, and thus is familiar only to anglers in the central portions of the country. Beginning in southern Minnesota, Wisconsin, and Michigan, the yellow bass ranges southward to the Tennessee River drainage in Alabama and to Louisiana and eastern Texas. In this limited area it is found in selected lakes and the larger rivers. Efforts to transplant the species into new waters both within and outside the boundaries of this natural range have met with little success. Attempts to propagate the yellow bass artificially have also been unsuccessful. One of the primary habitat requirements of these fish apparently is extensive areas of shallow gravel and rock reefs.

The yellow bass closely resembles the white bass, having a moderately compressed body, forked tail, 2 dorsal fins, spines on the first dorsal fin, and 3 spines on the anal fin. Its clean-cut body is dark olive-green above, with silvery to bright golden-yellow sides and a white belly. About 6–7 dark, longitudinal stripes run the length of the body, 3 of which are above the lateral line. The stripes lying below the lateral line are broken or interrupted toward the tail. These broken stripes, the yellowish coloration of the sides, the absence of teeth on the base of the tongue, and the even length of the upper and lower jaws are characteristics that distinguish the yellow from the white bass. There are 51–55 scales along the lateral line and 10 softrays in the anal fin.

The life expectancy of a yellow bass is short. Few live more than 3–4 years, and 7 years is about maximum. Annual survival after the first year of life is about 20–40 percent. Average size varies with latitude and food conditions, but approximates 4, 7, 9, 10, and 11 inches at the end of years 1–5, respectively.

A yellow bass weighs $1/4$ pound at $7^1/_2$ inches, $1/_2$ pound at $9^1/_2$ inches, and $3/_4$ pound at about 11 inches. It becomes attractive to fishermen when it reaches a weight of about $1/_4$ pound, which usually is late in the summer of the second year or early in the third year of life.

Yellow bass are a favorite among panfish anglers in the central United States. They are active fighters for their size and provide good sport on light tackle. They may be taken on a variety of baits, including worms, minnows, flies, spinners, spoons, and small plugs. They

173

sometimes feed on the surface, but usually are caught in middepths or near the bottom.

The flesh of the yellow bass often is compared to that of the yellow perch, being white, firm, flaky, and delicious. It usually is considered superior to the white bass.

PIRATEPERCH FAMILY   Aphredoderidae

PIRATEPERCH *Aphredoderus sayanus*   This is the only living species of its family, although it is related to the troutperch. It is not a true perch.

It is a small fish with spiny rays and rough ctenoid or comblike scales. The vent or anus is located in the throat region rather than in the more usual position in front of the anal fin. It is a dark olivaceous fish with heavy specklings of dark over the entire body, except the belly. Breeding specimens show much iridescent purple. Most adults are 3−4 inches in length, but may reach a size of 5−6 inches under good conditions.

The pirateperch is found from Minnesota eastward to Ontario and southward to Florida and Texas. It is rather widely distributed in the North in sluggish weedy creeks. It is very common along the Atlantic coastal plain in swamps and backwater creeks.

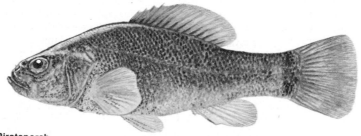

Pirateperch

The pirateperch spawns in the spring and both parents build a nest. They guard it and the young until the latter are $^1/_3$ inch long. It is a predaceous fish that attacks insects, crustaceans, and other small animals.

Peculiar to its life history is the location of the anus; the anus migrates forward as the pirateperch grows and eventually locates under the throat in the adult.

TROUTPERCH FAMILY   Percopsidae

TROUTPERCH *Percopsis cmiscomaycus*   Despite its name, this fish is neither a trout nor a true perch. It is easily recognized by a combination of an adipose fin on the back and spiny rays in the dorsal and

Troutperch

anal fins. The scales are rough or ctenoid. It is an olivaceous fish with lightish lower sides and underparts and with a series of spots forming a broken line along the lateral line. Its back is covered with less obvious and more diffuse spots. Most specimens are about 4 inches, and length seldom exceeds 6 inches.

The troutperch is widely distributed from the Yukon in the Northwest and Hudson Bay, southeastward to the Lake Champlain region, and south to the Potomac River in the East. In the Midwest it is found from the Great Lakes region southward to West Virginia, Kentucky, and Kansas. In the northern part of its range it is generally found in lakes, but in the South it lives in silty streams. Throughout much of its range it is seen only during the spawning season and is thought to stay in deepwater. A related species, the sand roller (*Columbia transmontanus*), occurs in the lower Columbia River drainage.

The troutperch is a spring spawner and may be found concentrated in tributaries of lakes and along lake shores, usually late in April and May. It feeds on small crustaceans, insects, and other aquatic animals. This species serves as forage for many gamefishes.

STICKLEBACK FAMILY Gasterosteidae

BROOK STICKLEBACK *Culaea inconstans* This fish is characterized by its naked body, a lack of a caudal keel, and the number of spines, which may be either 5 or 6. The pelvic fins are greatly reduced in size, and the caudal fin is rounded. Color is variable, but it is usually green to olive above, and white to cream below. Breeding color of the male is more intense. Maximum size is about 3 inches.

The brook stickleback is found throughout the north-central drainages of North America, from British Columbia to Hudson and

Brook Stickleback

175

James bays and New Brunswick to western New York and Pennsylvania, west to the Missouri River in Kansas, and throughout the Great Lakes. It occurs in clearwater, the coldwaters of weedy spring holes, boggy lakes, and streams, and in cold streams and springs.

Spawning takes place in April and May, and the nest is built and guarded by the male. Like other sticklebacks, this is a very aggressive species, driving away others from its territory. It eats small crustaceans and insects. In recent years, man-made alterations of the environment, such as dredging, filling, and pollution, have reduced its habitat.

FOURSPINE STICKLEBACK *Apeltes quadracus* This spiny little fish is identified by the 4 dorsal-fin spines, which may vary from 2 to 4, and another spine immediately in front of the soft dorsal fin. The body is naked and without the plates that identify the threespine stickleback, with which it might be confused because of the spine count. A distinct bony ridge occurs on either side of the belly. The soft dorsal and anal fins are almost identical in shape. The caudal fin is long and narrow, and rounded instead of concave as in the threespine stickleback. The fourspine is black or brown to olive-brown above, with dark mottlings, grading to paler or silvery below. The pelvic-fin membrane is red, giving the species the sometimes used name of bloody stickleback. The fish reaches a length of about $2^1/_2$ inches.

Fourspine Stickleback

NINESPINE STICKLEBACK *Pungitius pungitius* The large number of dorsal-fin spines identifies this species, there being 7–11, usually 9–10. A sharp caudal keel, a convex caudal fin, and a rather elongate body also help to distinguish it from other relatives. It lacks the bony plates of the threespine stickleback. Coloration is dull brown

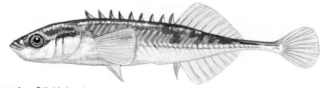

Ninespine Stickleback

above with faint bars or blotches and silvery on the belly. Variations in color and intensity depend on the season, sexual maturity, and habitat. The fish reaches a length of about 3 inches.

This is a coldwater stickleback, occurring more in circumpolar regions than others of the family. It ranges from northern Scandinavia to the Mediterranean and Black seas, from the Arctic Circle to Japan and northern China, and from Newfoundland to New Jersey. It also occurs in the cooler waters of the Great Lakes. Equally at home in fresh- and saltwater, it prefers quiet waters of creeks, estuaries, and salt marshes. In freshwater lakes it occurs at considerable depths.

THREESPINE STICKLEBACK *Gasterosteus aculeatus* The numerous bony plates on the sides of this fish (28 or more), the convex outline of the tail, and the 2 large dorsal spines followed by a smaller, third spine identify this member of the family Gasterosteidae. Its color is dull olive above, with faint bars or blotches, to white or silvery on the belly. This color varies depending upon the breeding season, state of sexual maturity, and habitat. The fish grows to about 4 inches long.

A widely ranging species, the threespine stickleback is found from Labrador to Chesapeake Bay and from northern Norway and Iceland to the Mediterranean and Black seas. It also occurs in northern China, southern Japan, and Baja California, as well as the Hudson Bay region and Lake Ontario. It occurs in salt- or brackish water, apparently readily adapting to either mode of life. While coastal forms are largely restricted to estuaries, a few may drift off to sea in clumps of floating weed. A year-round resident, particularly where grass or weed can be found, it moves into somewhat deeper water during the winter.

Spawning occurs in brackish or freshwater, from May to July, and is accompanied by one of the most elaborate nest-building and egg-care patterns known among fishes. In about 6 weeks, the young have grown to a length of about $3/5$ inch, when they closely resemble the adults.

The threespine is a pugnacious species, driving away other fishes from its territory with its sharp spines. Omnivorous, it eats small invertebrates, such as copepods, mysids, and young shrimps, as well as small fishes and fish eggs.

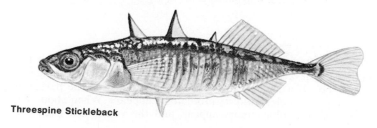

Threespine Stickleback

BOWFIN FAMILY Amiidae

BOWFIN *Amia calva* Also known as dogfish, grindle, grinnel, and cypress trout, the bowfin has a stout olive-colored body, a long dorsal fin, and a rounded tail. The top of the head is flattened; the mouth is large and filled with strong, sharp teeth. On the underside of the head is a distinctive gular plate. The sexes of the adults can be differentiated by a spot at the upper base of the tail. The male's spot is rimmed with orange-yellow; on the female the rim is lacking or the spot is absent. A feature of the bowfin's unique structure is an air bladder connected to the throat and used as a lung, enabling this fish to live in waters unsuitable for other fish. The bowfin attains lengths up to 3 feet and weights in excess of 20 pounds.

This primitive fish is the lone survivor of a large family now existing only as fossils in the rocks of Europe and the United States. It is found in most parts of this country from the Mississippi River drainage eastward to the St. Lawrence River and south from Texas to Florida. It usually inhabits shallow, weedy lakes and sluggish streams and is seldom found in fast currents.

Spawning occurs in the spring, April through June, depending on the water temperature of the locality, in quiet bays or inlets containing vegetation. The male builds a nest by biting off the vegetation in a small area and brushing it away with his tail and fins. When he has cleared away the weeds, a bed of soft rootlets, sand, or gravel remains for the eggs. Spawning takes place at night. After one or more females have spawned in the nest, the male guards the eggs for the 8–10 days required for hatching. As soon as the larvae hatch, they attach themselves to rootlets by an adhesive organ on the snout or lie on their sides in the bottom of the nest until they are about $^1/_2$ inch long. The male continues to stand guard; he hovers in a runway to the nest, his head projecting over it. When an unwelcome visitor approaches, he makes a noisy escape, probably to decoy the intruder away from the nest.

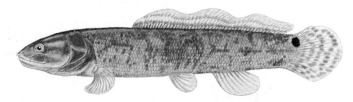

Bowfin

At about 9 days the larvae can swim and begin feeding. The adhesive organ ceases to be used, and the young follow the male in a close school. If a young fish becomes separated from the parent, it swims in close circles until its protector reappears. When about $1^1/_2$ inches long, the adult colors appear, and the young fish begins to protect itself by seeking cover individually. At a length of 4 inches or so, the juveniles cease to gather in schools.

Because the bowfin is a poor foodfish and because it feeds extensively on other fishes it usually is considered undesirable. But since the areas it prefers are likely to be overpopulated by stunted panfish or rough fish, the bowfin is often really an asset. It can be quite effective in holding fish populations in check.

Fishes compose upward of 80 percent of this voracious feeder's diet, with crayfishes making up much of the remainder. Many other items are eaten when they can be had easily.

GAR FAMILY   Lepisosteidae

An ancient group of predaceous fishes, gars can be recognized by a long, cylindrical body covered with heavy, diamond-shaped (ganoid) scales behind long, snoutlike jaws containing many sharp teeth. The dorsal fin is far back and is nearly opposite the anal fin. Possessing a modified gas bladder, used in part for breathing air, gars can thrive in very stagnant water.

Spawning occurs in the spring in shallow bays and sloughs. The dark green eggs are adhesive and attach to weeds or other objects. The young are solitary, and beginning early in life they lie motionless close to the surface; in shape and color they resemble floating sticks. Both young and old occasionally break the surface to expel gases and gulp air into the swimbladder.

ALLIGATOR GAR Lepisosteus spatula   The alligator gar is one of the monsters of inland waters. It often attains a weight of 100 pounds or more. The largest reported was 10 feet long and weighed 302 pounds. No other gar attains a size comparable. When it is young, the alligator gar can be distinguished from other gars by the double rows of large teeth on each side of the upper jaw; others have only a single row. Otherwise the snout is similar to that of the shortnose gar. Other distinguishing characteristics are the lateral-line scales; 62 usually are present. The body is long, slender, and olive- or greenish-brown above and lighter below. Sides are mottled toward the head with large black spots toward the rear and on the rear fins.

The alligator's range extends from northeastern Mexico, up the Mississippi River basin to near St. Louis, and up the Ohio River to Louisville, Kentucky.

The alligator gar prefers the backwaters, lakes, oxbows, and bayous along the large southern rivers. In some areas it is sought by fishermen because of the obvious sporting qualities of the huge adults. Fishes are its principal food.

FLORIDA GAR Lepisosteus platyrhincus   The Florida gar has been described as the Florida representative of the spotted gar. It is very similar to the spotted gar; the major distinguishing characteristic is the distance from the front of the eye to the back edge of the bony opercle. If that distance is less than two-thirds the snout length, the fish is a Florida gar; if the distance is more than two-thirds the snout length, it is a spotted gar. Both species are characterized by the relatively broad snout and the large round spots on the top of the head.

The Florida gar is found from South Carolina south through Florida. The spotted gar does not occur in most of its range. The Florida gar inhabits lakes and slow-flowing streams and is notably abundant in the Tamiami and other canals. It is gregarious and can usually be found swimming in groups of 2–10 or more.

Spawning occurs from May through July in backwaters and sloughs. A female averages 5,200 eggs. Other habits are similar to those of the shortnose gar.

Fishes make up the bulk of its diet, but freshwater shrimps compose 17 percent; insects, crayfishes, and scuds also are taken. In the canals where gars are abundant, largemouth bass have been reported to be adversely affected by their predation and competition. Over 2,000 gars have been taken from a 300-foot-long section of canal, and their total production has been estimated at 700–1,000 pounds per acre in some areas. Its lazy habits make it a very efficient utilizer of food: $2^1/_2$ times as much food is required for the more active bass as for this particular Florida gar.

LONGNOSE GAR *Lepisosteus osseus* This species is the most abundant and widely distributed member of the ancient gar family. Its very long slender beak, whose length is 18–20 times its least width, and a long cylindrical body covered with overlapping diamond-shaped scales distinguish it from all its freshwater relatives. The dorsal fin is inserted far back, almost over the anal fin.

It is found in the Mississippi River system northwest to Montana, through the Great Lakes except Lake Superior, to the St. Lawrence watershed of Quebec and south to northern Mexico. It grows to 5 feet.

SHORTNOSE GAR *Lepisosteus platostomus* The shortnose gar has a comparatively short beak whose length is about $5^1/_2$ times its least width. It has no spots on the head, but there are small round black spots on the fins. It has 60–64 scales in the lateral line. A very young fish has short jaws and a wide black stripe on the sides.

The shortnose is found in the Mississippi River drainage as far north as South Dakota and Minnesota to the north and west, in the Ohio River drainage, and southwestward to eastern Texas. It is more abundant in the southern part of this range. It prefers slow-flowing streams, lakes, and backwaters and avoids strong currents. Although it feeds by sight and thus prefers clearwaters, it is tolerant of muddy waters, and is found in such waters more frequently than some other species of gars. Length is to 4 feet.

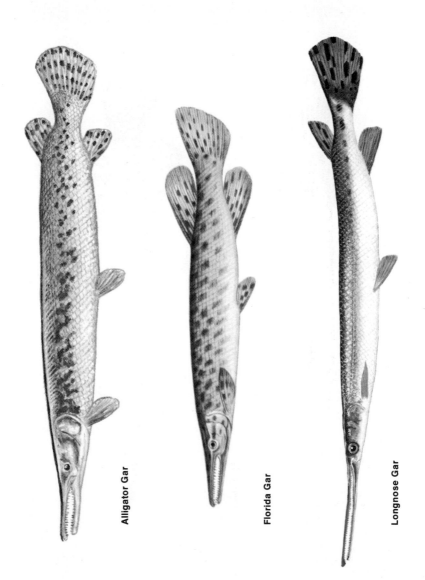

Alligator Gar

Florida Gar

Longnose Gar

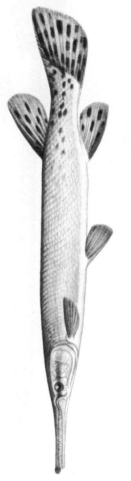

Shortnose Gar

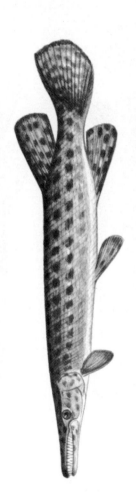

Spotted Gar

SPOTTED GAR *Lepisosteus oculatus* The spotted gar can easily be mistaken for the shortnose or the Florida gar. It can be distinguished from the shortnose gar by large round spots on its head and by the 54–58 scales in its lateral line, and from the Florida gar by the distance from the front of the eye to back of the opercle. The snout is much broader than that of the longnose gar. Its body appears heavier than in the longnose or shortnose gar. It is deep olive-green, with darker spots on the back. Its sides are lighter, and the fins are heavily blotched and spotted.

The spotted gar is found from Minnesota to Ohio in the North, and southward to Texas and northwest Florida. Length is to 4 feet.

NEEDLEFISH FAMILY Belonidae

The needlefishes are voracious elongate fishes with a superficial resemblance to the freshwater gar; however, they belong to the order that includes the halfbeaks, sauries, and flyingfishes. The jaws of needlefishes project into long, thin, and rather fragile beaks, usually with the upper jaw slightly shorter (more so in the young than the adults). A band of long pointed teeth, in addition to a band of shorter ones, arms the jaws.

Atlantic Needlefish

These are marine fishes; however, one species, the Atlantic needlefish, *Strongylura marina*, enters and ascends freshwater rivers from Cape Cod to Texas; it may reach a length of 4 feet.

PADDLEFISH FAMILY Polyodontidae

PADDLEFISH *Polyodon spathula* Also known as spoonbill, spoonbill cat, shovelnose cat, and boneless cat, the paddlefish is a living representative of an old group of fossil fishes. Its only near relative is a native of the Yangtze River in China. This species can be recognized by the long, flattened snout in front of a large head and mouth; the sharklike tail whose upper lobe is upturned and is longer than the lower; and the skin, which is scaleless except for a very few scales that are inconspicuous. The eyes are very small, and the gill covers have long, pointed flaps. Color is gray to bluish-gray in turbid water and grades to nearly black in clearwater. The skeleton is chiefly cartilage. One 200-pound specimen was recorded, but about 90 pounds is the usual maximum. Average weight of paddlefish caught by anglers in the Osage River, Missouri, is about 38 pounds.

Paddlefish are found in the large rivers and lakes of the Mississippi River system, including the Missouri River into Montana, the Ohio

River, and their major tributaries. They have thrived in large impoundments where extensive areas of gravel bars remain in large tributary streams to provide spawning areas and have declined in places such as the upper Mississippi River where the slowed waters of a continuous series of dams have caused siltation of these spawning areas.

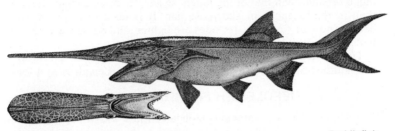

Under view   **Paddlefish**

Spawning occurs in April and May. The fish in lakes often make extensive movements to streams to find the gravel bars needed for spawning. This movement and spawning coincide with significant rises in the river level that allow the large fish to move over normally shallow riffles and provide current, which they appear to need for spawning. At this time they move in groups, often near the surface, where they frequently are hit by boat propellers. The eggs are scattered over the gravel bar and fertilized by accompanying males. Immediately upon fertilization the egg forms an adhesive coating, which causes it to sink and adhere to the first object it touches. Most adhere to the gravel, where they hatch in 5–10 days, depending on the water temperature. Upon hatching, the young fish depends on the attachment to the rock to hold the capsule as it wriggles free. When hatched, the young paddlefish has no indication of the snout that will begin to be apparent in 2–3 weeks, but the snout grows rapidly after that and soon is the most conspicuous part of the fish. It is proportionately longer on young fish than on those nearing maturity. The newly hatched larva begins to swim soon after hatching and does so continuously thereafter; thus it is removed from the gravel to the stream and, in many areas, to the lake very early in life. Growth varies greatly with the abundance of food, but a paddlefish usually grows 10–14 inches the first year and to about 21 inches the second. It is long-lived, up to 30 years in the Lake of the Ozarks, Missouri.

The paddlefish feeds by moving through the water with its huge mouth agape. If attracted by a swarm of plankton, it begins to circle and feeds actively through the swarm. Food is retained on large, comblike gillrakers; periodically the fish closes its mouth and gulps to swallow the accumulated food. The diet consists primarily of plankton and insect larvae. Small fishes have been reported taken infrequently. They appear to be ingested accidentally by adults, but have been noted more frequently among young fish during the only period of life when teeth are present.

STURGEON FAMILY Acipenseridae

This is a family of large fishes found throughout the northern hemisphere in the oceans and freshwater rivers. A total of 16 species is known, 7 of which occur in the United States.

The sturgeons are primitive fishes and were widely distributed in early geological history. They are characterized by a head covered with bony plates and the presence of 5 rows of bony scutes on the body. There are 4 small barbels anterior to the mouth; the mouth is protrusible in adaption to bottom feeding.

All sturgeons are slow-growing fishes, maturing at 12–22 years (according to species and sex), but they are long-lived, with individuals attaining 75 years or more.

ATLANTIC STURGEON *Acipenser oxyrhynchus* This species occurs from North Carolina to Nova Scotia. The anal fin is slightly more than half as long as the dorsal fin and almost entirely below it. There are 38 dorsal rays, 27 anal rays, 10 dorsal plates, and 29 lateral plates. The fish is olive-gray or brown in color and grows to 12 feet.

GREEN STURGEON *Acipenser medirostris* This species occurs from San Francisco to the Gulf of Alaska, but is limited to river mouths. The anal fin is almost as long as the dorsal and is positioned almost entirely behind the dorsal fin. There are 33 dorsal rays, 22 anal rays, 9 dorsal plates, and 26 lateral plates. The fish is olive-green with an olive stripe on the median line of the belly and on each side above the bony plates. Length is to 7 feet.

LAKE STURGEON *Acipenser fulvescens* The lake sturgeon is found from Hudson Bay and the St. Lawrence River through central Canada in the North, through Minnesota, Nebraska, Missouri, and southeast to northern Alabama.

It occurs in both lakes and streams of its range and prefers comparatively shallow waters. It ascends streams to spawn in the spring from April to June, but has been reported spawning in lakes. It grows slowly and requires 14–22 years to reach maturity, attaining a length of 8 inches the first year, 50 inches and 29 pounds at 20 years, and 65 inches and 69 pounds at 35 years in Lake Winnebago, Wisconsin. Females live longer than males and grow larger. Formerly abundant, the lake sturgeon now is scarce in many parts of its range.

PALLID STURGEON *Scaphirhynchus album* This species occurs in the Mississippi River drainage. It closely resembles the shovelnose sturgeon, but its belly is almost devoid of the bony plates that entirely cover the shovelnose. Length is to 4 feet.

Atlantic Sturgeon

Lake Sturgeon

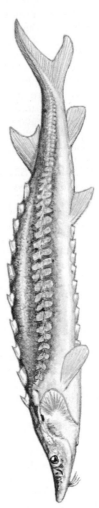

White Sturgeon

SHORTNOSE STURGEON *Acipenser brevirostris*   The shortnose occurs from Florida to Cape Cod. The front of the anal fin is below the front of the dorsal fin. There are 41 dorsal rays, 22 anal rays, 8–11 dorsal plates, and 22–33 lateral plates. The fish is blackish-olive above, with alternate black and pale bands on the sides and reddish color in the plates. Length is to 3 feet.

SHOVELNOSE STURGEON *Scaphirhynchus platorhynchus*   Occurring in the Mississippi River drainage, the shovelnose is distinguished by its slender caudal peduncle entirely covered by bony plates. Its color is brown, and the fish grows to 5 feet.

WHITE STURGEON *Acipenser transmontanus*   This is the largest fish found in inland waters of the United States. It can be differentiated from other sturgeons by its short, broad snout with 4 barbels, located much farther forward than those of other sturgeons, and by its gray color. The toothless mouth is small with thick lips, and is directed downward.

The white sturgeon is found along the Pacific coast from Alaska south to Monterey, California.

Many white sturgeons spend part of their lives in the ocean and ascend the larger rivers along the Pacific coast to spawn. In some headwaters, such as the upper Columbia River, they are entirely landlocked. Adults make a winter or spring migration to spawn in the spring over upstream gravel beds and return downstream in summer. The white sturgeon does not care for the eggs or young. It averages 19 inches long the second year, 40 inches the seventh, and matures at about 12 years when 50–53 inches long and 35–50 pounds in weight. Ages of the very large fish reported have not been determined, but growth rates of $2^1/_{10}$–$2^3/_5$ inches per year after fast initial growth the first 8 years indicate that 14- to 16-foot fish are 60–75 years old.

In freshwater it takes crustaceans, mollusks, insect larvae, and other bottom organisms, which it sucks up as it works along the bottom.

The roe of an 800-pound sturgeon weighs 50 pounds and is valued for caviar. The largest fish reported taken weighed 1,800 pounds. The white sturgeon is prized as a foodfish. These trophy fish have been overfished in the past, and careful regulation of harvests has been necessary to ensure maintenance of a fishable population.

SLEEPER FAMILY   Eleotridae

The sleepers are of worldwide tropical and subtropical distribution, and at least 7 species occur in southern United States freshwater and tidewater streams and canals, ranging from South Carolina through Central America and to Brazil. In contrast to the marine gobies (Gobiidae), in which the ventral fins are united to form a suckerlike disk, the ventral fins of the sleepers are completely separated. The

Bigmouth Sleeper

body is elongate, usually cylindrical anteriorly and compressed posteriorly. Sleepers have 2 separated dorsal fins; the first is composed of short, flexible spines and the second contains softrays, which may be preceded by a single spine. The caudal fin is rounded.

Many species of the Eleotridae are voracious and predatory, concealing themselves in weeds, rock crevices, or soft mud bottoms, where they move with great speed in capturing other fishes. However, sleepers are of small size, and the larger bigmouth sleeper, *Gobiomorus dormitor,* which is caught in southern states, seldom exceeds 20 inches in length. Sleepers take live baits and occasionally strike spinners, flies, and small plugs. They are fairly common in the Florida freshwater catch, but seldom are correctly identified. Large individuals have some food value.

LIVEBEARER FAMILY   Poeciliidae

These are small fishes most common in the southern United States. Fertilization is internal, the male depositing sperm in the genital tract of the female. Eggs hatch internally and the young emerge alive. Popular in aquaria, livebearers also provide forage for black basses and sunfishes, particularly in the Gulf states area.

GAMBUSIA *Gambusia affinis*   Commonly known as mosquito fish, the gambusia is abundant in the southern United States into Mexico and is found in southern Illinois, Indiana, and California. Sexes differ in size, the male seldom exceeding 1 inch and the female attaining 2 inches. The female's reproductive period extends over 15 weeks. A single mating furnishes spermatozoa for a series of broods. The gesta-

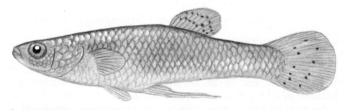

Gambusia (Mosquito fish)

188

tion period is 21−28 days. The gambusia feeds to a large extent on the larvae and pupae of mosquitoes. Called potgut minnow by fishermen, it is a common food of the largemouth bass.

SAILFIN MOLLY *Mollienisia latipinna*   This livebearer is found in the wild along the coast from South Carolina into Mexico. It is also bred as an aquarium fish and is the species most usually called the Mollie. A wild specimen has a body that is light olive-green above and lighter below. It has 6−8 rows of dots forming horizontal lines. The dorsal fin has rows of spots and is very long and high. It is almost as long as the back and is especially high in some males. Maximum length is 3−4 inches.

Sailfin Molly

The eggs are fertilized internally by the male, and the milt may be stored so that one fertilization is sufficient for 4−5 broods. The eggs hatch within the mother, growing to the same maturity as the young of fishes that are hatched from eggs do when they have absorbed their yolk sac; after this they are expelled ready to swim. They mature in 3−4 months.

FRESHWATER EEL FAMILY   Anguillidae

AMERICAN EEL *Anguilla rostrata*   The common American eel, sometimes called silver eel, is a catadromous freshwater fish and is closely related to the European eel, *A. vulgaris*. The American eel is elongate, almost snakelike in appearance, and the dorsal fin originates far behind the pectorals. This characteristic distinguishes it from the conger eel, whose dorsal originates slightly behind the tip of the pectorals. The eel has a pointed snout, a large mouth that extends as far back as the midpoint of the eye or past it; its gill slits are arranged vertically, the upper corners opposite the base of the pectorals.

On their spawning grounds, American eels mingle with the European species, which have made the longer westward journey. Although the breeding grounds overlap, the larvae of the American species al-

American Eel

ways work back to the west side of the Atlantic and those of the European to the eastern side. This trip takes about 1 year for the American eel, which approaches a length of 6 inches by the time it reaches the brackish waters along our Atlantic coast. The European eel, however, takes 3 years to make its longer journey, which may be as much as 5,000 miles. Young eels appear along our shores in spring, entering tidal marshes and estuaries in tremendous numbers along the coast from the Gulf of St. Lawrence to the Gulf of Mexico. The males remain in tidewater; the females ascend the rivers until sexually mature.

Eels grow slowly, and full-grown adults may be 5–20 years old. When fully grown, the female eels, traveling mostly at night, drop downstream. They and the maturing males that have been living in the river mouths cease feeding, change from an olive to a black color, and move out to sea. Once they leave the shore, the eels drop wholly out of sight. Only the discovery of newly hatched larvae over the deep parts of the oceanic basin, south of Bermuda and 1,000 miles east of Florida, shows where their destination lies. Evidently the eels die after this single spawning, for no spent eels have been found and no large eels ever run upstream again.

LAMPREY FAMILY Petromyzontidae

Lampreys are not eels, but eellike forms with a sucking-disk mouth structure or buccal funnel; they lack true jaws and have a soft, cartilaginous skeleton. There are 14 species found in North American waters occurring as anadromous and strictly freshwater populations. Most are small (6–9 inches) and of only indirect interest to anglers because of the parasitic role of some species in relation to gamefishes.

The adults of nonparasitic lampreys have a nonfunctional digestive tract. These species are small, seldom over 7 inches in length, and generally known as brook lampreys. Most common are the northern brook lamprey (*Ichthyomyzon fossor*), southern brook lamprey (*I. gagei*), Allegheny brook lamprey (*I. greeleyi*), mountain brook lamprey (*I. hubbsi*), western brook lamprey (*Lampetra richardsoni*), and American brook lamprey (*L. lamottei*).

PACIFIC LAMPREY *Entosphenus tridentatus* This species differs from the sea lamprey in having only a single dorsal fin, rather than a dorsal divided in two by a deep notch, and lacking the well-developed arrangement of rasping teeth on the sucking disk, there being only 5–6 cusps. It is dark bluish to brownish-gray and is seldom mottled. A length of over 2 feet is attained. It occurs from southern California to northwestern Alaska.

SEA LAMPREY *Petromyzon marinus* The sea lamprey is one of the best-known species. It has the dorsal fin separated into 2 parts by a deep notch, the second part confluent with the caudal fin. The mouth is merely a sucking disk lined with horny cusps, which are also present on the tongue. The closely spaced teeth are arranged in curved, radiating rows. Adults are dark tan to olive or red-brown, with chocolate blotches; spawning adults are purple or blue-black. The young ammocoetes are tan above and lighter below, occasionally with darker mottlings. This lamprey grows to 3 feet and nearly 3 pounds.

The sea lamprey occurs in saltwater from Greenland to Florida, and from northern Norway to the Mediterranean Sea, ascending freshwater to breed. Some occur landlocked in freshwater lakes. Following spawning, the young spend 5–10 years or more (individuals have been recorded to 13 years) buried in the mud, after which they transform and move downstream into the ocean or a lake. Adults spend about 2 years parasitizing various fishes, then return to freshwater. Nests are built in the stream bed, large depressions being made by the adult moving large stones with its mouth. Adults die following spawning.

The sucking disk is used by the lamprey to attach itself to its prey and to bore a hole through the skin with the rasp tongue, after which it sucks blood from the host. Lamprey scars are visible on many different kinds of fishes.

During spring runs, large numbers were formerly taken and used for food, their flesh being considered a delicacy. Adults are important to biology classes, and are sought by biological supply houses. Because the adults destroy valuable commercial species, particularly in freshwater, attempts have been made to control their numbers. Selective chemical poisoning has been effective in certain areas.

Sea Lamprey

SILVER LAMPREY *Ichthyomyzon unicuspis* This species is characterized by its single dorsal fin, which distinguishes it readily from the sea lamprey. It resembles other lampreys in general shape, but its

191

cusps have only 1 point, in contrast to many other freshwater lampreys. Like the sea lamprey, its cusps are arranged in radiating series, but are more widely spaced than in the sea lamprey and lack the arrangement of larger cusps around the tongue cavity. Its color is light tan to silvery-tan becoming bluish-black during the spawning season. It grows to a length of 14 inches, the young ammocoetes reaching a maximum of 7 inches.

The silver lamprey is found exclusively in freshwater throughout the Mississippi drainage and the Great Lakes to Hudson Bay and the St. Lawrence River. It is a parasitic lamprey, undertaking an extensive spring migration and nest-building activities. Adults spawn over sand and gravel bottom. After the young emerge from being buried in the gravel, they burrow into soft mud, where they remain for long periods.

In spring, at a length of about 4–6 inches, the ammocoetes drift downstream to take up a parasitic life on fishes in large bodies of water. They remain in these areas until late in the following spring. In recent years, siltation, pollution, and other man-made alterations in the environment have drastically reduced the numbers of silver lamprey.

COD FAMILY Gadidae

BURBOT *Lota lota* Also called cusk, ling, or lawyer, this is the only member of the cod family found in freshwater in North America.

The body is elongate, somewhat eel-shaped, with a barbel on each anterior nostril and a longer barbel in the middle of the chin. The small first dorsal fin is followed by a long second dorsal fin that is similar in shape to the anal fin. The small, numerous scales are embedded in the heavy skin, which is colored dark olive above with chainlike blackish or yellowish markings on the sides. This coloration is more marked in the young of the species. The burbot occasionally exceeds 30 inches, although the average size is less than $1\frac{1}{2}$ feet. While the average weight of the Great Lakes form is about 1 pound, the subspecies found in Alaska and Siberia may attain a length of 5 feet and a weight of 60 pounds. The common form is distributed from New England and the Susquehanna River system in the East, throughout the Hudson Bay drainage, and in the Columbia River. This is a coldwater species, occurring in lakes; it seeks deepwater in the summer and has been caught to depths of 700 feet.

Although it is not normally found in streams, it is abundant when present and is most often taken by the angler around large boulders and other shelter. The burbot occurs in both sluggish and swift streams.

Reproduction occurs under the ice, usually over sand or gravel bottom. During February, burbots enter shallow water 1–4 feet deep, where they spawn at night. A voracious feeder, the burbot takes fishes, crayfishes, and other animals, the feeding being carried on es-

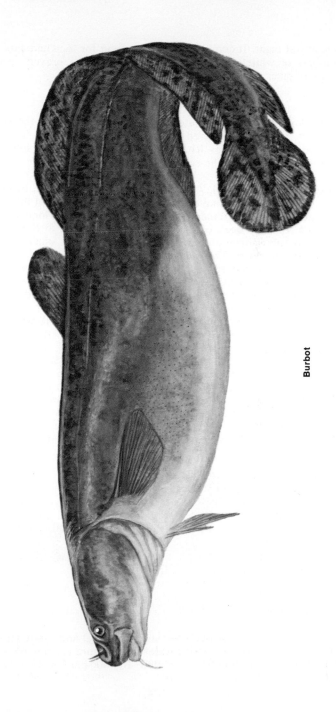

Burbot

sentially at night. It competes with lake trout for food and eats large numbers of whitefish and ciscoes. The burbot is preyed upon by northern pike.

DRUM FAMILY Sciaenidae

In addition to the freshwater drum, the red drum and the spotted seatrout, usually considered marine species, occur as freshwater populations in St. Johns River, Florida, and have been introduced into impoundments in the southwestern United States.

FRESHWATER DRUM *Aplodinotus grunniens* The freshwater drum has a rather oblong body with the back somewhat humped or elevated. The tail is rounded, the snout blunt, and the long dorsal fin extends from the peak of the humped back almost to the tail. The mouth is subterminal and horizontal, and there are small, comblike teeth on the jaws. The dorsal fin is nearly separated, with the forward part composed of 8–9 spinyrays and the rear portion containing 25–31 softrays. The anal fin has 2 spines, the second of which is long and very stout. The upper portion of the body is pearl-gray and sometimes gives off bronze, blue, and silver reflections. The sides are lighter and more silvery; the belly is milk-white.

Distributed principally in large rivers and lakes, the freshwater drum ranges from the Hudson Bay drainage of Manitoba and northern Ontario and from the Great Lakes (except Superior) east to Quebec and Lake Champlain, and south to the Gulf and eastern Mexico to Guatemala. The Missouri River drainage forms its western boundary, while to the east the fish's range extends almost to the Atlantic coast states. Although the species prefers clearwaters, it can withstand turbid waters better than many species and thus is found in abundance in some of the large, silty lakes and rivers.

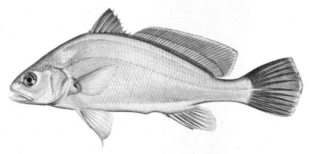

Freshwater Drum

Freshwater drums spawn over shallow gravel and sandy stretches of shore in April or May when water temperature is about 65°–70°F. The eggs, probably numbering 10,000–100,000 per female, are broad-

194

cast and adhere to pebbles. No parental care is given the eggs or young. Hatching may take about 2 weeks, after which the young stay in the shallows and begin feeding on minute crustaceans. The diet of adults consists primarily of mollusks, insects, and fishes in various combinations. Mollusks are probably preferred when they are present in sufficient quantity. This drum is particularly adept at obtaining and "shelling"mollusks. Searching the bottom mud and debris primarily by touch and taste, the fish picks out mollusks and then crunches or "shells" them with its large, strong pharyngeal teeth. The shells are spewed out, and the soft bodies are swallowed.

The size of the freshwater drums that are marketed commercially runs $1^{1}/_{2}$–5 pounds. Specimens as large as 20–60 pounds occasionally are reported.

RED DRUM *Sciaenops ocellata* This species is better known as redfish along the South Atlantic and Gulf coasts and as channel bass in some other localities along the eastern seaboard of the United States. It occurs along the Atlantic coast from Massachusetts to Texas. Specimens weighing more than 50 pounds are rare; many of the individuals taken weigh up to 40 pounds, but most weigh much less. The largest specimen on record weighed 90 pounds and measured 4 feet 7 inches.

The red drum can be distinguished from the black drum by the absence of chin barbels and the presence of a black spot on the base of the tail. The body is copper- or bronze-colored rather than silvery or gray. The red drum has 11 dorsal spines, 23 25 dorsal rays, 2 anal spines, 8 anal rays, and 40–45 scales along the lateral line. There are 8–9 gillrakers on the lower limb of the first arch. The upper jaw projects beyond the lower. The maxillary reaches to, or beyond, a vertical from the posterior margin of the orbit.

SPOTTED SEATROUT *Cynoscion nebulosus* One of the most popular inshore saltwater gamefishes in the southern United States, the spotted seatrout occurs from New York to Florida and throughout the Gulf of Mexico.

The body coloration of the spotted seatrout is dark gray above, with sky-blue reflections, shading to a silvery below. The upper parts of its sides are marked with numerous round black spots, the spots extending on the dorsal and caudal fins. The very young have a broad, dark lateral band and blotches of the same color on the back; the base of the caudal fin is black. Fins are pale to yellowish-green; the dorsal and caudal fins are spotted with black in the adult.

The spotted seatrout has 10 spines (rarely 11) in the first dorsal fin, 1 spine and 24–26 softrays in the second dorsal fin. The anal fin has 2 spines followed by 10–11 softrays. There are 90–102 scales in the lateral line. The body is elongate and somewhat compressed; the back is a little elevated, while the head is long and snout pointed.

MULLET FAMILY Mugilidae

The family of mullets is worldwide in tropical and temperate seas and is of considerable economic importance wherever found in abundance. Most species are marine, although many, particularly the striped mullet, invade brackish and freshwater. Here they may be seen making high, very ungraceful leaps, often several in succession. They do not dive back in the water head-first; instead, they rigidly maintain the position in which they began the leap and land with a splash.

STRIPED MULLET *Mugil cephalus* The striped mullet has a very wide distribution, being found on both sides of the Atlantic and Pacific oceans and in the Indian Ocean. In the Americas it is found from Brazil to Cape Cod, and as a stray to outer Nova Scotia; it also occurs along the West Coast from Monterey to Chile. It is common in coastal freshwater rivers.

Striped Mullet

The striped mullet has a spiny first dorsal with 4 spines and a soft dorsal fin with 1 spine and 8 softrays, the two well separated. The ventral fins are on the abdomen behind the point of insertion of the pectorals; the anal fin usually consists of 3 spines and 8 softrays, with only 2 spines in very small fish; the caudal fin is forked moderately deep. The soft dorsal and anal fins are almost naked (scaled in most other American mullets), but the body and head are clothed with large, rounded scales. Adults are bluish-gray or greenish above, silvery on the lower part of the sides and below; the scales on the sides have dark centers that form longitudinal lines. The lining of the body cavity is black. The striped mullet grows to 30 inches or more and over 15 pounds in warmer waters.

Mullets feed chiefly on vegetable matter, but they feed also on eggs and small marine animals such as snails. They nibble at marine plants or scoop up mud and, after sucking out the edible portion and straining it through long gillrakers, reject the residue. Most have a muscular, gizzardlike stomach that enables them to grind their food before it starts through an exceptionally long digestive tract.

196

TARPON FAMILY Elopidae

LADYFISH *Elops saurus*   This is a fairly common fish occurring in the Atlantic, Indian, and western Pacific oceans. It is most abundant in the warmer parts of its range and very common around southern Florida and in the Caribbean. Despite the various names applied to this species, such as chiro and ten-pounder, ladyfish seems to be the most acceptable. The name ten-pounder is misleading as this fish seldom reaches a weight of much over 5–6 pounds. Large ladyfish of 8–9 pounds have been reported but are rare in the western Atlantic.

The ladyfish is slender, finely scaled, and generally silver in color with a blue-green back. Dorsal rays number 20, anal rays 13, pectoral rays 16–19, and pelvic rays 13–15. Scales are very small, about 100–120 along the lateral line. The body is quite elongate. The pectoral fins are inserted low on the body. The dorsal fin is single, on the middle of the back, the last ray not produced into a whiplike filament as in the tarpon. Pelvic fins are slightly in advance of the dorsal fin, about midway between pectoral and caudal fins. Caudal fin is deeply forked. Upper jaw reaches well beyond vertical from posterior margin of the orbit.

The ladyfish occurs in shallow water close to shore over sandy and muddy bottom. It is usually taken in bays and estuaries, but it also enters freshwater streams in Florida.

TARPON *Megalops atlantica*   This species belongs to a family of very primitive bony fishes. Its nearest relative is the oxeye herring of the Indo-West Pacific. Like the ladyfish and the bonefish, it possesses an eellike, leptocephalous larval stage. It occurs on both sides of the Atlantic; on the western side it has been taken as far north as Nova Scotia, although it does not regularly occur north of Cape Hatteras.

The color is usually dark blue to greenish-black dorsally, shading to bright silver on the sides and belly. Specimens from inland waters sometimes display brownish or brassy colors.

Other distinguishing characters of the tarpon are body with almost vertical sides; dorsal outline of head nearly straight and horizontal, the back somewhat elevated; ventral outline strongly curved anteriorly; depth 3.4–4.3 in standard length. Scales large, firm with crenulate membranous border; 41–48 in lateral series. Lateral line complete, decurved anteriorly, the pores branched. Head moderately short and deep, its depth at middle of eye not quite twice its width at the same place. Mouth superior; mandible projecting far beyond the gape, entering dorsal profile in advance of mouth.

Dorsal fin high anteriorly with 13–15 softrays, the last ray greatly elongated; origin of fin about equidistant between base of caudal and anterior margin of eye. Caudal fin deeply forked, the lobes about equal in length, generally somewhat longer than head. Anal fin somewhat elevated anteriorly with 22–25 softrays, the last ray elongated in

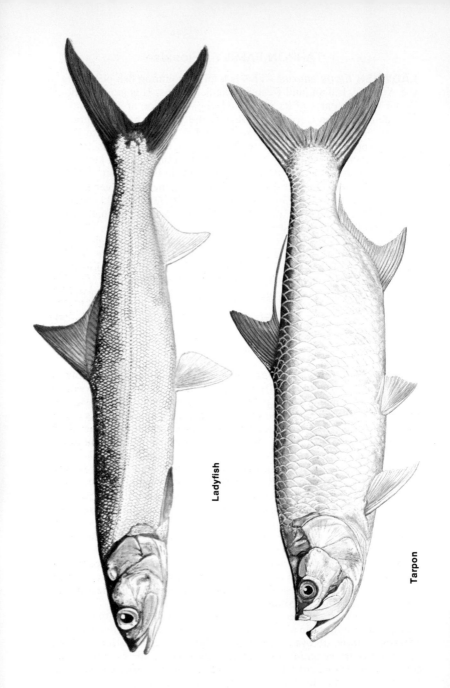

Ladyfish

Tarpon

adults, its base 4.6–5.6 in standard length. Pelvic fin rather large, inserted more than an eye's length in advance of origin of dorsal and somewhat nearer to base of pectoral than to origin of anal. Pectoral fin rather long with 13–14 softrays. Axillary scale of pectoral rather small, only about a third of the fin length.

The tarpon's rate of growth is relatively slow. It probably does not attain sexual maturity until it is about 6–7 years old and attains a length of about 4 feet. Individuals weighing 100 pounds are probably 13–16 years of age. The young fish are common in small brackish or freshwater streams. As they grow larger they move into the larger streams and estuaries. They are carnivorous and are known to feed upon mullets, silversides, marine catfishes, and blue crabs.

The tarpon is one of the most prolific of all fishes; a single large female may contain more than 12 million eggs. Spawning probably takes place in shallow, estuarine waters any time from May to September, at least in Florida. It is able to tolerate a wide range of salinity, often being found in purely freshwater. It seems to prefer the lower salinities of estuaries and the mouths of large rivers. It reaches a very large size; an individual over 8 feet long with an estimated weight of 350 pounds was taken from the Hillsborough River Inlet, Florida.

SNOOK FAMILY   Centropomidae

FAT SNOOK *Centropomus parallelus*   This is the second largest of the West Indian snook. It occurs in Florida as far north as Lake Okeechobee and throughout the American Atlantic tropics. The fat snook occasionally reaches a total length of about 20 inches, but larger individuals are rare. The largest known specimen measured 28 inches in total length. The robust body is heavier than in the other species at the same length.

The fat snook has 79–92 lateral scales, 10–13 gillrakers, usually 11–12 on the lower limb of the first arch, not including the rudiments. There are 6 anal rays and 14–16 pectoral rays, usually 15. The second anal spine does not reach beyond the vertical from caudal base. Pectoral fin does not reach to vertical from the tip of pelvic. The pelvic fin reaches to or beyond the anus. Maxillary reaches to or beyond vertical from the center of the eye.

The greater number of lateral scales and the more robust body distinguish this snook from the others. A closely related species from Brazil, *C. constantinus,* has fewer lateral scales (68–79). Another relative, *C. poeyi,* from the vicinity of Veracruz, Mexico, usually has 9 dorsal rays instead of 10.

SNOOK *Centropomus undecimalis*   This important marine gamefish occurs in most of Florida and in southwestern Texas. As a stray, it has been reported from as far north as Delaware. The snook is found throughout the American tropics on the Atlantic and Pacific

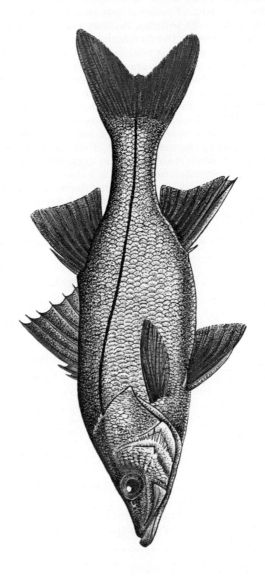

Fat Snook

sides. This is, by far, the largest and most common species of snook. One of the heaviest specimens on record measured 4 feet 7 inches in total length and weighed 50 pounds 8 ounces. A related species, the black snook, occurs on the Pacific side of tropical America.

The snook is long-bodied but thick through the middle, with the upper snout depressed and a protruding lower jaw. The color is variable according to habitat, but is usually a brownish or brown-gold on the back shading to a lighter color on the belly; it has a pronounced black lateral stripe along the sides that extends to the tail. The lateral scales number 67–78, gillrakers 7–10, usually 8–9 on the lower limb of the first arch, not including rudiments. Anal rays are 6, pectoral rays 14–16, usually 15. Second anal spine not reaching to vertical from caudal base, pectoral fin not reaching to vertical from tip of pelvic, pelvic fin not reaching to anus, maxillary reaching to or beyond vertical from the center of the eye.

This species is distinguished from the other Atlantic snook by the fewer gillrakers, the shorter second anal spine, and the pelvic fins not reaching to the anus.

This snook occurs along the coast in saltwater, in addition to bays, estuaries, canals, and freshwater streams. Small, immature individuals, less than 1 year old, usually occur in the marginal areas of coastal lagoons and estuaries. Adults occur well inland, being caught in Florida's Lake Okeechobee with some frequency.

The common snook feeds primarily on fishes, but crustaceans are also an important food item. The spawning season extends from June to November. This species may reach the age of at least 7 years, and nearly all specimens are mature by the third year of life. The common snook and probably the other species of snook are very sensitive to cold. The minimum temperature tolerated is about 60°F.

This snook is presently being considered for more widespread introduction in Florida freshwaters.

SWORDSPINE SNOOK *Centropomus ensiferus* This is the smallest and rarest of the snook. It occurs in extreme southern Florida and southward throughout the American Atlantic tropics. Full-grown adults probably do not attain a total length of much more than 12 inches. The common and scientific names refer to the long, second anal spine. Two related species, *C. armatus* and *C. robalito,* occur on the Pacific side of tropical America.

The swordspine occurs in estuaries and in the lower course of freshwater streams and canals.

It has 49–59 lateral-line scales. Gillrakers number 12–16 on lower limb of first arch, not including rudiments; anal rays 6; pectoral rays 14–16, usually 15. Second anal spine reaching beyond vertical from caudal base; pectoral fin reaching to vertical from tip of pelvic; pelvic fin reaching to or beyond anus; maxillary not reaching beyond vertical from center of eye.

In addition to its smaller size, this snook is distinguished from the other Atlantic species by the longer second anal spine and the fewer lateral-line scales.

TARPON SNOOK *Centropomus pectinatus* In the United States, this species is confined to Florida, from the Caloosahatchee River southward, It occurs throughout the American Atlantic tropics. Although larger than the swordspine snook, the maximum known size attained is about 16 inches in total length. The common name refers to the upturned snout, reminiscent of the tarpon. A very close, nearly identical relative, *C. grandoculatus,* occurs on the Pacific side of tropical America.

The tarpon snook occurs in bays, estuaries, and the lower course of freshwater streams and canals.

The tarpon snook has 62–72 lateral scales. Gillrakers number 15–18 on the lower limb of first arch, not including rudiments; anal rays 7; pectoral rays 13–15, usually 14. Second anal spine not reaching beyond vertical from caudal base; pectoral fin not reaching to vertical from tip of pelvic; pelvic fin reaching beyond anus; maxillary not reaching to vertical from center of eye.

The greater number of anal rays, fewer pectoral rays, and more upturned snout distinguish this species from the other Atlantic snook. Also, the body is much more compressed.

Snook, 6-pound Male

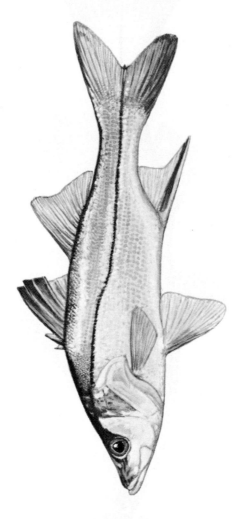

Swordspine Snook

Tarpon Snook

INDEX OF FISHES

Page numbers set in *italics* indicate the main entry of a fish, and page numbers in **boldface** indicate illustrations. Page numbers for passing references to fishes are set in roman type.

208